THE TRIAL OF CHRIST

A TWENTY-FIRST CENTURY LAWYER DEFENDS JESUS

DEE WAMPLER

WINEPRESS WP PUBLISHING

The Trial of Christ
A Twenty-first Century
Lawyer Defends Jesus

Jesus Christ

Printed in the United States of America.

WinePress Publishing, PO Box 428, Enumclaw, WA 98022.

Arrested

Unless otherwise noted all scripture quotations are taken from the Holy Bible, New International Version, Copyright © 1973, 1978, 1984 by the International Bible Society. Used by permission of Zondervan Publishing House. The "NIV" and "New International Version" trademarks are registered in the United States Patent and Trademark Office by International Bible Society.

Tried

ISBN 1-57921-185-2
Library of Congress
   Catalog Card Number: 99-63468

Cover:
   Jesus' First Fall
   by Ben Stahl
   Sarasota Museum of the Cross

Mocked

Crucified

© S P Co.
1942

Acknowledgements

"She will give birth to a son, and you are to give him the name Jesus, because he will save his people from their sins."

—Matt. 1:21

Jesus Christ was the maker of one of the few revolutions in world history which lasted. It has been objected that no authentic life of Jesus can be written because our information is insufficient and cannot ever be anything else. His public career can, to a considerable extent, be reconstructed. The evidence is hard, very hard, to decipher. But something substantial is there for the finding.

In my endeavor to find out the truth about Jesus, I have discovered the most loving, dramatic life ever lived.

As Joachin Jeremias, one of his greatest modern interpreters exclaimed:

"Our task is a return to the actually living voice of Jesus. How great the gain if we succeed in rediscovering here and there behind the veil the features of the Son of Man!"

The first person to plant the seed that I should lecture and write on The Trial of Christ was Rev. Stanley V. Michael of the Assemblies of God Headquarters, Springfield, Missouri. He loaned me Chandler's book, *The Trial of Christ*, waited four years until I read it, and nurtured me with quiet encouragement. My wife Anne put up with my study and research for 10 years, and encouraged me as my best friend. Rev. Michael Obel, Immanuel Reformed Presbyterian Church, Eve Keene, and Paul T. Herzog assisted with scriptural research. Joe S. Passanise assisted with legal research. Rev. Jim Anderson, former President of Calvary Bible College in Kansas City, Missouri, and Dr. David A. Lewis, Springfield, Missouri, spent one month with me in Jerusalem visiting the crime scene.

Along the way, Pastors John M. Edie, James Reimer, John Marshall, and Gene Gibbons Second Baptist Church; Rev. Bob and Donna Strand, Park Crest Assembly of God; Rev. Jess and Paula Gibson and Rev. Lindsey M. and Jane Robison, Cornerstone Word Church, all of Springfield, Missouri, have given encouragement, as did Cary Summers, former President of Silver Dollar City, Branson, Missouri, Rev. Hayes Wicker, First Baptist Church, Naples, Florida, Rev. John and Darlene Graham, Word of Faith Fellowship,

Ozark, Missouri. Ken Cowan and Steve McGuire assisted with photography, layout, and design.

My personal secretaries Maxine Reid and Becki Thomas worked ten years with transcription. Tina Nuccitelli and Jennifer Strickland helped with research foreign language translations.

Finally, the love and support of my parents Homer D. and Lualice Wampler who watched me research this book but did not live to see its publication.

FOREWORD

. . . we have seen his glory, the glory of the one and only Son, who came from the Father . . .

—JOHN 1:14

"Nativity" by Phillippe de Champaigne (1602-1674) Lille, Jusee des Beaus-Arts

Some 40 years after Julius Caesar was murdered in the Senate House at Rome, a little boy was born in a tiny village near the southeastern corner of the shores of the Mediterranean. More stories have been told about this little boy than any other human being. One of these stories tells how he came to die. It is likely that half the members of the human race, whether they are Christians or not, have heard of Jesus and how he came to die on the cross by a judgment of a Jewish court and Roman judge nearly 2000 years ago.

Millions have heard the story, discussed it, and examined it for many purposes, in many ways. Few were there on that long ago Friday in Jerusalem who suspected what was happening. No one knew the world would never be the same again.

Outside the Hall of Judgment the mob howled, "Crucify Him! Crucify Him!", unaware those words would echo through the centuries to come. Repeatedly, Governor Pontius Pilate found "no fault in this man," but gave into the mob anyway, unaware the consequences of his weakness would be felt throughout history.

It was a great mystery to the men who knew Him, and remains a great mystery. There is no way to explain how it was possible to be man and God at the same time.

No one can know in advance what is true, and at the same time profess to be searching for it. Even the best detective in the world could not be completely successful in finding out exactly what happened on that day so long ago.

As a criminal trial attorney I will try to explain what happened.

Dee Wampler

INTRODUCTION

TRUTH. We all search for it. Some secretly, others openly. Philosophers have attempted to explain the truth of life, the universe, morality, science, origin of man, goodness and mercy without reference to God as the source of that truth, but it is a hopeless and empty search.

The facts concerning the trial of Christ will help you decide who he is. In the courtroom prior to impaneling a jury, we have an opportunity to ask the jurors questions known as "voir dire." The purpose is to search the juror's mind concerning any prejudices or presuppositions that they have concerning the subject matter to be litigated.

As a prosecuting attorney, I located witnesses and carefully organized pieces of physical evidence to show the jury. To secure a conviction and a verdict of "guilty," the prosecutor's proof must be strong—beyond a reasonable doubt. This awesome burden can only be met by careful investigation, organization of facts, and reconstruction of the crime scene. The jury needs a front row seat to the commission of the crime. There must be no doubt or pang of conscience to keep them from voting "guilty" and returning home for a sound night's sleep.

As a defense attorney, it is not easy to defend one whom you know is guilty. My job is to ensure a fair trial. I do not judge the accused. He will have his ultimate judgment day. I hate the sin but love the sinner.

Witnesses and evidence brought against an accused are carefully examined and only the finest, purest, most relevant facts are considered by the jury. If there is any reasonable doubt their duty is to acquit, rather than run the risk of punishing an innocent man.

It is the lawyer's duty never to take reported facts for granted but to delve into the evidence, ascertain its source and validity, and make sure of its credibility before conceding the fact.

A career spent analyzing critical evidence to be used at trial would make anyone a "Doubting Thomas." Likewise, there is nothing wrong in reading the Bible critically and cross-examining the Scriptures. My favorite Scripture verse challenges me:

"Test everything. Hold on to the good. Avoid every kind of evil."
—1 THESS. 5:21-22

Because of my legal training to refuse evidence at face value, I believe little of what I hear and only a small portion of what I see until I test it and am sure it is true.

Lawyers are notoriously preoccupied with technicalities. I would have preferred to have minutes taken at the proceedings and have preserved documents and trial transcripts for my historical research. The Evangelists did not intend to give a completely full record of the actual events. The Gospels give us the historical account of Jesus of Nazareth as the fulfillment of the divine promise to be the Savior of man.

This book has been an ever-growing labor of love—an adventure in scholarship. I became more emotionally committed to the task as the years progressed, enjoyed the research journey's interminable lecturing and writing. I compared notes with world scholars. Absolute proof of every detail recorded here is not possible. I have checked sources against each other to develop a feel for the "probable or possible," and visited the "scene of the crime" in Jerusalem.

In the last century, 60,000 books have been written on the life of Jesus; more than on any other person in history. Very few have paid attention to his trial. It is as if the trial was not really a part of the story of his life. Of those written on the trial, less than a half dozen have been written by lawyers. Most wrestle with the age-old problem of trying to make Jesus relevant in our time—to see Jesus with our own eyes.

Thirty years after the death of Jesus, hundreds, perhaps thousands, of people believed firmly that he had lived and was divinely commissioned to establish a new universal kingdom.

My sole armament is a lifelong belief that Jesus is God; an unquenchable curiosity to which I've become enslaved; and belief that Jesus truly loved everyone, and proved it.

This book is far from what I wish it to be. It is not complete because a great deal of what happened during the trial is lost in antiquity.

The death of Christ by crucifixion was divinely ordained. The Psalmist wrote about it a thousand years before the event. But never in our history has there been a travesty of justice equal to that observed in the trial of Christ.

There can be few people in the world who do not have some feeling of curiosity about Jesus. What kind of person must he have been to have had such an enormous influence? Was the rise of the church and the growth of Christianity due solely to his extraordinary personality?

But if this book has helped one person to understand Jesus a little better and to appreciate his mission, then it was worth the effort.

Before reading this book, I ask you: If it could be proved to you by the evidence that Jesus Christ really is the Son of God, would you believe it? If you reject part of the Bible as not being true, is that rejection based on a study of the Bible and concluding on a rational basis that it is not true, or is the Bible rejected out of ignorance because it has never really been studied by you?

> "We did not follow cleverly invented stories when we told you about the power and coming of our Lord Jesus Christ, but we were eyewitnesses of his majesty."
>
> —2 PETER 1:16

In a discussion that Christ had with Pilate just before his death on the subject matter of truth:

> "Pilate therefore said to him, 'So you are a king?' Jesus answered, 'You say correctly that I am a king. For this I have been born, and for this I have come into the world, to bear witness to the *truth*. Everyone on the side of *truth* listens to me.'"
>
> —JOHN 18:37

Jesus Christ is willing to have his claims examined with our minds. It is a command from Christ that we examine his claims, not only with our hearts but with our minds. It is a command from Christ to examine history and archeology, and any other facts that such study would lead to the truth, and that truth would lead to Christ. Are you willing to accept this challenge?

Dee Wampler

Attorney at Law
Springfield, Missouri

Contents

For he who said, "Do not commit adultery," also said, "Do not murder." If you do not commit adultery but do commit murder, you have become a lawbreaker.

—JAMES 2:11

CHAPTER ONE

The Law Today

SINCE OUR NATION was founded in 1776, law and jurisprudence have been based on English common law. Tracing further back, it is easy to find early Roman law. And of course, although it may be politically incorrect, a large part of law derives from and is influenced by the Bible and the teachings of Jesus.

In the Twenty-First Century, our idea of what is fair has been formed by centuries of case law and decisions (known as "precedents"). We review prior cases which have been decided in a court and apply these precedents to current cases.

The *Fourth Amendment* in the Bill of Rights places a limit on government power. Police, prosecutors, or informants are not allowed to conduct illegal activities. Police are not permitted to cross the threshold of your house except by prior court approval with a written search warrant, properly sworn and authenticated, specifically stating the crime charged, the place to be searched and the things to be seized.

The *Fifth Amendment*, one of the most controversial amendments in our Bill of Rights, guarantees that an accused *need not speak* during a police investigation or at trial, and his silence will not be used against him. If any utterance would tend to provide a link in a chain which might help to incriminate the accused, then the accused has the absolute *right to remain silent*. No person can be compelled or ordered to speak. Neither he nor his lawyer has any duty or obligation to say one word. The judge and jury are bound by law not to take as any evidence of guilt that the accused elected to remain silent.

The *Sixth Amendment* gives an accused the *right to know the* nature of the *charges against him*. He cannot be expected to defend against charges unless they are specific and he knows the date, hour, place and specific crime he allegedly committed. The government, through its prosecutor, must state in writing in advance of trial (to give the accused an effective opportunity to prepare a defense) the exact nature of the charges. Even if the accused is convicted, an appellate court may later say that the criminal charge was not specific enough and the case may then be thrown out and the accused set free.

He has a right to confront his accusers, to know their full names and addresses in advance of trial, to interview them or place them under oath on the witness stand. If they have previously spoken to police and reports have been made, the accused is entitled to see those reports and prior statements in advance of trial, to use them to impeach and question the credibility of the witness.

He has a right to know if the prosecution witnesses have a motive to lie, have been paid money, have previously perjured themselves, have been convicted of prior crimes, or have a bad reputation. The accused has the right to bring this damaging evidence before the jury so the "triers of fact" can weigh and determine whether the witness is telling the truth. Complaining witnesses are placed under oath and if they are co-conspirators or have a reason to lie, the jury is instructed by the judge to take their testimony lightly. If they lie, they can be charged with perjury.

He has the right to cross-examine eyewitnesses and test the credibility and truthfulness of their testimony. If the case against him is circumstantial or indirect, the accused enjoys the *presumption of innocence* unless all the circumstantial evidence points inescapably towards guilt and away from other reasonable explanations or hypotheses of innocence.

He has the right to have a sufficient amount of time to consult with his family, friends, and lawyer, locate favorable witnesses, and investigate the background of unfavorable witnesses to test their truthfulness in court. He has the right to have sufficient time for sober reflection as to what statements he might make in court and what defense he might present. In the courtroom all the parties and their lawyers carefully plan strategy and trial techniques. To a lay person, it may seem that things happen accidentally or

Gethsemane
Raiser Friedrick Museum, Berlin
Religious News Service

extemporaneously. The opposite is true. A jury trial is often like a large iceberg. Ninety-nine percent of the ice is under the water and cannot be seen but it provides the foundation for the one percent of the iceberg that can be observed. The sure way to win a criminal trial is by careful preparation of each and every detail with full investigation, legal briefing, and thought given to cross-examination of every witness.

If the accused is acquitted of a charge, it is forbidden the government to reaccuse on the same or similar charges. The provisions of "double jeopardy" have been in the common law for many centuries. Once the accused is acquitted, he is free to go. If he is convicted, he has the absolute right of appeal to a higher court where other judges will carefully review the evidence and transcripts of witnesses. Under calm and cool deliberation, they will later decide whether the original judge and jury made the right decisions or whether, due to the emotions in the courtroom, the accused was in some way denied a fair trial or other basic human rights.

If important trial errors which might have affected the jury's decision were made, a new trial may be ordered in which the case is tried "de novo." Sometimes the accused is acquitted and the judgment of conviction is reversed outright.

When witnesses testify, it is required that their testimony be proven or *corroborated*. If their testimony cannot be sufficiently verified by other witnesses or substantiated by proof of independent facts, the jury will tend to disbelieve that witness, especially if the accused testifies to the opposite. In a trial, if it is one witness' word against another without any other supporting documents or proof, normally the accused will be acquitted.

The burden of proof in a civil case is a much smaller one by a preponderance of the evidence, but in criminal law it is beyond a reasonable doubt. In a criminal case, even strong suspicion of guilt is not enough. The burden is always greater in criminal cases because taking a person's liberty and freedom has been more important than taking his property. In America, the right of personal freedom and liberty, to associate, to speak, to write, to advance a particular idea has always been protected unless it advocates the violation of a specific law or it advocates treason or the overthrow of the government. A person's freedom cannot be taken from him lightly, unless there is a verdict against him, unanimously agreed to by all twelve jurors beyond a reasonable doubt.

As our legal system has evolved, there is an excruciatingly long period of time from the date of arrest until a case is ultimately concluded by an appellate court, for instance. The average length of time involved in appealing a death sentence is ten years.

Even in most felony cases, the average length of time for a trial and appeal is two to three years, because the belief is that no stone should be left unturned before a man's liberty is taken. Every possible reason for acquittal is carefully investigated and tested.

Once an accused is taken into custody he must be treated humanely, advised of basic constitutional rights, (the "Miranda Warnings"), and given decent treatment. He cannot be deprived of any essentials of life. He must be given an adequate jail, access to an attorney or law library, adequate food, heating, lighting, clothing, and the usual amenities of life. No prisoner can be mistreated, threatened, coerced, or have improper pressure brought upon him.

This brief synopsis of current criminal law, somewhat familiar to all, provides a basis for studying the law 2000 years ago. Many of the principles are the same.

Many people that lived at the time of Jesus were very intelligent. They had good basic laws that were supposed to be fair. Although many people were illiterate and could not read, many could speak several languages. The law was recited, learned, studied, memorized, and passed down by oral tradition. Families did home schooling. Detailed laws and customs were in place to ensure that government was competent.

But the laws, as all things made by man, were not perfect. Some elected officials, like today, were weak, incompetent, and corrupt. They desired to be politically correct and stay in office.

The Jerusalem Sanhedrin knew better. Within their power, they could have afforded Jesus a fair trial. But instead of obeying their laws, they conspired to commit judicial murder.

Is there independent proof today that Jesus Christ really lived and was crucified? Or is our sole proof the Bible? Let's examine the evidence.

Preach the Word; be prepared in season and out of season; correct, rebuke and encourage - with great patience and careful instruction. For the time will come when men will not put up with sound doctrine. Instead, to suit their own desires, they will gather around them a great number of teachers to say what their itching ears want to hear. They will turn their ears away from the truth and turn aside to myths.

—2 TIM. 4:2-4

CHAPTER TWO

Proof

TRIAL LAWYERS RISE OR FALL on their ability to untangle facts from the mere appearance of facts. As attorneys we are honor bound never to assume as true an alleged reported fact. To succeed before a jury we must be able to analyze what is represented as fact to learn its true source and validity and assess its credibility.

Ironically, untangling facts about Jesus' trial and conviction from the appearance of facts is more demanding than preparing for and trying any jury trial. The material that might qualify as evidence about Christ's legal troubles can overwhelm even the most experienced scholar. But any post-mortem on the trial of Christ stands or falls on whether historical facts are untangled from tradition and faith, whether reliable texts are separated from unreliable ones. Only then can we reach a sound verdict on the trial of Christ.

But it is a worthy labor. Apart from the challenge of probing whether or not a man who claimed to be both human and divine was fairly tried, convicted and executed, the result of this trial touched the lives of nearly a third of the world. It touches the lives of Jews whose heritage, in part, reflects a violent encounter with this Jewish carpenter. It touches the lives of Muslims who look to him as a prophet. It touches the lives of millions in numerous eastern religions who see in Jesus a supremely self-actualized man. And it touches the lives of progressive humanists whose world and life view arose in the 18th century from a secularizing of his teachings.

Still, Jesus seems an unlikely focus of all the attention. He appeared a full 2,000 years ago, unknown outside his nondescript village and ignored or scorned inside it. For a few brief years this itinerant preacher traveled through Palestine, what is now northern Israel but then a part of the Roman Empire.

He appeared to accomplish little; he wrote nothing ever published; he led no more than a small number; he earned no fortune; he neither married nor fathered a child. Friends had to bury his body in a tomb that was borrowed.

But within three centuries of his execution the empire that executed him revered him for exactly who he claimed to be. And today his name is on someone's lips every second of time. Indeed, the western world bases its calendar on his birth.

It is the Christian belief that Jesus of Nazareth is the Savior of the world. Millions of Christians throughout the world believe Jesus died to save sinners from the just wrath of God and to teach us how to live. The price he paid was the supreme sacrifice, a painful and humiliating death on the cross of Golgotha. Christianity further holds that on the third day after his death he arose from the borrowed tomb. The Christ of religious faith is not the subject of this book. He does not need books written about him. This book is written with the hope that something will be learned about the other Christ—the Christ of history, tried, convicted, and executed for a crime he did not commit.

CHRISTIAN SOURCES: BIBLICAL

Evidence about this Christ of history abounds. Sources range from the religious to the secular, from the ancient to the contemporary. Some of the evidence for the Christ of history is Christian, foremost of which is the New Testament. But there are other Christian sources, including literary and personal testimonies to the reality of Jesus of Nazareth. There is powerful and abundant evidence for the Christ of history among ancient secular writers, and there is the evidence of archeology.

The Bible

A wealth of modern archeological data is providing a revealing glimpse into the times of Jesus:

1. In 1961, the inscription found at Caesarea Maritima confirmed that Pilate was the Roman prefect in Judea;
2. In 1968, the discovery of the crucified man outside Jerusalem whose wounds were strikingly similar to those described in the crucifixion of Jesus;
3. In 1990, the tomb of Caiaphas was discovered near Jerusalem;
4. The ninth century B.C. stone inscription was unearthed bearing the name of David.

The sands are yielding secrets hidden for thousands of years that shed surprising new light on the historical veracity of those sacred writings. Many consider biblical archeology to: "prove the Bible true," but in fact the Bible has ended up being an invaluable tool in understanding and interpreting the artifacts and ruins. Archeology and the Bible have been matching well. Without the Bible, for instance, we wouldn't even know that there were Philistines.

There are still scores of sites in Israel, from the Church of the Nativity in Bethlehem to the Church of the Holy Sepulcher which have been verified with solid physical evidence.

In the future, a new golden age of biblical archeology awaits. Radar imaging may speed the process and is showing promise in scanning beneath the earth's surface for buried ruins such as the discoveries in 1992 of Juris Zarins, the lost city of Ubar, and the recent discoveries of additional caves, holding more Dead Sea Scrolls at Qumran.

These important finds have caused anxiety for skeptics. There are many more mysteries to be solved—it's just a matter of time.

The Bible is a remarkable book; to the pagan it is often meaningless, to the skeptic an enigma, and even for the believer its secrets are not revealed at first sight.

"For everything that was written in the past was written to teach us, so
that through endurance and the encouragement of the Scriptures we might
have hope.   —ROM. 15:4

"But these are written that you may believe that Jesus is the Christ, the
Son of God, and that by believing you may have life in his name."
                                                        —JOHN 20:31

The Bible is unique among works of literature. It was written over a
1,600 year period in 66 books by 40 diverse authors. Two of them were
half-brothers of Jesus who did not believe his claims until after he was
resurrected. The Bible was written in different places, including the thrones
of kings and in dungeons and jails. It was written on three different conti-
nents, Asia, Africa and Europe and in three languages, Aramaic, Hebrew
and Greek. In spite of the diversity of its authors and the fact that most
writers did not have access to each other or other writings, there is total
consistency in the facts and theology of the Bible. Not one author criticized
the other. There are no dissenting opinions or footnotes.

The New Testament tells the story of the "New Covenant" between
God and the new people of God, "the church." It centers on the life and
teachings of Jesus and his sacrificial death. Jesus fulfilled the expectations
of Christians as expressed in Jewish Scriptures that a "Messiah" or "Christ"
designated by God would deliver Israel.

The New Testament begins with four "Gospels," or messages of Good
News, of Jesus' ministry, execution and resurrection. Each Gospel is not a
biography but is written more like a sermon or call to faith.

The Gospels say little about the first 30 years of Jesus' life and never
describe his physical appearance. There are stories of healing and confrontations and each contains an abbreviated account of his last days in Jerusalem. The book of Acts tells of the early church and how apostles spread
beyond the Jews to the Gentiles, through Paul.

While there are probably as many views about the date the New Testament documents were completed as there are scholars, there are two generally accepted views. A few see the writings completed before A.D.70 when
Roman soldiers sacked Jerusalem. Another view from the tradition of German higher criticism sees the writings completed around or after the turn
of the second century.

But whatever date one chooses, the New Testament is immensely dependable as history. In the words of British scholar F. F. Bruce, "There is no body of ancient literature in the world that enjoys such a wealth of good textual attestation as the New Testament."

The New Testament was written in Greek and later translated to Latin in the second century on thin and fragile papyrus. There are hundreds of modern discoveries of papyri relating to daily life at the time of Christ.[1]

Although the original writings of the New Testament were written on thin paper-like sheets made from papyrus reeds that grow along rivers of the Middle East (like the Nile River), later copies were written on durable animal skins called vellum. There are thousands of these documents available. In fact, it has only been in the last two centuries many of the most valuable manuscripts have been located and studied.[2]

In 1844, Constantine Tischendorf, a German specialist in ancient languages, made one of the most valuable discoveries—the *Codex Sinaiticus*, the earliest near complete Biblical text.[3] Written on expensive vellum, Sinaiticus required the skins of 360 young sheep and goats. There is little doubt that this was produced under the patronage of Christianity following Constantine the Great's conversion in the fourth century.

The earliest piece of the New Testament so far discovered is a torn papyrus page containing fragmented remnants of John 18:31-33 on one side, and 18:37-38 on the other. It is dated by its writing style to about A.D. 125. Those verses contain the trial of Jesus before Pilate and the latter's famous question: "What is truth?"

Archeologists found fragmentary manuscripts in the rubbish dumps from 1897-1904 in the ancient town of Oxyrhynchus. These papyrus writings contained the sayings of Jesus on pages dated to the years A.D. 200 to 250.

Matthew

Matthew, whose name means "gift of the Lord," was a tax collector who left his work to follow Jesus (Matt. 9:9). He was one of the twelve Apostles and the author of this Gospel.

He probably wrote in Palestine in the early church period, possibly A.D. 50, when the church was largely Jewish and the Gospel was preached to Jews only. It was written in Greek, although the passages show that Matthew's Gospel is Jewish.

Mark

Although there is no direct internal evidence of authorship, most believe this Gospel was written by the Apostle John Mark, associated with Peter in early non-biblical tradition.

Mark explains Jewish customs, translates Aramaic words, and seems to hold a special interest in persecution and martyrdom, subjects of concern to Roman believers. His Gospel may have been written because of the persecutions of the Roman church in A.D. 64-67.

Mark's Gospel portrays in a simple and vivid way Jesus' ministry emphasizing his actions rather than his words.

Luke

The author's name does not appear in the book, but unmistakable evidence points to Luke. This Gospel accompanies the book of Acts, and the language indicates both were written by the same person and addressed to the same reader, Theophilus.

Luke was probably a Gentile, a Roman official of wealth and status, well educated in Greek culture, a physician by profession. His writings reflect a studied, self-conscious commitment to historical accuracy.

The book probably was written in Rome, in Greek, between 59-63, or A.D. 70-80. The main theme of the Gospel is the way Jesus fulfilled biblical prophecies.

John

The author is the Apostle John, prominent in the early church, who knew Jesus' life well. It was based on the recollections of an eyewitness. Tradition dates the book to A.D. 85, though it may have been completed before A.D. 70.

Some believe John's aim was to set forth a version of the Christian message that would appeal to Greek thinkers, but his primary intention was evangelistic. He wanted to understand and believe, and his purpose may have been to build up believers as well as win new converts.

The Gospel writers were not professional historians nor were they interested in giving an exhaustive account of everything Jesus said or did. But as more and more New Testament manuscripts have been unearthed, we have learned the New Testament Gospels are based on historical fact. These discoveries have corroborated not just the Gospels, but the rest of the New Testament writings.

For those interested in finding evidence of the historical Jesus, the first stop clearly should be the four Gospels.

Prophecies

Approximately 25 percent of the Bible consists of prophecies. The penalty for a Jewish prophet was death if he was wrong.

Within the Old Testament, there are over 300 prophecies alone concerning the Messiah that were fulfilled by Jesus Christ. These prophecies were written from 450 to 2000 years before his birth. These Messianic prophecies were so vivid, that before the discovery of the Dead Sea Scrolls it was argued that ordinary men could not have written them. The Dead Sea Scrolls established that prophecies were written hundreds of years before the birth of Christ. A few of these prophecies include:

1.　". . . your king comes to you, righteous and having salvation, gentle and riding on a donkey . . ." —Zec. 9:9

Kings don't ride donkeys, they ride chariots. Christ fulfilled this prophecy on Palm Sunday when he entered Jerusalem on a donkey. He came as a suffering servant, and not as a conquering king.

2.　"He was despised and rejected by men, a man of sorrows, and familiar with suffering. Like one from whom men hide their faces he was despised, and we esteemed him not." —Isa. 53:3

From Gethsemane his disciples "left him and fled." —Matt. 26:56

3.　". . . He had no beauty or majesty to attract us to him, nothing in his appearance that we should desire him." —Isa.53:2

Jesus was born in a stable, worked in his youth as a carpenter, was raised in Nazareth and was an itinerant preacher.

4.　"Surely he took up our infirmities and carried our sorrows, yet we considered him stricken by God, smitten by him, and afflicted. But he was pierced for our transgressions, he was crushed for our iniquities; the punishment that brought us peace was upon him, and by his wounds we are healed. We all, like sheep, have gone astray, each of us has turned to his own way; and the Lord has laid on him the iniquity of us all." —Isa. 53:4–6

Above: Jesus drives out the pigeon sellers and overturns
the tables of those exchanging and trading coins.
Artist unknown, 1928
Pentecost Evangel

Below: Christ in the Garden of Gethsemane
By Delacroix
Church of St. Paul
St. Louis, MO

5.   "And I will pour out on the house of David and the inhabitants of Jerusalem a spirit of grace and supplication. They will look on me, the one they have pierced, and they will mourn for him as one mourns for an only child, and grieve bitterly for him as one grieves for a first-born son."
   —ZEC. 12:10

These prophecies were fulfilled when Christ's body was pierced and crushed by being nailed on the cross and when he was whipped by the Roman soldiers.

6.   "He was oppressed and afflicted, yet he did not open his mouth; he was led like a lamb to the slaughter, and as a sheep before her shearers is silent, so he did not open his mouth." —ISA. 53:7

"Then Pilate asked him, 'Don't you hear the testimony they are bringing against you?' But Jesus made no reply, not even to a single charge—to the great amazement of the governor." (Mt. 27:13)

7.   "He was assigned a grave with the wicked, and with the rich in his death, though he had done no violence, nor was any deceit in his mouth."
   —ISA. 53:9

Jesus was assigned to be with wicked men because he was scheduled to be buried with two thieves in a common burial plot outside of Jerusalem. But Joseph of Arimathea, a rich man, asked Pilate for Christ's body to prevent him from being buried in a grave with wicked men.

Some have calculated that the mathematical probability of just seven of the 300 prophecies being fulfilled by chance is 1 in 1017. It is impossible to calculate the mathematical probability of all the prophecies coming true. Among extra-biblical sources of Christian evidence for the historical Jesus are several key personal testimonies.

CHRISTIAN SOURCES: NON-BIBLICAL TEXTS

Justin Martyr
   In particular, Christian apologists, Justin Martyr (A.D. 100-165) and Tertullian (A.D. 160-220),[4] asserted in the second century that official archives could prove Jesus legal troubles.[5] These two early fathers of the

Christian church wrote before the Gospels became the prevailing standard. There is evidence Pilate reported the case of Jesus to the Emperor, a letter by Emperor Maxim, in A.D. 311, known as "Memoirs of Pilate," confirms the existence of official records on Jesus.[6]

Justin Martyr wrote twice on the subject, once to the Roman Senate in A.D. 140 and once to Antonius.[7] Justin exemplifies the apologists who manifested an early effort of the Christian church to reconcile faith and reason. He was martyred in Rome in A.D. 165. Born in Palestine, he worked as a philosopher and convert to Christianity. Only three of his many writings exist, two *Apologies*, and *Dialogue with Trypho Judaicus*, (135 B.C.). In *Apology* he wrote:

> "And these things were so done, you may know from the acts made in the time of Pontius Pilate."

Justin Martyr in his *Dialogue* wrote that Jews had seen in Jesus the "son of a carpenter," a sorcerer who could heal the sick.[8] He wrote to the Jew Trypho: "You crucified him." Several other sayings were attributed to Jesus.

In *Dialogue with Trypho*, 17, Justin links Jesus with the Temple incident:

> "He appeared distasteful to you when he cried among you, 'It is written, my house is a house of prayer; but you have made it a den of thieves.' He overthrew also the tables of the money-changers in the Temple . . ."

Papias wrote *Expositions of the Oracles of the Lord* (140 C.E.), but it survives only in fragments and is quoted by Origen and Eusebius. According to Papias, Mark wrote, "accurately all that he remembered of the words and deeds of Christ, but not in order."

Eusebius (A.D. 263—339) was the first to attempt a history of the church on a grand scale. Born in Palestine, imprisoned for his faith, he was Bishop of Caesarea (A.D. 313) and later became a close friend of Emperor Constantine for whom he composed many flattering speeches. His writings include *Chronicles, To Justify Christianity*, and *Church History*.

Church History was the first full length, continuous narrative history from a Christian point of view, giving an account of Christianity in its first three centuries of trial and persecution from the coming of Jesus to the final triumph of Constantine.[9]

Ireneaus

Ireneaus (A.D. 130-200), probably was born at Smyrna a few miles from Ephesus, may have accompanied Polycarp on his journey to Rome (A.D. 154), and was elected as bishop of Lyons in A.D. 178. His literary and religious work survives from early Christian literature.[10] His famous treatise against heresies (A.D. 185), and *In Proof of the Apostolic Preaching* discovered in 1904, list conclusively events of early Christianity.

In various writings he wrote of Christ:

> "For he has made known to us in all wisdom and insight the mystery of his will, according to his purpose which he set for in Christ as a plan for the fullness of time, to unite all things in him, things in heaven and things on earth."[11]

Ignatius

The second bishop of Antioch, Ignatius, left the Christian church seven letters composed en route to martyrdom in Rome. He was put to death during the reign of Trajan and was so enthusiastic to become a martyr he begged the Christians in Rome not to prevent his expected execution. His seven letters are not a systematic treatment of Christian thought, but a witness to his concerns. There was no New Testament at that time, but he certainly knew the Gospel of Matthew and Paul's first letter to the Corinthians:

> "Just as where Jesus Christ is, there is the catholic church."[12]

Ignatius wrote that Jesus Christ:"

> . . . was really born, and ate, and drank . . . was really crucified and died."[13]

Ignatius wrote his letters from A.D. 110 to 117. He wrote:

> "Be ye deaf, therefore, when any man speaketh to you apart from Jesus Christ, who was of the race of David, who was the son of Mary, who was truly born, and ate, and drank, was truly persecuted under Pontius Pilate, was truly crucified and died in the sight of those in heaven and those on earth and those under the earth; who moreover was truly raised from the dead, his Father having raised him, who in like fashion will also raise us also who believe in him . . ."[14]

Ignatius was the first writer known outside of the New Testament to mention the virgin birth of Jesus.

Clement of Rome

Little is known of Clement, one of the early bishops of Rome who died around A.D. 100 and knew Peter and Paul. His name is linked to a letter known as *1 Clement*, an open letter from the church at Rome to the church at Corinth.

The letter sheds interesting light on church life soon after the age of the Apostles, the martyrdoms of Peter and Paul. He quotes extensively from the Old Testament and from the writings of the Apostles.

Marcion

Marcion was born in Sinope, Pontus, on the Black Sea. The son of a bishop, he arrived in Rome about A.D. 140. His garbled Christian views were firmly repudiated by the early church, and he was excommunicated. Tertullian wrote *Against Marcion* in A.D. 207, and regarded him a formidable foe of the true Christian doctrine. Marcion believed that Jesus Christ was not born of a woman but suddenly appeared in the synagogue at Capernium in A.D. 29 as a grown man. His view of Christ was similar to that of the Docetists. He believed that Christ was tried and crucified, and that his resurrection was necessary for salvation.

Marcion rejected the entire Old Testament, but he did accept the 10 letters of Paul.

Nag Hammadi Library

In 1945 a remarkable library of books, discovered in the desert of Southern Egypt, boosted the reliability of the New Testament documents. This collection, the Nag Hammadi library, was found about 370 miles south of Egypt in the town of Hammadi. Among its fifty or so tractates was a copy of the Gospel of Thomas found in a sealed jar. Of the 114 sayings and parables in the Gospel of Thomas, half have parallels in the synoptic Gospels. The versions of the Gospel of Thomas were written in Coptic, the language of ancient Egypt.

The library consists of twelve books, plus eight leaves removed from a thirteenth century book. We learn the history of Gnosticism from the books which takes up about where the history of the Essenes, as documented in the Dead Sea Scrolls, breaks off.[15]

The Gospel of Nicodemus

The Gospel of Nicodemus must have been written to supplement the Gospel accounts on points they did not entirely agree, or to "satisfy either the curiosity or the imagination of the faithful".[16] Some theologians claim the writing is accurate and authentic, while others disagree.[17]

Nicodemus, a Pharisee, twice mentioned as a friend of Jesus (John 3:1; 19:39), is said to have recorded in Hebrew all he had seen and heard concerning the conduct of the chief priests. That record was lost, but Ananias, an officer of the guard being learned in the law, made a search for the reports of that period and assures readers he found "these acts in the Hebrew language and according to God's good pleasure translated them into Greek for the information of all those who call upon the name of the Lord Jesus Christ." This version (A.D. 425) leaves divided opinions as to whether or not Ananias is really the author.

ARCHAEOLOGICAL SOURCES

Archeology confirms the existence of key New Testament figures like Pontius Pilate and the high priest Caiaphas in the trial and execution of Jesus. In 1961, researchers found a three foot by two foot Roman dedicatory inscription bearing Pilate's name on the sandy mounds by the Mediterranean shore at Caesarea in the ruins of a temple built in honor of Tiberius. This plaque recorded a building commissioned by "Pontius Pilate, Prefect of Judea," is the first and only archeological remnant of the fabled Roman governor.[18]

An unusual burial custom developed—the reburial of the bones of the deceased in smallish, rectangular bone boxes called "ossuaries." About a year after the burial when the flesh had decayed, the bones were deposited with bones from previous burials in a repository. Some scholars explain the Biblical phrases *"gathered to their fathers," (Judges 2:10; 2 Kings 22:20), "buried with his fathers" (2 Kings 8:24), or "slept with his fathers (2 Kings 13:13)*, is what is meant by such burials. Ossuaries were used in the late Second Temple Period ending with the Roman destruction of the temple.

In 1990, the remains of Caiaphas were discovered by workers excavating for a park and road development in the Jerusalem Peace Forest. The single cave burial tomb belonged to a small family but the large number of ossuaries indicates use over a relatively long period. The disarray of the tomb indicates the cave was robbed in antiquity.

The outstanding feature of this tomb is the unique occurrence of the name "Caiaphas" to represent the well known high priestly family.

The name "Yehosef bar Qafa" (Joseph, son of Caiaphas) is written on the side. The ossuaries were decorated with geometric designs and plant motifs. No human faces appear, strictly interpreting the second Commandment forbidding graven images (Exod. 20:4; Deut. 5:8).

One-half mile south of Jerusalem at the southeast end of the Hinnom Valley lies an important archeological site containing burial caves dating to the Herodian Period (37 B.C–A.D. 70) known as Akeldama or "Field of Blood" (Matt. 27:3-9; Acts 1:18-19). It includes the likely burial place of the family of the high priest Annas. Eusebius (A.D. 335), Emperor Constantine, and Jerome (A.D. 400), all identify this place with confidence as the Field of Blood.

In the early 1980's large-scale excavations began at Sepphoris, three miles northwest of Nazareth. Archeologists discovered a striking new perspective on the kind of society in which Jesus grew up. Though not mentioned in the Gospels, it plays a prominent part in the first century Jewish history of Flavius Josephus. Gleaming marble theaters and surrounding public buildings are powerfully persuasive symbols of the new, Roman way of culture, economics, and life.

JEWISH SOURCES

Josephus

A Pharisee of priestly descent, Josephus courted Roman favor and lived in Rome after Nero's persecution of the Christians and during Domitian's reign. Eusebius, Origen and other writers often cite Josephus' work.[19] Josephus may have mentioned Jesus without believing he was the Messiah.[20]

Josephus, born shortly after Jesus died, was a general in charge of Galilee during the Jews revolt against Rome, and was a keen participant in, and an observer of the tumult of the time. As a follower of the Pharisees, he was thoroughly versed in the teachings of the written and oral law. As a committed Jew, he was highly sensitive to the sufferings and helplessness of the Jews in the grip of Imperial Rome.

Josephus did all of his writing in Rome, and his writings gave valuable information about the Jews from the Maccabean revolt to the fall of Masada. He wrote to justify his own conduct and to commend what was most attractive in Judaism to the Romans. He condemned the Zealots and praised his patrons Vespasian and Titus.

Josephus first wrote *The Jewish War*, then *Antiquities of the Jews*, and finally his autobiography, *The Life*. He admired Thucydides and Polybius, grand historians of the time, was a student of political power and a master of historical narrative. From his writings we can construct the framework within which Jesus' life, trial, crucifixion and resurrection were played out.[21]

Josephus, writing his famous four volume work *Antiquities of the Jews*, (A.D. 81-96), speaks of Jesus twice, once casually in connection with the stoning of James "the brother of Jesus who is called Christ," and again in a longer passage:

"About the same time came Jesus, a wise man, if one call him a man at all. For he was a performer of miracles and a teacher of all men, who received the truth with joy. He attracted many Jews and many Greeks. He was the Christ. Pilate sentenced him to die on the cross, having been urged to do so by the noblest of our citizens; but His followers did not forsake him, for he appeared to them on the third day, being alive again, just as God-sent prophets had predicted this and a thousand other miracles concerning him. And up til now the people of the Christians, who are named after him, have not disappeared."[22]

Great debate over ancient writings never come to rest, especially the notorious Testimonium, the supposed "testimony" to Jesus' ministry in death in Josephus' *Antiquities*. Some experts conclude that Josephus' version is the result of later Christian editing by scribes.[23]

The Testimonium is silent on why Jesus is put to death. It could be that Josephus simply did not know, that he suppressed references to the Jewish Messiah, keeping with his general tendency. It could be Josephus understood Jesus' huge success to be sufficient grounds.

Josephus records the martyrdom of the Apostle James, the brother of Jesus, who was stoned to death by the Jews after having been convicted by the Sanhedrin.

From his works we construct the framework within which Jesus' life, trial, crucifixion, and resurrection were played out. We can resurrect the historical Jesus by drawing a portrait from the intricate of time, place, and structures.[24]

Historians carefully confirm the Greek *Testimonium Flavianum*, a revision of the original Josephus text from *Antiquities*, that: Jesus lived in the time of Pilate and was ordered crucified by him; he did "paradoxical" deeds; he exercised the function of teacher and found many disciples among the Jews; and he frequently sojourned at the Mount of Olives and had done so shortly before his death.[25]

Philo

Philo, an orthodox Jew,[26] who is referred to as "Philo the Jew" or "Philo of Alexandria," was born about 30 B.C. His lifetime extended from Herod the Great. He describes a visit in A.D. 40 by a delegation of Jews from Alexandria to the Roman Emperor Caligula. Though he was a contemporary of Jesus of Nazareth and in constant touch with the tense situations amid which Jesus' activity would have taken place, he does not mention Jesus. He does refer to Pontius Pilate and the incident involving the placing of "shields coated with gold" in Herod's palace.[27]

He came from a wealthy family, later gained an appointment as a Roman procurator in Palestine in A.D. 46, and was made prefect of Egypt by Nero. He turned Roman legions upon the Jews and during one of the riots 50,000 Jews were killed.

Philo lived when the temple was still standing and visited it at least once. Philo states that "not to commit any sin at all" is the property of God and perhaps also of a "divine man." This passage is of considerable interest and possibly refers to the sinlessness of Jesus.[28]

Philo knew nothing of oral tradition on which Talmudic law was ultimately based, knew the Pentateuch,[29] knew no Hebrew, and was simply a practicing Jew.

The Dead Sea Scrolls

In the spring of 1947, a bedouin boy while tending his goats tossed a stone into a cave at Qumran on the northwest corner of the Dead Sea. Hearing the stone strike something, he found a number of scrolls in large clay jars. The jars had protected them from the harsh climate.

Scholars soon realized the scrolls contained ancient documents hidden away prior to the Roman siege of Jerusalem. The discovery was of immense significance, from the study of the first century Judaism and early Christianity, portraying the view of Jews contemporary with the New Testament era.

The scrolls contained differing forms of Jewish text of Scripture as Jesus or Paul would have known. Apart from Esther, at least a portion of every book in the Hebrew Bible was found at Qumran, including all of the book of Isaiah.

The Great Scroll of the book of Isaiah, which was a thousand years older than any copy then in existence, was identical except for a few variations.

The greatest scroll was the Temple Scroll which has a special history.[30] It was found in Cave No. 11. The Temple Scroll is the longest of all Dead Sea Scrolls, about nine meters and contains the description of the plan of the temple and many other discoveries. It was first published in 1977 and in English some years later.

The scrolls at the Qumran plateau were written between 250 B.C. and A.D. 50. The evidence provided by coins found at the site, together with signs of the destruction of the buildings by the Romans in A.D. 68, make these findings quite firm.[31]

The scrolls are legalistic, obsessive about ritual cleanliness, and harshly exclusive.

We are aided by the science of paleography (the science of dating ancient manuscripts according to the stage of evolution of the actual writing or script), and Carbon 14 testing.[32]

All the scrolls have been acquired by Hebrew University. Some are on display at the Shrine of the Book in Jerusalem.

The scrolls are the most intriguing source of evidence for understanding early Christianity. Unlike the New Testament which has undergone centuries of ecclesiastical editing, the huge cache of Hebrew and Aramaic texts is the only contemporary manuscript evidence of religious thought from first century Judea. Consisting of some 800 separate documents—oracles, commentaries, legal codes, Scripture, and speculations about the eminent arrival of a messiah—the scrolls are an unparalleled opportunity for scholars to examine the beliefs of at least one group of Jesus' contemporaries.

Talmud

The circle being drawn around credible historical facts about the life and death of Jesus also includes material from Jesus' own religious tradition. As a Jew himself, Jesus ministered primarily to fellow Jews.

His Jewish community was a religiously fertile one. Eminent religious lawyers like the great Rabbi Hillel applied the Pentateuch and other sacred

Jewish writings to contemporary problems and questions and collected their insights. Eventually these insights, written in what are called "Baraitas," were edited and codified in the "Mishnah." Later, Jewish leaders commented on the Mishnah and, in turn, collected those commentaries into the "Gemara." Eventually, after 300 years, the Mishnah and Gemara formed the two parts of the "Talmud," the fundamental code of Jewish civil and religious law and, for observant Jews, supplement the Old Testament.

At points the Mishnah confirms Christian writings. The Talmud agrees that Jesus was born without a father and that he performed miracles.

Some writings in the Baraitas refer to a certain "Ben Stada," later identified with Jesus of Nazareth. One part of a Baraita provides strong indication that as a small boy Jesus and his parents fled Palestine for Egypt because of a cruel king and that when grown Jesus attracted a large following.

Another section speaks of Jesus' death:

> "On the eve of the Passover they hanged Yeshu (of Nazareth) and the herald went before him for 40 days saying, '(Yeshu of Nazareth) is going forth to be stoned in that he hath practised sorcery and beguiled and led astray Israel. Let everyone knowing aught in his defence come and plead for him,' but they found naught in his defence and hanged him on the eve of Passover."

Following this Baraita, came remarks of the Amora "Ulla":

> "And do you suppose that for (Yeshu of Nazareth) there was any right of appeal? He was a beguiler, and the merciful one hath said: No thou shalt not spare neither shalt thou conceal him. It is otherwise with Yeshu, for he was near to the civil authority."

> "Tradition tells us on the eve (of the Sabbath) of the Passover Yeshu (of Nazareth) was hanged. A crier went before him for 40 days: He should be stoned, because he has bewitched, and seduced, and alienated Israel. Let everyone who knows of a justification for him come and establish it for him. But no justification was found for him, and so he was hanged on the eve of the Passover."[33]

These Baraita show that ancient Jews thought their ancestors were involved in and even responsible for the death of Jesus.

Archko Volume

One book, a hoax, claims to have found in an Istanbul library the report of Caiaphas to the Sanhedrin concerning the execution of Jesus.[34] The report purports to contain Caiaphas' description of Jesus:

> "He took but little care of his health or person; cared not for his own relatives. He traveled mostly on foot in the company of his disciples and some suspicious women, and lived on the charity of his friends. He seemed to take no notice of the political affairs of his country; would as soon be governed by one nation as another. In fact, it seemed if he had any preference it was for the Romans. It seems that he became so infatuated that he really thought he was the head of the Kingdom of Heaven. This manner of preaching, along with his presumption, aroused his enemies to a powerful pitch, and it was all I could do to keep the Zealots from mobbing him in the Temple. They had no confidence in a doctrine that set the Jewish laws at naught, and mocked the priesthood of God, and they with the Sadducees and Scribes were not willing to submit to a man who acknowledged no authority higher than himself, and was seemingly endeavoring to overturn everything that they had held more sacred and dearer than life . . . indeed, the conduct of Jesus was so strange and incompatible with the interests of the Jews as a nation, that it seemed to me that he was a subject employed by the Romans to keep the Jews submissive and obedient to all their tyranny and abuse."

The Jewish rabbinic law probably directed two court clerks to write down the speeches pleading for acquittal and conviction. No proof of such recordings in the case of Jesus have emerged.

SECULAR SOURCES

Tacitus

If one totaled up the non-Christian sources of information on Jesus, a single page would hold it all.[35] Other than two passages in the *Antiquities* of Josephus, and the three Latin writers, the New Testament gives us, for all practical purposes, the history of Jesus.

Publius Cornelius Tacitus (A.D. 55-115) in *The Annals* relates how Nero escaped blame for the burning of Rome by blaming the Christians. Tacitus wrote of the fire at Rome and the ensuing persecution of Christians:

Above:
Christ Driving the Money Changers from the Temple
El Greco
The William Hood Dunwoody Fund.

Below:
The Crucifixion
Clemente
Germany

A disaster followed, whether accidental or treacherously contrived by the emperor, is uncertain, as authors have given both accounts, worse, however, and more dreadful than any which have happened to this city by the violence of fire. It had its beginning in that part of the circus which adjoins the Palatine and Caelian hills, where, amid the shops containing inflammable wares, the conflagration both broke out and instantly became so fierce and so rapid from the wind that it seized in its grasp the entire length of the circus. For here there were no houses fenced in by solid masonry, or temples surrounded by walls, or any other obstacle to interpose delay. The blaze in its fury ran first through the level portions of the city, then rising to the hills, while it again devastated every place below them, it outstripped all preventive measures; so rapid was the mischief and so completely at its mercy the city, with those narrow winding passages and irregular streets, which characterized old Rome. Added to this were the wailings of terror-stricken women, the feebleness of age, the helpless inexperience of childhood, the crowds who sought to save themselves or others, dragging out the infirm or waiting for them, and by their hurry in the one case, by their delay in the other, aggravating the confusion. Often, while they looked behind them, they were intercepted by flames on their side or in their face. Or if they reached a refuge close at hand, when this too was seized by the fire, they found that even places which they had imagined to be remote, were involved in the same calamity. At last, doubting what they should avoid or whither betake themselves, they crowded the streets or flung themselves down in the fields, while some who had lost their all, even their very daily bread, and others out of love for their kinsfolk, whom they had been unable to rescue, perished, though escape was open to them. And no one dared to stop mischief, because of incessant menaces from a number of persons who forbade the extinguishing of the flames, because again others openly hurled brands, and kept shouting that there was no one who gave them authority, either seeking to plunder more freely, or obeying orders . . .

Nero fastened the guilt and inflicted the most exquisite tortures on a class hated for their abominations, called Christians by the populace. Christus, from whom the name had its origin, suffered the extreme penalty during the reign of Tiberius at the hands of one of our procurators, Pontius Pilate, and a most mischievous superstition, thus checked for the moment, again broke out not only in Judaea, and the first source of the evil, but even in Rome, where all things hideous and shameful from every part of the world find their centre and become popular. Accordingly, an arrest was first made of all who pleaded guilty; then, upon their information, an immense multitude was convicted, not so much of the crime of firing the city, as of hatred against mankind. Mockery of every sort was added to their deaths. Covered with the skins of beasts, they were torn by dogs and perished, or were nailed to crosses, or were doomed to the flames and burnt, to serve as a nightly illumination, when daylight had expired.

Nero offered his gardens for the spectacle, and was exhibiting a show in the circus, while he mingled with the people in the dress of a charioteer or stood aloft on a car. Hence, even for criminals who deserved extreme and exemplary punishment, there arose a feeling of compassion; for it was not, as it seemed, for the public good, but to glut one man's cruelty, that they were being destroyed.[36]

Both Josephus and Tacitus were aristocratic historians, the former from the Jewish priestly elite, the latter from the Roman consoler nobility. Tacitus was profoundly faithful to the senatorial ideals of the Roman republic, Josephus to the priestly ideals of the Jewish theocracy.

Pliny

Pliny the Younger, Governor of Bithyna, writing to Emperor Trajan in A.D. 112 reports that Christians were rapidly spreading "superstition and . . . were in the habit of meeting on a certain fixed day before it was light, when they sang a hymn to Christ, as to a God, and bound themselves by a solemn oath not to commit any fraud . . ."

The Roman writer Lucian scorned Christians and described Christ as "the man who was crucified in Palestine because he introduced this new cult into the world."[37] These remarks came from men who were very hostile toward Christianity and not well informed about it. Yet it shows Christianity was widespread by the early second century A.D. and the historical existence of Christ was accepted as a fact, even by his enemies. They viewed him as a religious fanatic who had gained more of a following than he deserved.[38]

Greek and Latin historians of the first and second centuries also wrote of Christ. The famous Roman philosopher and politician Celsus mentioned Jesus by name:

"Celsus says expressly that Mary had been divorced by her husband, a carpenter by trade, for adultery; and she gave birth to Jesus secretly, that poverty forced him to earn his living in Egypt as a day laborer, that he learned magic there, and that he returned and by virtue of skill publicly declared himself God."[39]

Sarapion's Letter

Among the oldest secular reports on the death of Jesus is an ancient private second century letter from a Syrian, Mara bar Sarapion, from Samosata, addressed to his son studying in Edessa[40] He speaks quite freely of "our gods" and bases his statement that "the wise king is not dead." The name of Jesus is not used, and it is probable the writer was not familiar with his name. Some scholars place the letter in the first century:[41]

"What good did it do to the Athenians to kill Socrates, for which deed they were punished with famine and pestilence? Or what did it avail the citizens of Samos to burn Pythagoras since their country was covered over with sand in one moment? Or what did it avail the Jews to execute their wise king, since their kingdom was taken from them from that time? For God justly avenged those three wise men . . . the Jews were slaughtered and driven from their kingdom, and lived dispersed everywhere . . ."[42]

Acts of Pilate

Students of the New Testament should study the "other gospels," not accepted into the Canon of the New Testament, because they are helpful in the study of early Christianity. The so-called *Acts of Pilate* may have been invented to deal with Jesus' death and resurrection and may be a forgery.[43]

Pilate probably made a full report of the proceedings to Rome. Pilate left his office involuntarily just before the Passover in A.D. 36. There was no procurator holding power of life and death in his hand in Judea until the ascension of Herod Agrippa, in A.D. 41. Some believe the vacancy during this period was ordered on account of the condemnation of Jesus.[44]

No reason exists to assume the procurator of Judea had to send a report to Rome about trials for high treason, especially when the accused was without the rights of a Roman citizen.

Imperial Rome received dispatches from the provinces at regular intervals. These included reports of major events, trials and executions ordered by Roman governors. A Roman official probably made a record of the trial at the time, but it has been lost. Reportedly, Archives of Jesus' trial existed in the middle of the second century but have been destroyed.[45]

Suetonius

Gaius Suetonius Tranquillus (A.D. 69—140), Emperor Hadrian's secretary wrote history, natural history, and grammar.[46]

In his book *Life of Claudius*, Suetonius mentions "Chresto" or "Christus," an instigator of the uprisings in Rome under Emperor Claudius who reigned A.D. 41-54. But this can hardly be linked to Jesus since there were no Christians physically present in Rome during the reign of Claudius, and Christians were "a . . . sect professing a new and mischievous religious belief."[47] Emergent Christian communities took great pains not to create disturbances. Suetonius assumes Chresto was residing in Rome and still alive, and his report obviously referred to rebellious Jews, not Christians.

Undeniable Proof of Christ

Non-Christian sources in our historical search substantiate three important facts:

1.   That Jesus was crucified on the strength of a sentence pronounced by Pilate, the Roman governor;

2.   That Pilate's action against Jesus took place at the instigation of the Jewish authorities; and

3.   Since the Jews in the trial cannot have been confined to mere denunciation to Pilate, they participated decisively in the events which led to the execution.

Jesus' death by execution under Pilate is as sure as anything historical can ever be.

Consider what we know about Jesus if we knew nothing at all from Christian sources. We would know about Jesus from Josephus and Tacitus. These two writers agree on three points: There was a movement, an execution, and the movement continued to spread.

We learn of the environment in which Jesus lived, the political conditions, and the religious and ethical ideals which prevailed. We learn from Josephus, Tacitus, Suetonius, and the Talmud Mishrash that Jesus did live and die in Judea during the Roman occupation.[48] It is simply impossible for a purely fabricated presentment of the figure of Jesus to have so firmly gripped people's imaginations.

In the New Testament we find "facts plus faith."[49] Yet, none but the most cynical skeptic denies that the New Testament is a good source of facts. Said John Stuart Mill:

> "It is of no use to say that Christ as exhibited in the Gospels is not historical, and that we do not know how much of what is admirable has been super-added by the tradition of his followers. Who among his disciples, or among their proselytes, was capable of inventing the sayings ascribed to Jesus, or of imaging the life and the character revealed in the Gospels?"

Should we believe the New Testament books when they describe the death of Jesus? We should, as well as the Old Testament, since they are inspired of God: *"All scripture is given by inspiration of God"* (2 *Tim. 3:16, nkjv*). They were written and circulated while many eyewitnesses were still alive who could correct them if any mistakes had been made. There is no evidence that anyone at the time had any doubts about the death of Jesus.

In a court of law, we believe the testimony of an "eyewitness" over "hearsay" testimony of someone who was not there at the time. John was an eyewitness.:

> "This is the disciple who testifies to these things and who wrote them down. We know that his testimony is true. Jesus did many other things as well. If every one of them were written down, I suppose that even the whole world would not have room for the books that would be written."
> —JOHN 21:24-25

John " . . . came as a witness to testify concerning that light, so that through him all men might believe..as a witness to the light . . . ."

—JOHN 1:7-8

Clearly, there is ample evidence to fairly render a verdict on the trial of Christ.

Christianity is the only religion in the world based upon historical evidence. The Bible doesn't call us to "blind faith" but always to a faith in those things established by evidence. And the evidence for Jesus is overwhelming. No one can disbelieve in Christ because of the lack of evidence.

Jesus Christ founded the largest religion in history. Christianity is twice as large as its closest competitor. Today there are 1,320,000,000 who claim to be Christians.

Beginning with a handful of hesitant followers in the obscure Roman province of Judea, Christianity has grown to become the nominal faith of approximately one-third of the planet's population. It is spread more widely and deeply rooted among more people than any other religion in the history of mankind. From the attacks of Celsius and Lucian of Samosata in the second century to those of Voltaire in the 18th century, Karl Marx in the 19th century, and Adolph Hitler in the 20th century, Christianity has not only held its own but continued to expand. It has an amazing ability within the faith to periodically reform and renew itself.

The hallmarks of apostolic Christianity were simplicity, community, evangelism, and love. The community of love was sealed by baptism. Early Christians were aggressively evangelistic, sharing their new-found life in Christ with others less fortunate.

But the key to understanding the growth of early Christian movement was the resurrection of Christ. Their master had conquered death and appeared to many of them in person. They had discovered a different way of life, forgiveness of sin, peace with God, hope for the future, a higher ethical code, and life after death.

The scope and extent of Christian growth in the past 2000 years is breathtaking—the renewal, reform, periods of evangelism and missionary activity. It was Jesus' final command to his followers to *go into all of the world and preach the Gospel*, to "make disciples of all nations."

Some people say Jesus was a myth: He never really existed. The historical evidences of his existence are greater than those in support of any other event in ancient history—no candid scholar could reject them without also renouncing his belief in every event recorded in ancient history.[50]

The four biographies of Christ in the Scripture and the testimony of Gospel historians is more accurate and detailed than that of any other secular historian.

Secular historians and writers of antiquity who refer to Christ or Christianity include: Eusebius, Marcion, Origen, Tertullian, Clement, Tacitus; Suetonius; Pliny the Younger; Epictetus; Lucian; Aristides; Galenus; Lampridus; Dio Cassius; Hinnerius; Libanius; Ammianus; Marcellinus; Eunapius; Zosimus and Minucius Felix. Others who have written books against Christianity (which name Christ) include: Lucian; Celsus; Porphyry; Hierocles; and Julian the Apostate.[51]

There has never been anyone like Jesus Christ.[52] The more his life is studied the more impressive it is. No person has walked the face of the earth that has had such an influence—and his influence is still growing today. Jesus Christ was the greatest person this world has ever known and the greatest human who ever lived in this world.

No one who witnessed the death of Jesus would have guessed that someday this image of a man being crucified on a cross would become an emblem of the world religion. Yet, wherever you travel in the world today you are likely to find this image.

The fact that Jesus existed is beyond question. For the historian, however, there remains the problem of who he was and where he came from. What did he want? Why was he followed and by whom? What crime did he commit to be convicted and sentenced to death?

ENDNOTES

[1] Cobern, Camden M. *The New Archeological Discoveries*. (Funk & Wagnalls Co.: London: 1917), pgs. 3-97. The Chester Beatty Papyrus I, at the Chester Beatty Museum, Dublin, Ireland, also known as Papyrus 45 is the earliest existent copy of the four Gospels, dating to 200- 250 CE. It has one chapter of John, eight of Luke, and ten of Mark. The sequence was well known between 180 and 200 CE by Ireneaus. In the second century Christians, Marcian and Tatian, also wrote about it. Crossan, John Dominic. "Why Christians Must Search for the Historical Jesus," *Bible Review*, Vol. XII, No. 2, April 1996, pg. 38.

[2] Wilson, Bill. *The Best of Josh McDowell*. (Here's Life Publishers: San Bernadino, CA: 1990), p. 44.

[3] Some missing pages were found only recently at St. Catherine's Monastery. Wilson, Ian. *Jesus the Evidence*. (Harper & Row: 1984), p. 13.

[4] *First Apology*, pgs. 35-48. Tertullian was the first major Christian author to write in Latin (A.D. 196-212). He lived in Carthage, capital of the Roman province of Africa.

[5] Sherwin-White. *Roman Society and Roman Law in the New Testament*, pgs. 100-155.

[6] Scheitweiler, F. *New Testament Apocrypha*, Vol. I., pgs. 444-447.

[7] Published in English by W. Reeves in Leipsig, Germany, in 1709.

[8] *Dialogus Cum Trypho Judaicus*, by Justin, Ch. 69.

[9] Chestnut, Glen E. *The First Christian Histories*. (Editions Beauchesne: Paris: 1977), p. 31.

[10] Cobern, Camden M. *The Archeological Discoveries*, 2nd Ed. (Funk and Wagnalls Co.: London: 1917), p. 256.

[11] Goergen, Donald J. *The Jesus of Christian History*, Vol. 3. (The Liturgical Press: Collegeville, MN: 1992), pgs. 46-49.

[12] Ignatius. *Smyrn*, 8.

[13] Ignatius. *Trall*, 9.

[14] Ignatius. *Trall*, 9.

[15] *The Nag Hammadi Library in English*, James M. Robinson, General Editor. (Harper: San Francisco: 1978).

[16] Goguel, M. *Jesus and the Origins of Christianity*, Vol. I, p. 158.

[17] Von Dobschuetz, E. *Der Prozess Jesus Nach Den Akten Pilate*, Vol. 3, p. 89.

[18] Pilate is often erroneously referred to as a "Procurator" (an economic leader) but, as we now know he was a Prefect (a military commander).

[19] Origen was the greatest scholar and most prolific author of the early church, born into a Christian family in Alexandria in A.D. 185. His *Hexapla* was a great piece of biblical scholarship. His major first work on theology *First Principles* set forth the Christian doctrine systematically: God, Christ, and the Holy Spirit.

[20] Brown, Raymond E. *The Death of the Messiah*, Vol. 1. (Doubleday: New York: 1993), p. 374.

[21] Rivkin, Ellis. *What Crucified Jesus?* (Abingdon Press: Nashville: 1984).

[22] Josephus. *Antiquities of the Jews*, 17.3.3. (Harvard University Press, 1926). *Antiquities* was rewritten and copied by Christian scribes, and even though they may have re-written the text, it remains highly probable Josephus included Jesus in his account of the period. Josephus discussed John the Baptist and other prophetic figures such as Theudas and the Egyptian.

[23] Meyer, John P. "Jesus and Josephus: A Modest Proposal," *The Catholic Biblical Quarterly*, Vol. 52, No. 1, Jan. 1990, p. 80.

[24] Rivkin, Ellis. *What Crucified Jesus?* (Abingdon Press: Nashville, TN: 1984), p. 15.

[25] Bienert, W. *Der alteste nichtchristliche Jesusbericht*. (Halle: 1936), pgs. 258-263.

[26] Williamson, Ronald. *Jews in the Hellenistic World: Philo*. (Cambridge University Press: 1989), p. 3.

[27] Philo, *Legum Allegoriae*, Period 299.

[28] Williamson, Ronald. *Jews in the Hellenistic World: Philo*. (Cambridge University Press: 1989), p. 45.

[29] Goodenough, Erwin R. *An Introduction to Philo Judaeus*. (Yale University: New Haven, CT: 1940), p. 14.

[30] Yadin, *The Temple Scroll: The Hidden Law of the Dead Sea Sect.* (London: Weidenfeld & Nicholson: 1985).

[31] De Vaux, R. *Archeology and the Dead Sea Scrolls*; Thiering, Barbara. *Jesus and the Riddle of the Dead Sea Scrolls.* (Harper: San Francisco: 1992), p. 8.

[32] Milik, J.T. *Ten Years of Discovery in the Wilderness of Judea.* (London: SCM: 1959), p. 58.

[33] It is questionable who wrote this Baraita, it is anonymous and the date is indecisive. Many suppose it was written at the time of Rabbi Akiba and Bar Kokhba when many Christians were being punished because they would not renounce the Messiahship of Jesus.

[34] McIntosh, Dr. and Twyman, Dr. "The Archeological Writings of the Sanhedrin and Talmuds of the Jews," *The Archko Volume*, Ch. 5, pgs. 97-116 (translations of the manuscripts in Constantinople from the Vatican Library).

[35] The Christian Roman Emperor Justinian destroyed the created famous library in Alexandria—which contained much of the wisdom of the world—in A.D. 500. Very few of the mighty books survived, and very few of the priceless parchments written by sages. Thus, humanity had been forever denied access to the gathered learning, knowledge, science, literature, poetry, and enlightenment of ages previous to Christ—all in the name of "preserving the purity of Christianity from the corruption of pagan writings." Caldwell, Taylor and Stearn, Jess. *I, Judas.* (Atheneum: New York: 1977).

[36] Tacitus, *The Annals*, XV:38 and 44.

[37] Lucian. *The Passing of Peregrinus.* William Hernemann Ltd.: London: 1936, pgs. 13-15.

[38] Packer, James I., Tenney, Merrill C. and White, William, Jr. *The Bible Almanac.* (Thomas Nelson Publishers: Nashville: 1980), p. 511.

[39] Mendelssohn, H. *Jesus: Rebell oder Erloser.* (Hamburg, Germany: 1981), p. 16.

[40] Aufhauser, J. *Antike Jesus Zeugnisse*, 2nd Ed., 1925, pgs. 5-11; Cureton, William. *Spicilegium Syriacum*, (1855), pgs. 43-48.

[41] Brown, Raymond E. *The Death of the Messiah*, Vol 1. (Doubleday: New York: 1993), p. 382.

[42] Frickey, Weddig. *The Court-Martial of Jesus.* (Grove, Weidenfeld Press: New York: 1987), p. 45.

[43] Craveri, M. *The Life of Jesus.* (Grove Press: New York: 1967), p. 407.

[44] Ayway, Srinivasa S. "The Legality of the Trial of Jesus," *Madras Law Journal*, Mylapore, India. (Platt & Peck Co.: New York: 1915), p. 116.

[45] Justin Martyr, Apol. 1.35.9; Tertullian, Marc. 4.17 19; Eusebius, Hist. Eccl. 2.2.1-4.

[46] Rolfe, J.C. *Suetonius*, Vol. 1. (Harvard University Press: 1913).

[47] Suetonius. *Nero.* (G. P. Pulmans Sons: New York: 1935), p. 111.

[48] Herford, R. Travers. *Christianity in Talmud and Mishnah.* (London: 1905), pgs. 401-436.

[49] Hunter, Archibald M. *The Work and Words of Jesus.* (Westminster Press: Philadelphia: 1950), p. 16.

[50] Lawson, J. Gilchrist. *Greatest Thoughts About Jesus Christ.* (Richard R. Smith, Inc.: New York: 1919), p. 160.

[51] Kennedy, D. James. *Why I Believe.* (Word Publishing: Dallas) p. 96.

[52] Many school administrators forbid mention of and direct teachings of the Bible in American classrooms. What a pity! The most historical and authoritative book ever written is somehow denied to our children whose intellect is directed in more "politically correct" directions. Josephus, Flavius. *Antiquities of the Jews*, XIV 10.11.4. *The Jewish Wars*, I VII 5. According to Josephus, "Owing to perpetual wars, the Jews were no longer capable of revolting against anybody."

"Where is the one who has been born king of the Jews? We saw his star in the east and have come to worship him."

—Matt. 2:2

Chapter Three

The Times

THE LIFE AND DEATH of Jesus remains a tantalizing mystery. It is known that he was born in the tiny village of Bethlehem some 40 years after the death of Julius Caesar. His death is documented in the Gospels and by oral tradition, but the search for the truth and the meaning of that awful Friday continues. My study, as a criminal trial attorney, is focused on the events leading to the trial and death of Jesus. *But what about the world that Jesus was born into?* The mystery of his life and death can be partly solved by a look at the environment Jesus lived in.

At the time of Christ the Roman Empire was over 700 years of age and growing. The banners of Rome snapped in breezes along the Rhine and Danube Rivers, the Atlas Mountains of North Africa, across Portugal, Syria, Belgium, Egypt, and over much of the civilized world.

History

Rome

Founded by Romulus in the middle of the eighth century B.C., the Roman monarchy survived for two and one-half centuries until it became a republic. That republic grew because of a stunningly successful—and durable—military.

The Roman army lasted longer than any other military institution in history. It began with citizen soldiers and ended with long term professionals. It started with the protection of Rome and climaxed with the conquest of the world.

It was ever changing from decade to decade. When its infantry was defeated by barbarian horsemen the Roman legion acquired horses. When the spear was outgunned by the slingshot, Rome trained cohorts to use the new weapons. It copied and invented. In time of war it recruited all males between 17 and 60 who could walk, and all those under the age of 47 had to fight in the field.

It failed only once in it's long march against Hannibal.

The real strength of the army lay in its heavy infantry. In a legion of 4500 men, each man had a large medal shield, a metal helmet, and a leather cuirass which protected the soldier from neck to naval. Half carried short Spanish thrusting and cutting swords; the other half carried throwing spears.

A legion, commanded by a tribune, was broken into groups of 120 men and like a chess piece each advanced into battle to fight and retire. Spaces were left in between so that those in front could retreat while alternate groups advanced through the gaps. One group sent forth a shower of spears and then another group followed using short swords.

The policy of ancient Rome was to extend and hold her possessions by force of arms. Her trophies were the treasures of conquered provinces and chained captives, and her theory was "Might makes Right." Her invincible legions conquered the civilized world. "Wherever you are, remember that you are equally within the power of the conqueror," said Cicero to the exiled Marcellus.

Not only did Rome's well organized army survive, so did its political system.

Even after Caesar was assassinated, caesarism remained. Surviving consul Antony took the reins of state but faced a rebellion led by Brutus and Cassius. In 42 B.C. at Philippi the forces of Antony and Octavian were successful in battle which ended with the deaths of Brutus and Cassius. The Republic was at an end.

On September 2, 31 B.C., Actium witnessed one of the most momentous battles in history. The forces of Octavian, Caesar's adopted grandson, were victorious. Antony and Cleopatra fled to Egypt where the following year they committed suicide. The Roman world now only had one master, Octavian, who controlled 60 legions and 900 warships.

The Roman ship of state began to move slowly but inevitably toward the degeneracy and depravity that signaled doom. That degeneracy was reflected in Rome's leader at the time of Christ. Tiberius Caesar was a morbid, jealous, and capricious tyrant. The slightest suggestion of treason in any part of his empire roused his suspicious temperament to intense activity. Tacitus records fifty-two cases of prosecutions for treason during his reign, many for flimsy and trivial causes. Tiberius appointed Pilate to the small post of procurator of Palestine on the endorsement of Pilate's wife and a certain confidant and spy named Segasejamus.

By the beginning of the Christian era the Roman religion had fallen into contempt. The family institution declined. The marital relationship was a mockery and a sham. The humane spirit vanished from Roman hearts and slavery was the curse of every province of the empire. Corruption and barbarism pervaded every form of Roman life. The city of Rome was a hub around which revolved the wheel of the empire, a marvel of cultural laxness, business efficiency, gutter politics, of enormous strength but cheap chicanery.

Palestine

Some six decades before the birth of Jesus, Roman legions brought a final end to the freedom of the Jewish state. In 63 B.C., General Pompey entered Jerusalem after a three month siege and ended a period of independence where Jews had governed themselves for the first time in centuries. This freedom arose from the leadership of Judas Maccabaeus and his brother Jonathan years earlier. Known as the Maccabaen Wars, these conflicts went well for the Jews until 134 B.C. when Syrian forces began defeating Jewish forces. The Jews could no longer hold their capital.

When the Romans entered the city, they spared none. Men, women and children, old and young, tender girls and aged women, were all slaughtered like sheep. In the winter of 63, the orgy of slaughter counted the death of 12,000 Jews.[1]

When Pompey profanely set foot in the Holy of Holies in the Temple, he was astonished by what he found. He was amazed by its magnificence—the censers of solid gold, the spice cups, the libathion cups and lamps, and the heaps of offertory money, none of which he touched. On the other hand, the Roman general was haunted by what was not in that sanctuary, as much as by what was. There was no visible god, no idol, no statue, no Delphic oracle, no inscription. The sanctuary was empty. Pompey expected to find there a mighty god, some monstrous deity of the sort worshiped by the Egyptians—but he found an empty sanctuary, a temple dedicated to an Unseen and Invisible God.[2]

By the time Herod the Great came to the throne (37 B.C.) the royal city and the entire land of Israel was a wilderness. During the 30 years which elapsed before Herod was designated puppet king, more than 100,000 Jews were killed, the pick of the nation, healthy, mainly young men, and the most enthusiastic who had refused to suffer the foreign yoke.

In the political ferment which followed the death of Herod, there was a great and wild fury that spread itself over the nation. There were riots, reprisals, and Romans killed dissidents and rebels whenever they appeared. Over 2,000 Jews were crucified, the usual Roman method of executing criminals.

Palestine was in a state of political turmoil. Since this small and insignificant nation was on the far edge of the Empire, the Romans were not greatly concerned about being compassionate, or cruel. Herod's rule was brutal, but effective. The Jewish subjects despised him partly for his half-Jewish blood, partly for his introduction of foreign practices and idols, and partly for his excessive cruelties. No single member of his family was strong enough to control the entire kingdom so the territory was divided among his three sons, Philip, Antipas and Archealus. The important part of Herod's kingdom was assigned to the eldest son, Archealus, who inherited Judea with the capital city of Jerusalem. But ethnarch Archealus was unable to control the Jews in the place where opposition to Roman domination was most intense. He was so tyrannical and unjust, the Jews applied to Rome to investigate his conduct. He was recalled and exiled in Gaul.

Augustus made a decision which proved fateful for the Jewish nation. He refused to place any more of Herod's relatives on the throne and rejected the request of the Jews that the nation be restored to independence. He converted Judea into a Roman province and appointed a Roman governor.

Jerusalem

No city in human history has been conquered more times than Jerusalem, destroyed and rebuilt as many as 35 times![3] Jebusites, Jews, Syrians, Romans, Arabs, Crusaders, Turks, British, Palestinians, and Israelis have all claimed her as their own. Jerusalem is "the city of our God" (Ps. 48), reflecting upon the epics of battle when the city has been threatened by formidable enemies.

It is impossible to speak of the Jews and their lives without considering the unique city to which the fate of Israel had been firmly bound for a thousand years. It means more than Paris means to the French, or London to the Commonwealth:

> "I rejoiced with those who said to me, 'Let us go to the house of the Lord.' Our feet are standing in your gates, O Jerusalem. Jerusalem is built like a city that is closely compacted together. That is where the tribes go up, the tribes of the Lord. . . ."   —Ps. 122:1–4a

> "If I forget you, O Jerusalem, may my right hand forget its skill. May my tongue cling to the roof of my mouth if I do not remember you, if I do not consider Jerusalem my highest joy."   —Ps. 137:5, 6

The dearest dream of all Jews from the four corners of the world was to visit it at least once. The famous expression, "next year in Jerusalem," is centuries old.

Jerusalem was more than a mere earthly city. This holy city was linked with every major happening in Biblical history since conquered by David 1,000 years earlier, and so it was to be again. Located in the country's heart, resting atop the Judean hills on a downward slope, 2,450 feet above sea level, the hills and valleys are noted frequently in Biblical sources, including Mount of Olives, Mount Zion, and Mount Scopus (first mentioned during Abraham's wanderings in the promised land). Joshua led the twelve tribes of Israel into the promised land of Canaan, as it was then known.

The first dwellings were constructed on the eastern slope around 3,000 B.C. During the Early and Middle Bronze ages, people lived in and around Jerusalem. The earliest mention of the name Jerusalem was in an Egyptian text dating to approximately the Middle Bronze Era (2,000 to 1,800 B.C.).

Jerusalem was twice laid desolate, once by Babylon and once by Rome. The siege of the city and its destruction was a decisive calamity for the

Above:
Christ on Calvary
Munkacsy

Right:
The Crucifixion
Matthias Grünewald
The National Gallery of Art
Washington D.C.

Jews. The *freedom fighters*, such as Barabbas, were called *bandits*. After the Great Uprising in A.D. 66 they were called *zealots*.

The books of Genesis, Joshua, and Judges mention the growth of Jerusalem (Gen. 14:18-29) and describe Abraham as being blessed by a king of *Salem* (Jerusalem).

King David (son of Jesse) moved the capital to Jerusalem (1004 B.C.) from Hebron because the valleys provided security walls, there was a constant water source, and it was a neutral area unoccupied by any of the twelve tribes. David left the task of building the temple to his son, King Solomon. In the fourth year of his reign (961 B.C.), Solomon built a temple and the twelve tribes had a political, religious, and cultural center in Jerusalem.

When Solomon died (922 B.C.), the kingdom underwent a period of dramatic change. Political infighting split the kingdom into two parts, Israel in the north and Judea in the south. In 586 B.C., the Babylonian king Nebuchadnezzar, ravaged Jerusalem, his armies burned down the temple, and the Jewish people were carried into a humiliating captivity in Babylon. This was the end of the *First Temple Period*.

Seventy years after the destruction of this temple, the Jews were permitted to return. Babylon had been overpowered by the Persian ruler, Cyrus the Great, and the Persians released the Jews. Two great charismatic rulers arose, Ezra and Nehemiah, and provided direction to build the Second Temple (516 B.C.).

During the *Second Temple Period*, the walls of the city of Jerusalem expanded to their greatest circumference. Jews were allowed to pray amidst the rubble of the Temple Mount during the first 60 years of Roman occupation.

The houses clung to one another, overlapping. There were no statues on street corners whereas in pagan towns it was impossible to move any distance without being obliged to acknowledge some god or another. The streets were exceedingly narrow, people would jostle one another which caused a great deal of shouting and dispute. Trader's stalls lined the streets in open air markets.

The town was rich in odors and noise—the shouting of the tradesmen to attract customers—the cry of water carriers bearing their skins on their backs, the public criers calling to make official announcements, the shouting of guards making way for condemned men being taken to "the place of the skull," animals being driven toward the temple bleated and lowed.

Jesus loved Jerusalem, the Holy City.

Herod's secret police would ferret out the opinions of the populous. Police largely employed spies. Spies beset the people, alike in town and country, watching conversations and the unrestrained confidence of friendly intercourse. Herod himself was said to have acted in that capacity, and to have lurked about the streets at nighttime in disguise to overhear or entrap unwary citizens. The city was under martial law.

RULERS

Herod the Great

Herod the Great ruled Israel for thirty years just before Jesus was born, from 37 B.C. to 4 B.C. His reign was oppressive and opulent. In the course of his thirty-three-year rule, a day did not pass that someone was not put to death. In 37 B.C., he killed forty-five of the noblest in Jerusalem who belonged to the Maccabaen family and confiscated their property. In 29 B.C., he had strangled his own wife Mariamne,[4] his mother-in-law Alexandra, and three-hundred men who were suspected of being their supporters. He changed the high priests as he might change his clothes.[5] He killed all of the Sanhedrin except one member,[6] and to fasten a firmer grip upon the high priest even kept the priestly vestments under his own supervision.[7]

Thousands of Pharisees were put to death for refusing to swear the oath of allegiance to the Emperor and to Herod. During his day, citizens were forbidden to assemble together, or walk together, or hold public meetings.

Josephus records that during Passover a Roman guard lifted his robe and exposed himself to the people. They began throwing rocks at the guard, a riot ensued, and 20,000 deaths occurred.

To these afflictions from a cruel king were added hardships from natural causes. In 31 B.C., an earthquake in Judea killed 30,000 people and a large number of cattle. Famine six years later brought starvation, plague, and pestilence.

Some young Jews had strong Messianic longings, were hot blooded, enthusiastic, and collected together in parties of zealots to hasten the redemption and "bring near the end." People were weary of enduring and expected considerable political change. Scarcely had Herod closed his eyes in death when there immediately broke out such riots as the Jewish nation had ever before witnessed.

His character was typical of an age that produced many men of intellect without morals, ability without scruple, and courage without honor. He raised at great expense a theater and an amphitheater in Jerusalem, adorned them with monuments to Augustus and other pagans, introduced

Greek athletic and musical contests and Roman gladiatorial combats at which the populous became enraged.[8]

Herod beautified Jerusalem with other buildings in what seemed to the people a foreign architectural style and set up in public places Greek statues whose nudity startled the Jews as much as the nakedness of the wrestlers in the games. He built a beautiful three-aisled royal portico or colonnade along the entire length of the south side of the temple.[9] There are vaulted areas to the west thought to be areas where animals were kept for sacrificial purposes while stalls for money changers were located in the royal colonnade above the vaults.[10]

Just before "the Great" died, he left Jerusalem for Jericho to spend his remaining few days. Two of the most revered rabbis among the Jewish people, Judas and Matthias, believing that Herod was dead, put themselves at the head of a gallant and ruthless band determined to wipe away all traces of Herodian idolatry.[11] They hung the golden eagle, the symbol of Rome, over the gate of the temple. They and forty of their followers were captured. Herod, on his deathbed on March 12, 4 B.C., was carried on a couch to preside as judge and prosecutor, and the little band of rebels was burned alive.

The law of Israel forbade images and likenesses of living things, even if death should follow from their actions. By pulling the eagle down, the students would acquire virtue, glory, fame and honor.[12] They defended themselves and their actions on the basis of the Torah and happily accepted punishment for their *piety*.

As his death approached, Herod realized there would be joy in Israel when the news of his death broke. Calling together many of the leaders of Israel, he imprisoned them in the Hippodrome at Jericho with orders to his sister Salome that they were all to be slain upon his death so that mourning would be great. She wisely did not carry out her brother's orders.

Five days before his death he executed Antipater, one of his sons, and changed his will a fourth time by naming his fourth wife Malthace the object of his bounty.

With the blood of tens of thousands of Jews on his hands and the destruction of his second wife Mariamne and three of his sons on his conscience, the old king died. It was into this distraught world Jesus was born as Herod Antipas succeeded his father on the throne.

Of Herod the Great, a certain historian remarked, "He stole along to his throne like a fox, he ruled like a tiger, and died like a dog." We cannot wonder in early Jewish literature why they wrote: "Now the day on which Herod died was made a festival."[13]

Herod Antipas

Antipas was as sly, ambitious, and cruel as his father had been, having learned from his father how to rule with an iron hand. He also put many innocent people to death and was a powerful man, but weak morally.

He was already married to an Arabian princess and had seduced his half-brother Phillip's wife Herodias, the granddaughter of Herod the Great.

Actually, Herod Antipas was not a king but only the tetrarch of Galilee and Perea. Rome had made him a ruler without giving him the honor of being a king. Because he was a murderer and an adulterer, he was a haunted man. Six years later he would be deposed by Rome and sent into exile.

Herod engaged in great building schemes, which employed tens of thousands of workers, he increased trade and made crown lands more prosperous, and ruthlessly suppressed all opposition, even minor protests.

Although Augustus remarked he would rather be Herod's pig than his son, if we compared Herod to the next four Roman emperors, Tiberius, Caligula, Claudius, and Nero, he would appear almost lenient and merciful and more effective as a ruler. He qualifies as a good king on balance because he raised Jewish Palestine to a new prominence throughout the world, continued his father's policy of obtaining benefits for Jews outside of Palestine, and did not allow a civil war. He kept Jewish citizens and Roman troops apart, and as long as Palestine was stable and strong, Rome left it alone.[14]

The lack of uprisings indicates Antipas was not excessively oppressive and did not levy exorbitant taxes by prevailing standards. Galileans in Jesus' lifetime did not feel that the things most dear to them were seriously threatened: their religion, their national traditions, and their livelihoods.[15]

Antipas did commit at least one major blunder. Herod had 10 wives and a good number of children. To accommodate Herodias as his new wife, Antipas planned to send away his former wife. John the Baptist openly criticized Antipas for marrying his brother's wife which led to his execution (Mark 6:27).[16] The populous saw Antipas' defeat by Aretas, an Arab king, as being divine retribution against the tetrarch for executing the Baptist.[17]

The Baptist was executed by Antipas causing popular resentment. An unnamed wife whom Antipas abandoned in favor of Herodias caused her royal father to come after Antipas with an army:

"In the ensuing battle, the whole army of Herod was destroyed . . . but to some of the Jews, the destruction of Herod's army seemed to be divine vengeance, and certainly a just vengeance, for his treatment of John surnamed the Baptist."[18]

Resentment for the Baptist's death probably persuaded Antipas not to move against Jesus. Although he threatened Jesus' death, it was not worth risking any further discontent among the peasantry.

He wanted to avoid possible trouble but felt unable to take action because he had no evidence of Jesus causing political trouble. Jesus' attitude towards the "fox" was one of disdain.

Pontius Pilate

Of all the people who play a prominent role in the career of Jesus, Pilate is the best known to us from secular history.

Pilate was the fifth prefect of Judea, appointed by Emperor Tiberius. He held office for 10 years from A.D. 26-36. In some way, not clearly known, he was subject to the legate of Syria.[19]

The governor exercised the unlimited jurisdiction of the military imperium."[20] His judicial activity would mainly concern Roman citizens, but it was also clear "if the interests of Roman sovereignty were involved, no doubt he would also at all times have summoned provincials to his court.[21]

When Pilate became governor of Judea (A.D. 25), the first thing he did was demonstrate his contempt of Jewish laws:

1.   He made a "graven image" (Exod. 20:4) which displayed the Emperor on military insignia. The people marched from Jerusalem and the surrounding countryside to Caesarea, where Pilate herded them into a large stadium where they remained for six days and nights refusing to leave. Josephus recorded: "Pilate could but admire such constancy in the observance of law, and he gave orders for the standards to be brought back from Jerusalem to Caesarea."[22]

2.   Pilate decided to provide Jerusalem with an extra supply of water. Looking for financing, he turned to the temple treasury, (known as the *Korbonas*) not by negotiating with the wardens of the treasury but by sequester. He robbed the sacred treasury to build an aqueduct to carry water from the Pool of Siloam to the other parts of Jerusalem.[23]

3. In May, A.D. 36, Pilate killed a number of worshipers at prayer in the temple. His last act as governor was to intercept, with cavalry and foot soldiers, a procession of Samaritans to their holy place the Mount of Gerizim, killing many and putting prisoners to death.

That Tiberius left Pilate in office for the extraordinarily long term of years attests to the fact that he probably represented Roman justice well.[24]

Pilate was a loyal servant of the Emperor. As reported by Philo, "energetic steps to exterminate the whole Jewish race" were to be taken. Pilate was strong minded, ruthless and dependable enough to be entrusted with a mission of that nature. His aversion to the Jewish cult caused him to be "naturally inflexible and stubbornly relentless, committing acts of corruption, insults, rapine, outrages upon the people, arrogance, repeated murders of innocent victims".[25]

Pilate married Claudia Proculla the daughter of Julia (the third wife of Tiberius) and granddaughter of Augustus Caesar. Julia was one of the most shameless women of her age, and her father Augustus on account of her lewdness banished her from Rome. Claudia was the illegitimate offspring of an intrigue with a Roman knight during the period of her banishment. Claudia won the favor of Tiberius and was allowed to be married to Pontius Pilate who thereafter received the emperor's commission as procurator of Judea.[26]

Vitellius, legate of Syria, probably at his seat at Antioch, heard charges Pilate had permitted the unprovoked slaughter of suspected Samaritan rebels. Vitellius had heard enough of the governor's aggravations and took firm action. He sent his friend Marcellus to Jerusalem to take charge of Jewish affairs and ordered Pilate returned to Rome to answer for what was charged against him by the Jews and Samaritans. Pilate never resumed his post, arrived too late to stand trial before Tiberius who had died.[27] On the Emperor's death in March, A.D. 37, a new governor was sent by his successor.

There are indications Pilate did not die a natural death.[28] Various traditions and false writings have circulated concerning his death, but the facts are shrouded with uncertainty. Some scholars claim he committed suicide.

Vitellius visited Jerusalem in September, A.D. 36, refunded to the inhabitants some taxes on the sale of agricultural produce, and was determined to be conciliatory.[29]

In the Bible, Pilate is presented as weak and vacillating.[30] He recognized the charges against Jesus were fraudulent, and wanted to release him, but his judgment was swayed by the insistence of an angry mob. He was coerced, even frightened, into giving into the Jews.

But Josephus and Philo record that Pilate was determined to rule as he saw fit. He did not show the least concern for Jewish public opinion. He went out of his way to harass Jews and crush their resistance violently. He used force to obtain his ends and made no effort to reach even a reasonable compromise.

Roman sources paint a picture of Pilate as an individual of extreme "venality, plunder, ill behavior, crime, one summary execution after another and mindless cruelty." He was "unbending and recklessly hard, naturally inflexible, a blend of self-will and relentlessness."[31] Tertullian said Pilate was a "Christian in his conscience."

When Jesus spoke of the 18 worshipers upon whom the tower in Siloam fell (Luke 13:4), some believe it could have been during the construction of the aqueduct but many believe it was a brutal attack ordered by Pilate in which innocent people were murdered.[32]

It was said Pilate always refused what the Jews desired of him and would always do what they implored him not to. When the crowd threatened Pilate by saying, "If you let this man go, you are no friend of Caesar," (John 19:12), one wonders if a person who questioned Pilate's patriotism and loyalty would be allowed to live if he reminded the governor of his duties as a Roman imperial officer. The last thing a Jew would need to do gratuitously would be to remind a Roman governor he was to punish "anyone . . . who opposes Caesar."

PEOPLE AND CULTURE

Taxes and Poor

Every town levied its own taxes for the maintenance of public roads, city walls, synagogue, elementary schools, public baths, the gates, and other general requirements. This burden of civic taxation was distributed easily and kindly. But Roman taxation, a symbol of foreign domination, was quite different—systematic, cruel, and relentless:

1. *Tributum Capitis*. The poll tax was two fold, consisting of income tax and head money on every male from 14-65 years of age.[33]

2. *Tributum Soli.* Landed property was subject to a tax of 1/10 of all grain and 1/5 of the wine and fruit grown.

3. *Annona.* Bridge and road money. Duty on all items bought and sold   in towns.

4. *Publicun.*[34] Regular taxes for the support of the Roman procurator, his household and court.

Some Jews bought the right to collect Roman taxes. The peaceable inhabitant, the tiller of the soil, the tradesman, or manufacturer was constantly exposed to their extractions at every bridge along the road and at the entrance to cities. Every bale had to be unloaded.

To avoid possible losses to the treasury, a regular census were taken to show the number of population and their means.

The Bible mentions the weight units of the kesitar, talent, beqa, mina, gerah and pim. The shekel, so named in the seventh century B.C., the most frequently mentioned unit, probably weighed roughly equivalent to an American half-dollar.

Ancient coins were produced by a process called "striking." The craftsman engraved the patterns for both sides on pieces of hard metal. He set the obverse die into an anvil and inserted a piece of metal called a "blank." The coin was struck with a sledge hammer. There were many opportunities for error and the quality of ancient coins varied greatly. No doubt much of the haggling in the temple market concerned the accuracy of scales used to weigh coins and the proper exchange rate.

The economic conditions of Palestine were affected by civil wars, Roman intervention with its financial burden, and re-migration of Jews. Herod brought a sophistication of the tax system and an increase in the levy. Herod's many public edifices caused financial drains and long-term commitments. A new valuation of property caused discontent when temple money was appropriated for the new water system.[35]

The Zealot movement stirred social unrest in A.D. 6, and by focusing resistance on the valuation of property and the counting of the population.

The Language

Palestine stood at the crossroads of the Roman Empire. Merchants, soldiers, travelers and pilgrims from far and wide crowded into the Holy City (Acts 2:9). Amid the babble of tongues three were prominent, Hebrew, Latin and Greek (John 19:20).

The nature of the Hebrew language requires some explanation. The native tongue of Palestine Jews at the time was Aramaic. Although rabbis and learned scribes spoke fluent classical Hebrew, the great majority of Jews thought it was a dead language. During the exile, they began to use Aramaic, a Semitic language related to Hebrew, as Italian is related to Spanish.

The translation was regularly read in original Hebrew, then in Aramaic translation for the benefit of Jews who knew little Hebrew. Perhaps because of pride or possibly because of simple indifference to scientific precision, Aramaic was popularly referred to as *Hebrew*. The Talmud, a commentary on the Jewish Law, was written in Aramaic.[36]

Latin was the official language of the conquerors. Few Palestinian Jews knew more than the most common of everyday Latin words such as *centurion, colony, denarius, legion* and *Praetorium*.

Greek was widely understood in Palestine (Matt. 4:15). In Galilee and Judea to the south, Jews would rub elbows with Greek speaking gentiles. To be successful in the marketplace bilingualism was an economic necessity. These three languages symbolize the three streams of diverse cultures. The Hebrew was *right*, the Greek was *ideal*, and the Roman was *practical*.

Jesus probably spoke Aramaic, the common language of the Galilean peasant. When evangelists made an effort to preserve his very words, they used the Semitic dialect.

Greek and Roman Social Life

The family is the unit of the social system and at its hearthstone all civilization begins. The law is shaped by the family.[37] The loosening of domestic ties is the beginning of the dissolution of the state. Whatever weakens the nuptial bond destroys the moral fiber of society. The degradation of women and the destruction of domestic purity were among the first signs of decay.

In the early stages of the Roman Republic, marriage was regarded not only as a contract, but as a sacrament, and there were no divorces granted for 520 years.[38]

Cicero divorced his first wife to marry a younger and wealthier woman. Cato was divorced several times. Pompey divorced his wife and married a younger woman, Julia, who was Caesar's daughter. Caesar himself was married five times. He divorced his wife Pompea because of rumors of her relationship to Clodius, a dashing young Roman soldier. Even though the rumors were false he proclaimed, "Caesar's wife must be above suspicion."

Slavery

Slavery existed in every province of the Roman Empire. Slaves outnumbered citizens. In Attica, according to the census of Demetrius Phalereus at the beginning of the fourth century B.C., there were 400,000 slaves, 10,000 foreign settlers, and 20,000 free citizens. During the reign of Augustus, one freeman died leaving 4,116 slaves.

A slave was the absolute property of the master. The owner could kill or torture his slave at will. There was no mercy or humanity shown to slaves. They worked on farms with chains about their limbs during the day and at night were lodged in subterranean apartments, badly lighted and poorly ventilated. The most cruel punishment awaited the slave who attempted to escape. The fugitavarii, a professional slave chaser, would run the slave down, brand him on the forehead and return him to his master. Often he was to be thrown into the amphitheater and consumed by wild beasts. Some slaves committed suicide rather than endure punishment for some transgression.[39]

If a slave murdered his master, all slaves under the same roof were held responsible. Four hundred slaves were put to death for the act of one who assassinated Pedanius Secundus during the reign of Nero. Augustus had his steward Eros crucified on the mast of his ship because the slave had roasted and eaten a quail that had been trained for the Royal Quail Pit. Once a slave was flung to the fishes because he had broken a crystal goblet.

A common saying of the day was: "We have as many enemies as we have slaves."

Luxury

In Ancient Rome their "peaceful inhabitants enjoyed and abused the advantages of wealth and luxury."[40] In conquest, Rome exacted heavy tribute from conquered nations and the wealth of the earth flowed into her coffers. The result was luxury and extravagance. Roman leaders would prepare for days for feasts and parties, trying to outdo each other.

The Golden House of Nero, its walls covered with gold and studded with precious stones, had banquet rooms decorated with gorgeous ceilings and were so constructed that flowers and perfumes could be showered from above onto the guests below. Romans displayed hosts of slaves who provided luxury, bands of musicians, dancing girls, elegant furniture, carpets glittering with gold and rich silver plates.

Some of the public bathing establishments were over 200 feet long. They were adorned with beautiful marble columns and were covered with exquisite mosaics.

Romans used food and drink with loathsome gluttony. There is no parallel in modern life. They would indulge appetites to the fullest extent, prolonging the pleasures of eating beyond the requirements and capacity of nature and were in the habit of taking an emetic at mealtimes.[41]

Of course, not all Romans were rich or indulgent. There were extremes of wealth and poverty. Rome was filled with idlers, vagabonds and paupers from all quarters of the globe. Hundreds of thousands of farmers had been driven from their lands. Homeless and poverty stricken people wandered to Rome to swell the ranks of adventurers who crowded the streets. Augustus was compelled to make annual donations of money and provisions to 200,000 people who wandered helplessly about the streets. This abject poverty was a harbinger of destruction to the state.

The Arts

At the time of Christ, the appetites of the common man had grown so depraved that gross spectacles were regarded as common place. Realities were demanded from the actors on the stage and the hero who played the role of the robber Laureolus was actually crucified before the spectators and was then torn to pieces by a hungry bear. The burning of Hercules on Mt. Oeta and the emasculation of Atys were staged by the actual burning and emasculation of condemned criminals.

Painting and sculpture also served to corrupt and demoralize Roman and Greek people by embodying in marble obscene myths. Lewd and lascivious acts were frequently proclaimed as sacred because they were sanctioned and committed by the gods themselves.

"As impurity formed a part of the religion, people had no scruples in using the temple and its adjoining buildings for the satisfaction of their lusts."[42]

Houses of prostitution were licensed and controlled. Brothels outside the city opened for business after dark. Prostitutes even solicited business in sections of the city, such as the Temple of the Goddess Isis. At one point Ovid found them under the city porticoes in the theater, at the circus maximus—"as numerous as stars in the sky."

Male prostitutes were also available. Homosexuality was condemned by a law which winked at it. In Jerusalem, the punishment was stoning.[43]

Gladiatorial Games

Gladiatorial combat was the culmination of Roman barbarism and brutality. The amphitheater had gorgeous ceremonials and bloody butchery. The contests originally began at funerals and were intended to honor the dead in 264 B.C. At the burial of D. Janius Brutus, three pairs of gladiators fought in the cattle market. In 216 B.C., 22 pairs engaged in combat in the forum. In 174 B.C., 74 pairs fought for three days. Later, political matters were discussed and questions of state determined at these events.

Since the contests were popular, generals and statesmen arranged them on a gigantic scale as a means of winning the favor of the people and for amusement. Augustus inaugurated gladiatorial shows in which 10,000 combatants fought. Wild beasts were brought into the arena. Pompey arranged for a fight among 500 lions, 18 elephants and 410 other ferocious animals brought in from Africa. The Flaminian Circus was flooded in A.D. 5. and Augustus brought in 36 crocodiles. Caligula brought 400 bears to fight an equal number of African wild animals.

In A.D. 106 Trajan celebrated his war victories on the Danube. The games lasted four months and 10,000 gladiators fought and 11,000 animals were slain.

Julius Caesar celebrated his triumph by a real battle in the circus. On each side were arrayed 500 foot soldiers, 300 cavalry men and 20 elephants bearing soldiers in towers on their backs. An actual battle was fought in which men were killed. To vary the entertainment, Caesar arranged a lake to be dug out on Mars Field and placed battleships upon it that represented Tyrian and Egyptian fleets, which then fought a naval battle. One thousand soldiers and 2,000 oarsman fought merely to furnish a Roman holiday. Emperor Claudius had 19,000 men engage in a bloody struggle at Lake Fucinus.[44]

Gladiator fights were announced by posters on the walls of the city. On the day of the performance a solemn procession of gladiators walking in couples passed through the streets to the arena to arouse the spectators to a high pitch of excitement. All male citizens looked alike with short hair, sandals, and loose fitting white togas. The amphitheater was kept cool and fragrant by frequent sprays of perfume. If a gladiator was wounded the words, "hock habet," were shouted whereby the wounded man begged his life from the people.

Attendants were at hand with hot irons to apply to the victim to see that death was not simulated. Servants then ran into the arena and scattered sand over the blood-drenched ground.

Gladiators were trained with the greatest care in schools. The most famous was in Capua, Italy, where Spartacus, a young gladiator of noble ancestry, caused an insurrection that soon spread throughout all of Italy and threatened the destruction of Rome.

Spartacus and his group took refuge in the crater of Mt. Vesuvius in 73 B.C., but they were finally defeated and those who were captured crucified. The entire way from Capua to Rome was marked by crosses on which 10,000 bodies were suspended.[45]

Throughout Italy, amphitheaters existed for gladiator games, but the most celebrated is the Coliseum in Rome. The building was begun in A.D. 72 with three rows of arches. The last two rows were finished by Titus after his return from the conquest of Jerusalem. Twelve thousand captive Jews were employed in this work as the Hebrews were employed in building the Pyramids of Egypt. Contrary to popular legend, Jews were never thrown to the lions at the Coliseum.

The Emperor Commodus fought in the Coliseum. He insisted on calling himself Hercules, dressed in a lion's skin and had his hair sprinkled with gold dust.

Infanticide

The destruction of newborn infants was the deepest stain on the civilization of the Romans. Every Spartan child was *exhibited* immediately after birth to public view and if found to be deformed or weak, he was left to perish on Mt. Taygetus. The Roman father was bound by no limitations but could cast his offspring away to die by pure caprice. It was a parental privilege. On the day of the death of Germanicus in A.D. 19, all children born on that day were left to perish as a manifestation of general sorrow.[46]

The Death Sentence

Life was not held sacred in Rome. Execution was an everyday event. The method used was an extremely important matter. It was not the nature of the offense that would yield a death sentence, but the standing of the offender in society determined the type of execution he faced.

The most humane variety was decapitation. The worst was being thrown to wild animals. Slightly less severe was burning. Although the pain was severe, this remained a manner of death in which the dignity of the accused was somewhat preserved.

There was occasionally the option of the arena. This was not preferred because death was still inevitable and the taunting and torment one might be subjected to while "losing" could diminish whatever glory one had attained in previous confrontations. Jews, and later Christians, were often forced to participate naked. The "games" were bloody, grotesque events. Some were forced to fight stacked battles with gladiators. Tacitus described Nero's cruelty: "Mockery of every sort was added to their deaths. Covered by the skins of beasts, they were torn by dogs and perished." The games were originally sacrifices of prisoners of war to please the spirits of their own fallen warriors. The games were seen by rabbinical eyes as idolatrous, and any Jew who watched in the stadium was thought to be "guilty of bloodshed."[47]

Crucifixion was the most detestable event anyone could face in the Empire. It was thought to be a fate worse than death, a painful, treacherous suffering. Only after every shred of dignity was stripped from a victim would he be allowed a slow painful death. Josephus referred to crucifixion as the "most miserable, the worst of all deaths,"[48] thought to be a punishment below the dignity of a Roman citizen and usually limited to foreigners and slaves. The general citizenry saw crucifixion as "a horrific, disgusting business."[49]

Crucifixion may have originated in Egypt where the victim was not nailed but tied. Other ancient sources, note that the Assyrians, Scythians, Taurians, and Carthaginians all practiced some form of crucifixion. Herodotus, in his *History*, reports that Darius crucified 3000 inhabitants of Babylonia. The Greeks instituted crucifixion long before the Romans:

> "In the Greek speaking world, criminals were at times fastened to a flat board (*tympanum*) for public display, torture, or execution. This form of punishment closely resembled crucifixion whenever the victims were nailed to the planks. Alexander the Great repeatedly resorted to crucifixion. On one occasion he had 2,000 survivors from the siege of Tyre crucified."

Crucifixion had certain advantages over other of the ultimate punishments. Being thrown to beasts required an arena and penned animals. Burning required burnable materials, which were in short supply. But crucifixion could be performed almost anywhere.

A recent body of knowledge comes from the archeological evidence uncovered in a single find at a burial tomb near Giv'at ha-Mivtar in Israel.

Left: Christ before Pilate, Gaudenzio Farrari, 16th Century

Above: **Ecco Homo**
Tintoretto

Above: The Temptation of Christ, Titian
(Tiziano Vecellio). The Minneapolis Institute
of Arts

Right: Jesus on the way to Calvary, Simone
Martin. Louvre Paris

There the remains of a male crucified during the Roman period were accidentally discovered in 1968. Due to modern research it is possible to reconstruct a crucifixion.

The victims were crucified after being flogged. Scourging (*flagellatio*) was inflicted by Roman soldiers using "the dreaded and most feared instrument of the time," a leather whip with small weights of metal or bone at the end of each flagellum.[50] The number of lashes was determined in some cases by the executioner, but generally only a few lashes were inflicted. They made some attempt to be careful, not out of concern for the victim, but to not exhaust him too quickly to interfere with the remaining crucifixion. Scourging was, in rare cases, used as a form of capital punishment, in which the victim was whipped to death.

The victim was stripped and shackled by the wrists to a low column, causing him to assume a bent position. During the whipping, the weight of the metal or bone objects would frequently carry them around to the front of the body. The shoulders, arms, and legs would be lashed. Bits of metal would dig into the flesh, ripping blood vessels, nerves, muscle and skin. The simplest whips were either rods, or thorns and thistles. More complicated whips of chains or ropes were distinguished by attached weights and iron hooks that rip into flesh, called "scorpions" (I Kings 12:11, 14). A whip was made of dried ox sinews or tendons.[51]

There were three grades of beatings: fustus, flagella, and verbera,[52] and beatings were meted out for three reasons: as a warning to potential troublemakers which was done with rods (Luke 23:16-22), as a means of obtaining a confession (Acts 22:24-25), as a prelude to crucifixion—an intrinsic part of the capital sentence.[53]

Flogging was mentioned as brutal prelude to execution by both Philo and Josephus. In the violent anti-Jewish attacks instigated by the governor Flaccus:

> "(Jews) were arrested, scourged, tortured, and after all these outrages, which were all their bodies could make room for, the final punishment kept in reserve was the cross . . . (Flaccus) ordered the crucifixion of the living . . . and he did this after maltreating them with the lash in the middle of the theater and torturing them with fire and a sword."[54]

There was considerable scourging under Syrian monarch Antiochus IV (167 B.C.), Roman Procurator Gessius Florus (A.D. 64), and Titus during the siege and fall of Jerusalem (A.D. 70):

"They were ripped, their bodies were mutilated, and while they were still alive and breathing they were crucified, while their wives and the sons whom they had circumcised despite the king's wishes were strangled, the children being made to hang from the necks of their crucified parents.[55]

"They were accordingly scourged and subjected to torture of every description, before being killed, and then crucified opposite the walls . . . five hundred or sometimes more being captured daily . . . the soldiers out of rage and hatred amused themselves by nailing the prisoners in different postures; and so great was their number, that space could not be found for the crosses, nor crosses for the bodies."[56]

The condemned was made to carry the cross. Although traditional depictions of Christ show the entire cross being borne upon his shoulder, doctors who examined the crucified man from Giv'at ha-Mivtar, side with historical sources in noting that only the crossbar was carried. Due to the economics of crucifixion and a scarcity of wood, both portions of the cross would be reused. The crosspiece weighed 40-110 pounds. The procession would go to the place of crucifixion outside city walls. Quintillion writes criminals were always crucified by crowded highways to warn as many as possible, and since this busy space was on the noisy, busy road to Jericho and Damascus, it was an appropriate spot.

We know Jesus was crucified outside the city gate (Heb. 13:12), near the city (John 19:20), so that people passed by Christ on the cross (Matt. 27:39), while friends stood at a distance (Luke 23:49).

The cross itself took on a variety of forms: the *crux capitata* being the traditional cross of Christian art and literature and the *crux commissa*, which was the capital "T" cross that modern scholars cite as the most common. There was also the *crux decussata,* the cross of St. Andrew, which was a large "X" shaped figure. This was probably used the least frequently because it required more wood and was more difficult to anchor than the other two types.

Both wrists and feet were nailed. Archeological evidence shows these nails bear little resemblance to the nails of modern carpentry. Fifteen years ago about seven tons of Roman nails (almost a million nails) were found at the Roman fortress of Inchtuthill, Scotland. They range from 1 to 40 centimeters long, and although deteriorated give a good idea of what Roman nails were like. The man at Giv'at ha-Mivtar had his heel bones pierced by a nail. The tip had bent when it had entered the vertical beam of the cross, probably because it struck a knot in the wood. After moving a man from the cross it was impossible to remove the nail from the cross and it was left in post mortem. Another nail that offers some historical relevance is one which was, according to legend, found in the third century by Helen, the mother of Constantine. It is purported to be one of the nails used in the crucifixion of Jesus, and is on display in Rome.

Nailing the condemned to the cross, the soldiers took the arm and nailed just above the wrist between the radius and ulna which could hold the weight of the body. Although Christian art portrays Jesus as being nailed through the hand this is very unlikely because the weight of the body would tear through the hand.

> "The pain [of this damage] is described as a particular burning sensation that is so intense that even gentle contacts like clothing or an air draft cause utter torture. The condition can completely destroy the morale of even the most stoic of individuals. A study by Slesser revealed that the pain became more severe with increase in the temperature and that none of his patients [afflicted with a like condition] was able to tolerate direct sun rays."[57]

After nailing the wrists, the crossbeam would be raised upon the cross and the feet nailed straddling the cross, one to each side or they may have been nailed on top of each other through the heels. The feet would have had to support the great weight of the body. In some cases the victim was seated upon a small peg which ran between his legs. Its purpose was to prolong the suffering by allowing the victim to breathe more.

Only after all this did the worst stage begin. At first the victim, still having some strength, would attempt to raise himself by pushing against his nailed feet lifting himself long enough for gasps of air. Death was caused by "the painful process of asphyxiation in which the two sets of muscles used for breathing, the intercostal muscles and the diaphragm became progressively weakened."[58] Eventually, he could lift himself no more. His head would drop to his chest, and finally he would die. Because crucifixion damaged no vital organs, death could come very slowly, sometimes after several days of atrocious pain.

If the condemned was still alive after a given period, his legs would be broken at the calf (considered to be a merciful act) so he would sag upon his arms, be unable to lift himself for breath, and die of asphyxiation. Jewish tradition required burial on the same day before nightfall.

The martyrdom of Andrew was told before A.D. 200:

> "He commanded that Andrew be flogged with seven whips. Then he sent him off to be crucified and commanded the executioners not to impale with nails, but to stretch him out tied up with ropes, (and), to leave his knees uncut, supposing that by doing so he would punish Andrew even more severely . . . the executioners..tied up only his feet and armpits, without nailing up his hands or feet, nor severing his knees because of what the proconsul had commanded them, for Aegeates intended to torment him by his being hung and his being eaten by dogs if still alive by night."[59]

The Old Testament speaks of the *hanging* of criminals on a tree (Deut. 21:22), but this was a mere posthumous indignity. Degradation was also a part of the punishment.

The real cross was little longer than the victim whose head was near the top and whose feet often hung only 12 or 15 inches above the ground. Pictorial art showing the crucifixion of Christ *misrepresents* the crosses as too large and too high (similar to a telephone pole). The art is also false because it fails to show the projecting beam from near the center of the cross upon which the criminal sat.

Crucifixion was conducted by a carnifex (hangman) assisted by Roman soldiers whose duty was to watch until the condemned was dead, to prevent friends and relatives from carrying him away. The general custom was to allow the body to remain and rot upon the cross or to be devoured by birds of prey or wild animals.[60]

RELIGION

The Greek-Roman Religion
The Origin of the Gods61

The religion of the empire in which Jesus was executed came in fits and starts. The Romans acquired their gods by inheritance, importation and manufacture. A few of the many included: Ceres: Goddess of vegetation, renown for her purity and beauty, a goddess of the underground world is responsible for the germination of seed; Jupiter: God of light, the father and preserver of all, protector of city and state, symbolizes virtues of justice, good faith, and honor; Minerva: Daughter of Jupiter, goddess of the arts and all intellect. Her awl symbolizes wisdom, her helmet, her role as the goddess of victory; Apollo: God of the sun, the son of Jupiter, patron of artistic inspiration, source of all order and reason; Venus: Goddess of Rome, born of the sea. She presides over the destiny of Rome with love and beauty. Julius Caesar claimed direct decent from Venus.

The average citizen was enamored of the beautiful myths and exquisite statutes of Greek gods. The influence of such gods in daily life was overwhelming.

From Greece and from every conquered country strange gods were brought into Italy and placed in the Pantheon. When a foreign city was captured, the Romans, after a preliminary ceremony, invited the native gods to leave their temples and go to Rome. There they were assured they would have much grander altars and would receive a more enthusiastic worship. Gods could be enticed and induced to immigrate. In their wars, the Romans frequently kept the names of their gods secret to prevent the enemy from bribing them. When Romans needed a new god and could not find a foreign one to please them, pontiffs deliberately manufactured a deity for the occasion.

Although there are extreme cases of intolerance in Roman history, the general policy of the Empire was of tolerance and liberality. All religions were tolerated if they consented to live side by side in peace with all other religions—so long as none challenged the authority of Rome.

Romans were required to worship in the Roman faith and the state religion was binding for all the world as the dominant cult.

> "Such toleration or indifference, however, found its own limits at once whenever the doctrine taught had a practical bearing on society, interfered with the worship of the state gods, or confronted their worship with one of its own; as well as when a strange god assumed a hostile attitude towards Roman gods, could be brought into no affinity or corporate relation with them, and would not bend to the supremacy of Jupiter Capitolinus. The Roman Constitution required that foreign religions should live in peace with its neighbors, and that it should acknowledge the dominance and superior character of the Imperial Roman Religion. All these things Jesus refused to do, as did his followers."[62]

For a Roman, "the state" represented the essential ruling principle. Religious worship was in a form laid down by the state and was a "civic duty." Caesar controlled God.

The worship of the gods united the people of the Roman Empire. Roman worship was very elaborate and ceremonial, consisting of sacrifices, vows, prayers and festivals.[63] Every act of Roman public and private life was framed in accordance with the will of the gods. Caesar never mounted his chariot without repeating a formula three times to avert dangers.

Painful exactness in the use of words was required in an offering of a Roman prayer. A syllable left out of a word or mispronounced or the intervention of any disturbing cause of evil import would destroy the merit of the formula. The voice of prayer could not be disturbed by noises or bad omens. Musical notes were not objectionable and frequently flutes were played while the prayer was being offered to chase away disturbing sounds.

The religion of the Caesars at the beginning of the Christian era was described by Suetonius speaking of Tiberius:

> "While he was rather indifferent towards the gods and religious rights, given as he was to astrology, and being persuaded that all things operated under the influence of fate, he nonetheless dreaded thunder beyond measure."[64]

Piety and faith were not necessary to Roman prayer. Ceremonial precision, rather than purity of the heart, was pleasing to gods. Romans believed if divine law was obeyed to the letter, the gods were under obligation to grant their prayers. They were frequently in doubt as to the name of the god who controlled the subject matter of their petitions.

One mode of pleasing the gods was by sacrifice. Animals, fruits of the field, and human beings were used for this purpose. They adapted the sacrifice to the whims and tastes of the gods. A provision of the "twelve tables" was that "such beasts should be used for victims as were becoming and agreeable to each deity." Each god had an appetite and discriminating taste for a particular animal.

Close attention was given to the selection of the victims of sacrifice from the flocks and herds and any serious defect in the animal disqualified it. A calf was not fit for slaughter if the tail did not reach the joint of the leg. Sheep with cloven tongues and black ears were rejected. Black spots on a white ox had to be rubbed white with chalk before the beast was available for sacrifice.

Human beings also were sacrificed. In early Roman history gray-headed men of sixty years were hurled from the Ponssublicious into the Tiber river as an offering to Saturn. In 227 B.C., the pontiffs discovered that two tribes of Gauls and Greeks were getting ready to attack them. To avert the danger, the senate decreed that a man and woman should be buried alive in the forum as a human sacrifice to the gods.

In their approach to human sacrifice it was the custom to sprinkle the statute of Jupiter with the blood of gladiators. A priest caught the blood as it gushed from the wound of a dying gladiator and dashed it, while still warm, at the face of the image of the god.

Various methods were employed to ascertain the will of the gods. Chief among the tools of this art of divination was the flight of birds, the inspection of the entrails of animals, the observation of lightening, and the interpretation of dreams.

Decline of the Roman Faith

The invasion of Italy by Greek gods was the first serious assault on the Roman faith. As time advanced, old gods grew stale and new deities were sought. But the effect of repeated changes in deities destroyed the moral fiber of Roman religion. It also prepared folk to embrace a completely new religion according to Roman thinkers.

Cicero wrote:

"I thought I should be doing an immense benefit both to myself and to my countrymen if I could entirely eradicate all superstitious errors. Nor is there any fear that true religion can be endangered by the demolition of this superstition; for as this religion which is united with the knowledge of nature is to be propagated, so, also, all the roots of superstition to be destroyed; for that presses upon and pursues and persecutes you wherever you turn yourself, whether you consult a diviner or have heard an omen or have immolated a victim, or beheld a flight of birds; whether you have seen a Chaldaean or a soothsayer; if it lightnings or thunders, or if anything is struck by lightening; if any kind of prodigy occurs; some of which things must be frequently coming to pass, so that you can never rise with a tranquil mind."

By the time of Christ, Roman gods were no longer needed and worshipers were ready to repudiate them. Augustus even chastised Neptune,
the sea god, because he lost his fleet in a storm and forbad the image of the
god to be carried in the procession of the next circensian games.

In fact, Greek and Roman intellectual leaders had long been in revolt
against the absurdity of the myths which formed the foundation of their
popular faiths and were outraged at the enforced obedience to the divini-
ties that Homer had handed down to them. Five hundred years before
Christ a great lyric poet of Greece, Pindar, denounced the vulgar tales told
by the deities.

At the beginning of the Christian era, the religion of Rome was privately ridiculed and repudiated by nearly all statesmen and philosophers
of the Empire although they publicly professed it on grounds of public
policy. Seneca, a contemporary of Jesus, advised observance of rights on
patriotic grounds stating:

> "All which things a wise man will observe as being commanded by
> the laws, but not as being pleasing to the gods.
> All that ignoble rabble of gods, which the superstition of ages has
> heaped up, we shall adore in such a way as to remember that their wor-
> ship belongs rather to custom than to reality."

The contemptuous scorn of cultured Romans was revealed in the writings of Cicero. He refers to the famous Cato, who said that he could not
explain why all the people did not laugh in each other's faces when they
began to sacrifice.

But this religious cynicism produced an equal and opposite legal reaction. The imperial rules knew that an assault upon a religious system was
an assault upon an entire social and moral organization.

Jesus espoused a religion that scorned an authorization from Rome to
worship its god. This scorn was an affront to the dignity and a challenge to
the laws of the Roman commonwealth. Such conduct was treason against
the Constitution of the Empire:

> "The substance of what the Romans did was to treat Christianity by
> fits and starts as a crime."[65]

The Romans regarded their religion as an:

" . . . engine of state which could not be shaken without the utmost danger to their civil government. The institution of the fathers must be defended; it is the part of wisdom to hold fast the sacred rights and ceremonies."

The Law of Judaism

Judaism, though not widely practiced in the empire, was nonetheless respected as unique. Its uniqueness lay in its claim to be the singular disclosure of the Creator of the universe. Unlike Roman cults, Judaism claimed to have arrived full-blown from the mind of the God Yahweh—not imported from a conquered people and not invented by man.

God's revelation was complete and all embracing. Everything that men were to do and be, he had revealed to them. The law (Torah) was God's greatest gift to men, the source of the laws and the whole legal system.

Jewish life, culture, and traditions were adapted from Jewish law that molds the character and contours of Jewish lifestyle. The Torah study is a form of worship itself. Learning Torah is a "mitzvah" and becomes an exciting goal in its own right. It discerns the will of God and is a mind boggling venture into the world of ideas.[66]

Keeping the law was man's paramount obligation. The Jew was to do it with no ulterior motive, because he loved God and wished to do God's will. Failure to obey God's revealed will, especially deliberate violation, spelled disaster. As God revealed the law, the law revealed justice. For centuries the ancient adage stood:

" . . . cease to do evil; learn to do well;"

—Isa. 1:16–17

Sacrifices

The Bible contains five types of required sacrifice: *burnt offerings*, *cereal offerings*, *peace offerings*, *sin offerings*, and *trespass offerings*.

1. *Burnt offerings:* None is eaten by anyone, as the fire consumes it all, usually male animals without blemishes. The animal was slaughtered and burnt, symbolizing the nation's desire to rid itself of sinful acts against God.

2. *Cereal offerings:* Israelites sacrificed cereals and vegetable produce mixed with oil and salt who brought them to the priest who either burned or ate it.

3. *Peace offerings:* A ritual meal called the Peace Offering (involving male animals) was shared with God, nearly identical to the burnt offering, but part was eaten by the priests and worshipers.

4. *Sin offerings:* Sacrifices for sin "paid off" through the worshiper's ritual faults against the Lord, which was payment for unintentional faults.

5. *Trespass offerings:* Similar to sin offerings except it was an offering of money for the sins of ignorance connected with fraud, such as if you had accidentally overcharged someone or charged too much.

Worship

Israel worshiped at different times, the most important events being:

1. *The Sabbath:* God instructed people to observe the Sabbath every seven days (Exod. 20:8).

2. *Passover:* All males were required to appear at the sanctuary for the Feast of Passover which celebrates the Death Angel's passing over the Hebrew households in Egypt, and the Feast of Unleavened Bread which commemorates the first seven days of the Exodus.

3. *The Feast of Weeks:* Observed fifty days after the Passover and marks the end of the harvest. Priests urge all to remember the needy at this time.

4. *The Feast of Tabernacles:* Commemorates Israel's wandering in the wilderness. All Jewish families eat or sleep for one week in a lean-to type enclosure with a room only of palm branches.

5. *The Day of Atonement:* A day set aside for the cleansing of sins, where the high priest symbolically transfers the sins of the people onto a goat (scapegoat), then led away into the wilderness to die.

Great Festivals

Pilgrimages to the temple in Jerusalem were linked with agricultural seasons:

1. *Passover* was the best known to Christians because Jesus' death and resurrection occurred during this feast. They are told to "remember" (Exod. 6:7) what God had done forever. In Jesus' time groups large enough to consume a lamb would gather together for the meal. Lambs were slaughtered in the temple the day before the Passover. Basic Passover rules included: remembering it annually (Exod. 13:3); eating unleavened bread (Exod. 12:18); cleansing all leaven out of one's house, which includes extensive house cleaning, putting away all dishes used during the year, purifying ovens, cleaning silver and utensils. "Remembering" means not just looking back in the past but it is a call to put ourselves back with those events and to recognize that they are also about us (Exod. 6:7).

2. *Pentecost* was a more popular festival than Passover. According to Josephus, an offering was brought fifty days after the "omer" offering. The omer was a grain offering that marked the beginning of the spring grain harvest. This festival marks its end. Two loaves of leavened bread were presented in the temple. Since destruction of the temple, there was no place to make the offerings. Today there are special rituals associated with Pentecost, but custom dictates Jews decorate their homes and synagogues with green plants and eat dairy foods.

3. *Tabernacles* was the third agricultural festival and celebrated for seven days the fall harvest (Exod. 23:16; Lev. 23:39). The people would dwell in huts during the festival and come to the temple waving branches of citron, palm, myrtle, and willow while singing praises to God.

4. All cultures celebrate the *new year*. Judaism marks it with solemn holy days usually referred to as "The High Holy Days." It begins with *Rosh Hashanah* and ends ten days later with the Day of Atonement, *Yom Kippur*, a period of serious reflection on the ways in which one has failed to be faithful to God during the past year.

The three blessings recited in the synagogue reflect the three fundamentals of Jewish belief: (1) God is king of the Universe; (2) God intervenes in the world to punish the wicked and reward the good; (3) God has revealed himself in the law at Sinai and will do so again at the end of days.

5. Unlike festivals which go back to early times, the festival of *Hanukah* originated in second century B.C. under the Maccabees. It commemorates the rededication of the Jewish temple. It is an eight day holiday, a minor feast in the Jewish calendar, except in countries such as the United States where it competes with the Christian celebration of Christmas. On each day a candle in the eight branched candlestick (the Menorah) is lit. Customs include playing games, singing special songs, and giving gifts of money to the children.[67]

Jews from outside Palestine (called "Diaspora") regularly made pilgrimages to Jerusalem to celebrate the great feast.

Synagogues and lodging facilities allowed people from a particular region to meet others who spoke the same dialect and to seek help and advise. Tombstones in Jerusalem attest to the influx of people from outside Jerusalem. Perhaps they came to spend their last days and be buried there.

The Old Testament commanded adult males make the pilgrimage to Jerusalem three times a year (Exod. 23:17; Deut. 16:16). Diaspora communities sent representatives with the half-sheckel tax for support of the temple required of all Jewish males. A Roman edict protected offerings as "sacred money" and mandated harsh penalties against anyone who might attempt to seize it.

The great pilgrimage and offerings strengthened ties between Jerusalem and Jewish communities outside Palestine. The spread of Christianity from Jerusalem into the Roman world followed the patterns already established in Jerusalem's relationships to Diaspora Judaism.[68]

In Jerusalem twice a week, three times every Sabbath and four times on the Day of Atonement, Jews met for the study of law and for prayer. The Pentateuch and the Prophets were read aloud in Hebrew, the reader often stopping to permit a paraphrase into Aramaic. Law was of the greatest antiquity, highly developed, and its essence was religious. The Bible supplied Israel with all the fundamental legal data just as the Koran is the law for the world of Islam.

Above Left:
Pilate Washes his Hands
Albrecht Altdorfer

Above Right:
Agony in the Garden
El Greco
The Toledo Museum of Art

Below Left:
Retreat of the Money Changers
Rembrandt Van Rijn

Uniqueness of Old Testament Laws

God told Moses how the people of Israel should live and these commandments are recorded in the first five books or Torah (Pentateuch) of the Old Testament. These laws teach us a great deal about Old Testament society and suggest how our own society should work.

God introduced his law by saying he chose Israel to be a nation with its own land, not a clan or a large family, and told the people how to live in harmony with him (the message of the Ten Commandments).

Biblical law was public law and was different from pagan laws which the king held privately as if they were his personal possessions. He did not publish these laws until he was ready to give up his throne. A person could even be arrested for breaking a law he had never known.[69]

God's laws were read by the priests to the people at regular times of the year and every citizen could learn the laws he had to obey (Deut. 31:10). In other societies citizens obeyed the laws because disobedience meant punishment. God's people were to obey his laws because they loved him. Love was the motive for obeying the law.

Biblical law sees all men as creatures of God, equal to one another and has important themes: (1) All crimes ultimately are crimes against God; (2) God expects all people to serve him in total submission; (3) All people have a natural responsibility to uphold the law; (4) Each person has an individual responsibility to God; (5) God's law protects human life; (6) God's law requires equitable punishments and penalties; (7) Rich people cannot buy their way out of punishment. God declares that every law breaker must suffer personally for his own crime; (8) God's laws are equally applicable and protect the poor as well as the rich.

The Deuteronomic Code covers a wide range of ethical and ritual concerns that Moses raised with the Israelites just before they entered the Promised Land.

Josephus writes, " . . . the Pharisees has passed on to the people certain regulations handed down by former generations and not recorded in the law of Moses."[70] An oral law was revealed to Moses along with a written law, and the oral law was faithfully transmitted from generation to generation, from school to school, and ended by being reduced to writing in the Mishnah and Talmud.

The existence of an oral law side by side with Biblical law is clear. From the fifth century B.C. on, Jewish scribes and doctors of the law meditated on this corpus juris divini into tractates (called *the Talmud*). The Talmud is composed of the Mishnah. The first Mishnah, the "Mishnah Rishonah," goes back three generations before the destruction of the temple to the days of Herod. Rulings were made on customs and traditions.[71]

The Talmud

The Talmud is a *corpus juris—a cyclopedia of all law*, consisting of two parts: The Mishnah and the Gemara. The Mishnah is the legal main text composed of six divisions. The Gemara is the commentary. The Talmud consists of 63 tractates, a mass of discussion, illustration, and commentary.

The oral law had been transferred verbally for centuries, growing in use and authority ever since the return of the nation from Babylon. Jewish writers refer to it without hesitation as including the code of criminal law in existence at the time of Caiaphas.

The four rules of *criminal* law were: strictness in the accusation, publicity in the discussion, full freedom granted to the accused, and assurance against all dangers or errors of testimony.[72]

The accused was to be free from private or personal investigation and not subjected to official questioning until he was brought for trial. An accused could only be convicted by the public testimony of two or three witnesses who testified on each detail of the crime (Deut. 19:15-18).

The Mishnah was the authorized codification of the unwritten or oral law, (tradition passed by word of mouth) drawing upon the Torah (regulations, customs, prohibitions, sanctions, rules, and orders from Scribes, the Great Synod, and the Sanhedrin).

The Mishnah does not identify its authors or contain a hint about what its authors conceive their work to be. Is it a law code or a school book? It does not attribute its saying to Biblical heroes, prophets, or holy men.

Two documents formed around the Mishnah are the Babylonian Talmud and the Palestinian Talmud.

The Mishnah is a six part code of descriptive rules and orders codified (subdivided into 63 Tractates and then 525 chapters) towards the end of the second century A.D. by a small number of Jewish sages, put forth as the Constitution of Judaism under the sponsorship of Judah the Patriarch, a head of the Jewish community at the end of that century. It stands alongside the Hebrew Bible for the last 1800 years.

Jewish Life

By the time of Jesus, Judaism splintered into factors. Jews holding different beliefs spent hours arguing difficult questions of law, history and politics. Many centuries had blurred the individual characteristics of the descendants of Jacob's twelve sons. Each nation inevitably preserved some characteristics while continuing a bitter rivalry among themselves.

To preserve the Torah, Jews established synagogues, instituted the office of *rabbi* and emphasized the need for a faithful *remnant* which guaranteed the survival of Judaism:

1. *The Synagogue* was a place where Jews could come together to pray, sing songs and discuss the Torah, making prayer the central act of synagogue worship.

2. *The Rabbinate.* Each synagogue had rabbis or teachers extremely well versed in the Torah and were allowed to expound their views. They organized and recorded the teachings of various rabbis.

3. *Remnant Theology.* Mainline Jews combated the drift toward paganism by stressing theology which declared that God would preserve a faithful remnant to be the seed of the new Israel.

Education

Long before it was ever written, the Old Testament existed only in the spoken word. The prophecies of Jeremiah were "said" for twenty-two years before ever reduced to writing.

Even when fixed in writing, the habit of oral transmission of thought was not lost. Rabbis continued to teach by word of mouth and their sentences were handed down the same way. The Tractate Gittin taught that writing them was unlawful.[73] The word *talmud* means *learnt by heart*. Christians handed down the *good news* solely by word of mouth.

Memory played an important part in the system. Rabbi Meir said, "The man who forgets something of what he has learned brings about his own ruin." A disciple's highest praise was that "he was like a well-cemented cistern, that does not lose a drop of his water." A visitor to a school today will see the method still used by Orthodox Jews and by Muslims.

The majority of Jews knew how to read and write. Christ speaks of the yod, the smallest letter of the alphabet, and when the woman was taken in adultery he is shown "writing on the ground with his finger."

Although the early years of children belonged almost entirely to the mother's care, education was also in the father's province. True Israelites attached more importance to moral education than anything else.

Train a child in the way he should go, and when he is old he will not turn from it.

—PROV. 22:6

As moral law merged into religious law, the father's first duty was to teach his children the commandments, repeated in the morning and at night in the prayer.

According to the Talmud, a system of primary education was not introduced until A.D. 65. Philo of Alexandria and Flavius Josephus indicate a methodical study of the books of Moses, the Prophets, and Psalms were general throughout Palestine. The sacred texts were literally drilled into the pupils' memory.

Galilean children were educated *in the fear of the Lord*. An ancient Jewish saying is, "God cannot be everywhere, hence he created mothers," and "Paradise is at the knees of the mother." As soon as children could talk, they recited prayers with their father twice a day and true to the divine prescription worshiped the Sabbath.

There were schools in the Palestine of Jesus' time, but they were a comparatively recent invention going back no more than 100 years. Public instruction came into existence in about A.D. 64. In his childhood, Jesus did not have the benefit of such a system.

The Temple

The temple in Jerusalem was enormous. Great dressed blocks of stone, still white from the chisel, glinted with golden bucklers. The overall magnificence was enhanced by lofty colonnades, broad flights of steps, and richly wrought doors.

The temple was a stunning work of architecture, with spacious porches and courts built on an immense terrace.[74] The white stone and gold appointments used on the sanctuary and the gates gave the temple a dazzling appearance in the sunlight. On three sides stood great porticos, open on one side, the roof supported by rows of pillars. In an elevated section of the city its appearance was magnified. Pilgrims coming to the city from outlying areas saw the temple white and gold in the sunlight long before they reached the gates of the city.

The temple took 46 years to build (Jn. 2:20), with 18,000 builders still in service in A.D. 63 when the labor force was finally dismissed.[75] They hauled material to the site, mammoth stone blocks for the walls, cedar limbs for the roof, and great columns of marble for structural support.

A diagram of the temple area shows it was divided into a number of chambers and courtyards. Only the officiating priest entered the court immediately in front of the temple where the great altar and the places for slaughtering sacrificial animals were located. Only males were permitted beyond the walls which separated the temple area from the Court of the Women.

Non-Jews were not permitted as far as the Court of the Women. Israelite men who were not in a state of ritual purity were confined to the Court of the Women. Persons suffering from leprosy or other diseases were barred from Jerusalem altogether.

> ". . . David captured the fortress of Zion, the City of David."
>
> —2 Sam. 5:7

David took Zion in a bloodless raid, renaming it Ir David, the City of David.

Joab, David's nephew and general (I Chronicles 11) had surprised the Jebusites by entering the town through a water shaft which can still be explored today. The forty foot long subterranean tunnel to the gurgling Gihon spring beneath the city was discovered by Sir Charles Warren in 1867.

The twelve acre city that David built is some 350 feet to the south of the walled Jerusalem of today. Archeologists have uncovered 21 strata belonging to the fourth millennium B.C., to the fifteenth century A.D.

With great flourish, the poet king had the Ark of the Covenant moved to Jerusalem, but it would fall to David's son and heir, Solomon, to build the temple atop the windswept Moriah plateau.

> ". . . you will be my witnesses in Jerusalem, and in all Judea and Samaria, and to the ends of the earth."
>
> —Acts 1:8

By the time Jesus passed through the Golden Gate, Jerusalem was the holy city of the Jews for more than ten centuries. The Bible chronicles the destruction of Solomon's Temple by Nebuchadnezzar (587 B.C.) and the painful exile of the Jews to Babylonia. The Holy City stretched well beyond David's hilltop fortress but its population was still less than 80,000.

The temple was incomplete when Jesus came to pray and preach. Herod, eager to outdo the great Solomon, had begun to expand the modest second temple built (515 B.C.) after Jews returned from Babylonia (539 B.C.).

Beyond the teeming, rectangular Court of the Gentiles lay a series of 13 gates through which only Jews could pass[76]. The most famous was the Bronze Nicanor Gate, so heavy it needed 20 men to open it, an event that signaled each new day. This area is close to where Jesus overturned the tables, and today is part of the open court of Islam's Dome of the Rock.

When Rome destroyed Jerusalem Temple, treasures were carted off and Jerusalem's land salted to keep it fallow. All that remained were the four outer retaining temple walls. One of them—the Western Wall—is sanctified by centuries of Jewish tears and prayers for the redemption of Zion and a return to Jerusalem. An irony of history is that the holiest shrine was not built by Solomon but largely by Herod, one of the most hated kings ever to rule the Jews.

Starting with David's transfer of the Ark of the Covenant to Jerusalem, and Solomon's construction of the temple to house it, the Jerusalem Temple developed from being the *leading* place, to become the *only* place where sacrifices could legally take place.[77]

The early Jerusalem church felt that animal sacrifices were proper, and Jesus' death at that time was in no way a substitute for the temple service. The church was "zealous for the Torah" (Acts 21:20) which included killing animals as sin offerings.

After the destruction of the temple, the Jerusalem church had something to take the place of animal sacrifices, and Jesus' death was a substitute with their link to the temple service.

The early followers of Jesus went to the temple regularly, where animals were sacrificed as sin offerings (Acts 2:46; 3:1; 5:12).

At the Passover Festival, tens of thousands of pilgrims traveled to Jerusalem. This was particularly striking since the normal population of the city was about 30,000.[78]

Special markets for the sale of the sacrificial animals, run by the family of Annas, somewhere near the temple were destroyed by popular movement in A.D. 67. There is plenty of evidence outside the Gospels for the existence of the trade of sacrificial animals in the Great Courtyard of the temple.[79] Traders took advantage of the demand for clean animals by raising the prices to exorbitant heights. Every Jew was supposed to spend a certain proportion of his income in Jerusalem.

The Men of God in the Service of the Temple

There was a popular saying in Jerusalem that there were as many priests and Levites in the temple as there were stones in its walls.

The temple was a vast organization and needed a considerable number of men, possibly 20,000, to run the national institution. As Moses organized it, there was the one tribe of Levi set aside for the service of religion. The hierarchial head was the high priest, with the total priesthood divided into 24 classes, some of higher standing than others.[80]

The first Scribe Temple rights necessitated the purchase of sacrificial animals such as sheep, cattle, doves, or the purchase of products such as wheat, flour, wine, corn, oil, and incense fruits. Each year 18,000 lambs were required for the celebration for the Feast of Passover. A significant number of merchants, trades people, and livestock owners earned their living from the economic activity generated from the temple.

There was a staff of scribes, physicians, incense-makers, weavers, bakers of shewbread.

Levites helped the priests to sacrifice, jointed and skinned the animals, took care of storehouses and holy vessels, and were the secretaries of the temple administration and clerks and ushers of the Sanhedrin. Levites served from the age of 25 to 50, and then retire after having made a fortune.

A study of documents and authorities discloses the names of all of the high priests at the time. Annas, who held office formally for seven years, even though out of office was frequently consulted on matters of importance and was the father-in-law of Caiaphas. For fifty years this family, including five sons, remained in power without interruption:[81] Eleazar (A.D. 23-24); Jonathan (A.D. 37); Theophilus (A.D. 39-42); Matthias (A.D. 42-44); Ananus (A.D. 63) (who illegally condemned the Apostle James to be stoned); Simon ben Camithus (A.D. 24-25); John (Acts 4:6); Alexander (very wealthy and loaned King Herod Agrippa 200,000 pieces of silver) (Acts 4:6); and Ananias ben Nebedus (A.D. 48-59) (who delivered the Apostle Paul to Procurator Felix, Acts. 23:2-24:1); Helcias (paid Judas Iscariot 30 pieces of silver as the price of his treason); Sveya, said to have had seven sons who devoted themselves to witchcraft (Acts 19:14).

Another class of men which belonged to God but not in a priestly capacity, were the scribes, the direct descendants of those who appeared in the Jewish community just after the exile. They studied religious questions and were described as *scribes* or *doctors of the law*, a type of *holy league* of intellect and piety of a unique type.

They defended the doctrines against paganism and were experts in matters of religion. They left the standing and privileges of the temple to the priests, and left political intrigues to the upper clergy, but provided true intellectual life and molded the thought of the nation. They had become members of the Great Sanhedrin and made it as much a *theological college* as a governing body and supreme court.

Any Israelite could become a doctor of the law by joining one of the schools that surrounded the most famous doctors. The students, sitting around the rabbi, would listen to his lessons for several years. They lived "in the law, for the law."

Nicodemus and Gamaliel were doctors of the law, virtuous and profoundly religious men.

Temple Revenue

The livelihood of the priests was provided in three ways: They received the choicest portion, often including the hides, of most of the animals sacrificed; they received the first fruits that farmers and shepherds were required to offer at the time of the harvest each year and that which parents presented at the birth of their first son which were to be of the highest quality, and they received tithes paid to the Levites (the lesser ranked clergy). Jewish law required one tenth of the total harvest of the most important agricultural products be turned over to the Levites and they in turn gave one tenth to the priests.[82]

The yearly half-shekel "Temple" tax, paid by all Jewish men was equivalent to two days pay for an average laborer.[83] The temple had one of the richest treasuries in the world and every Jew paid tribute.

The religion of the prophets teaches regard for the stranger and for people of other races. Isaiah called the temple "a house of prayer for all nations." Yet, a large sign in Greek letters was put up at the entrance of the inner court reading:

"Let no foreigner enter within the screen and enclosure around the holy place. Whosoever is taken so doing will himself be the cause that death overtakes him."

Josephus describes the opulence of the temple and the incredible wealth of its treasury with an enormous building and gates overlaid with gold, and over the entrance hung an enormous grape cluster made of gold.[84]

The families of the high priests possessed extraordinary wealth. Incredible sums were paid as dowries, and allowances for perfumes and jewelry. Widows of high priests were beneficiaries of extremely generous pensions paid out of the temple treasury, all of which corroborates the corruption.[85]

Josephus writes of the great political power of the temple establishment, and the high priest often directed other priests in the "trial of cases and litigation, and the punishment of condemned persons." The power of the ruling priest was by Roman design for it was the best way to guarantee tranquility and taxation.[86] Political and economic abuses flourished. The temple establishment had little competition as they were united by common purpose. They got along fairly well with the Roman government and "maintained a fairly consistent policy and pattern of collaboration in the Roman system."[87]

Bribery and violence characterized the temple establishment's rule. People were supplied with bribes and money. Wealth was used to attract those willing to receive bribes.

Socially and politically the fundamental conflict in Jewish Palestine was between the Jewish ruling groups and the Romans on one side, and the Jewish peasantry on the other.[88]

The First Christians

Pagans in the second and third centuries referred to Christians as the "third people" or the "third race" and saw them as something alien and sinister. "Away with the third race," was a favorite shout of the crowds in the circus.[89]

Nero made Christians scapegoats for the great fire of Rome calling them "notoriously depraved Christians," and Tacitus, reporting the incident, though no lover of Nero, shared his estimate stating Christianity was a "deadly superstition."[90] Celsius said Christians, "wall themselves off and break away from the rest of mankind."[91]

Nero's wife, Pomponia Graecina, was accused of having followed what Tacitus calls a "foreign superstition."[92] Tacitus uses the word *superstito* to describe Christianity in the account he gives of Nero's persecutions of Christians. Suetonius, a later writer, also uses the word "superstito" about the new faith.[93] Her family name is found in the catacombs in Rome so that kinsmen of hers were among the early Christians in Rome.[94]

Jesus' death had little visible effect on the life of Palestine. Pilate remained governor until A.D. 36. Pharisees and Sadducees continued to debate religious problems. Jews continued to pay taxes to the temple and to Rome.

Meantime, the eleven Apostles fled Jerusalem in fear, returned to Jerusalem only to celebrate the Feast of Weeks (Pentecost) seven weeks after the crucifixion. They soon chose a twelfth apostle, Matthias, to replace Judas Iscariot, and their lifestyle termed "The Way" resembled that of other Jewish sects at the time.

Most members referred to as "brethren" preached to all who would listen, speaking to small groups in temple courts and city streets, passing on memorized oral narratives.

More and more new converts were recruited among Hellenistic Jews who returned from all parts of the Roman Empire to settle in Jerusalem. They spoke Greek and used the Greek version of the Old Testament, "the Septuagint".

By A.D. 64, a network of Christian congregations were founded in cities from Damascus to Rome, from what is now northern Turkey to eastern Africa.

The teachings of Jesus were consistent with Hebrew Scriptures:

> "Do not think that I have come to abolish the Law or the Prophets; I have not come to abolish them but to fulfill them. I tell you the truth, until heaven and earth disappear, not the smallest letter, not the least stroke of a pen, will by any means disappear from the Law until everything is accomplished."   —Matt. 5:17-18

What then happened to cause such a split between Christian and Jewish communities? Initially it was a result of religious and social differences.[95]

When the Romans destroyed Jerusalem and the temple, the small sect of Jews known as Nazarenes took it as a sign that God had abandoned contemporary Judaism. For the rabbis' part, they were increasingly hostile to the way Jesus' followers rejected laws about circumcision, diet, and feast days.

Roman-Christian relations were even worse than Jewish-Christian relations. The majesty of Rome felt insulted and outraged. Persecution, torture and death was the inevitable result. The wisest of the Roman Emperors, Trajan, crucified early Christians, not because Christianity was spiritually false, but because it was intolerant and he believed its destruction necessary to the supremacy of the Roman state.

Trajan wrote Pliny, the former governor of Bithynia, congratulating him for the persecution of Christians:

> "You have adopted the right course..in investigating the charges against the Christians..it is not possible to lay down any general rule for all such cases. Do not go out of your way to look for them. If indeed they should be brought before you, and the crime is proved, they must be punished; with the restriction, however, that where the party denies he is a Christian, and shall make it evident he is not, by invoking our gods, let him be pardoned upon his repentance."[96]

Christianity was not on trial before Pilate but the author of Christianity was. Pilate learned the claim of Jesus to be "Christ a King." Clearly the teachings of Jesus were incompatible and a menace to the religion and laws of Rome.

Christians were described as "a lurking breed which avoids the light of day."[97] Nonetheless, the third race emerged into a very distinct existence and grew to defend itself against the pagan world. By their inflexible intolerance of other cults, Christians set themselves at odds with the "peace of the gods." Christians rejected all pagan cults without compromise, and incurred hatred, hostility, and reprisal in consequence.

Tertullian wrote:

> "The Son of God is crucified: I am not ashamed because it is shameful; the Son of God died: it is credible because it is absurd; the Son of God was buried and rose again: it is certain because it is impossible."[98]

A decisive shift in the balance between the Roman cultures and Christianity occurred in A.D. 250 in the Decian persecution in which the pagan popular suspicion lost enough power to allow Christians to live in security. The church went on to increase and multiply until a battle near Rome in A.D. 312, won by Constantine (and as he came to believe with the aid of the God of the Christians) conquering the western provinces of the Empire. Eusebius wrote:

> "Throughout the world a bright and glorious day, an unclouded brilliance, illuminated all the churches of Christ with a heavenly light."[99]

Christians were granted freedom to practice their religion and the church was restored the right to hold property. The co-emperor in the east, Licinius, joined Constantine to uphold the principle of religious freedom for all: "No one whosoever shall be denied the liberty to follow either the religion of the Christians or any other cult which of his own free choice he is thought to be best adapted for himself." Christianity was placed on equal footing with other religions.[100]

In just 300 years, Christianity became the official religion of the Roman Empire, in which Jews were still discriminated against and killed. By the time of Constantine, Christianity began to grow. Christians were no longer ashamed of the demeaning manner of Christ's death, and first began to display the symbol of the cross.

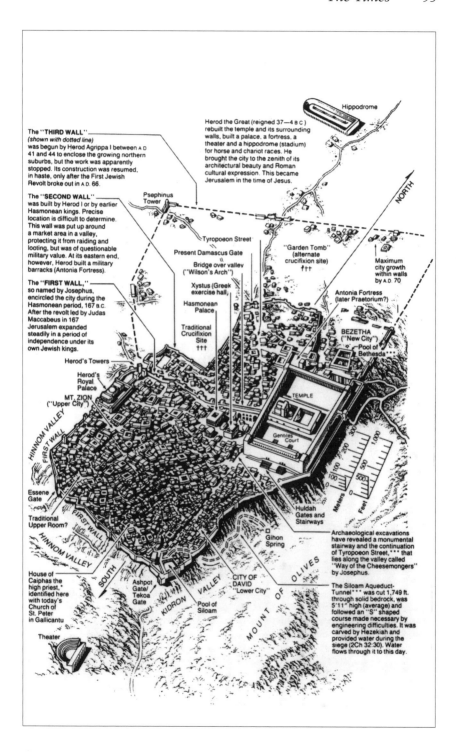

The "THIRD WALL"
(shown with dotted line)
was begun by Herod Agrippa I between A.D. 41 and 44 to enclose the growing northern suburbs, but the work was apparently stopped. Its construction was resumed, in haste, only after the First Jewish Revolt broke out in A.D. 66.

The "SECOND WALL"
was built by Herod I or by earlier Hasmonean kings. Precise location is difficult to determine. This wall was put up around a market area in a valley, protecting it from raiding and looting, but was of questionable military value. At its eastern end, however, Herod built a military barracks (Antonia Fortress).

The "FIRST WALL,"
so named by Josephus, encircled the city during the Hasmonean period, 167 B.C. After the revolt led by Judas Maccabeus in 167 Jerusalem expanded steadily in a period of independence under its own Jewish kings.

Herod the Great (reigned 37—4 B C) rebuilt the temple and its surrounding walls, built a palace, a fortress, a theater and a hippodrome (stadium) for horse and chariot races. He brought the city to the zenith of its architectural beauty and Roman cultural expression. This became Jerusalem in the time of Jesus.

Hippodrome

NORTH

Psephinus Tower

Tyropoeon Street

Present Damascus Gate

Bridge over valley ("Wilson's Arch")

Xystus (Greek exercise hall)

Hasmonean Palace

Traditional Crucifixion Site †††

"Garden Tomb" (alternate crucifixion site) †††

Maximum city growth within walls by A.D. 70

Antonia Fortress (later Praetorium?)

BEZETHA ("New City")

Pool of Bethesda***

Herod's Towers

Herod's Royal Palace

MT. ZION ("Upper City")

TEMPLE

Gentiles Court

Essene Gate

Traditional Upper Room?

Huldah Gates and Stairways

Gihon Spring

HINNOM VALLEY

FIRST WALL

FIRST WALL

HINNOM VALLEY

SOUTH

House of Caiphas the high priest,* identified here with today's Church of St. Peter in Gallicantu

Theater

Ashpot Gate/ Tekoa Gate

KIDRON

Pool of Siloam

CITY OF DAVID ("Lower City")

VALLEY

MOUNT OF OLIVES

Meters

Feet

100 200 300
500   1,000

Archaeological excavations have revealed a monumental stairway and the continuation of Tyropoeon Street,*** that lies along the valley called "Way of the Cheesemongers" by Josephus.

The Siloam Aqueduct-Tunnel*** was cut 1,749 ft. through solid bedrock, was 5'11" high (average) and followed an "S" shaped course made necessary by engineering difficulties. It was carved by Hezekiah and provided water during the siege (2Ch 32:30). Water flows through it to this day.

ENDNOTES

[1]   Josephus. *Antiquities of the Jews*, 14.10.11.4; *The Jewish Wars*, 1.7.5. According to Josephus, "Owing to perpetual wars, the Jews were no longer capable of revolting against anybody."

[2]   Josephus. *The Jewish Wars*, 1.7,6.

[3]   According to world renown author and biblical historian Dr. David Lewis, Springfield, MO.

[4]   Josephus records that after Mariamme had been put to death, Herod seemed inconsolable, cried and called her name incessantly, and even commanded a servant to call out her name as if she were alive. Josephus. *Antiquities of the Jews*, 15, 7:7. His agony has been immortalized in the words of Byron:

> "Oh, Mariamme! Now for thee
> The heart for which thou bled'st is bleeding;
> Revenge is lost in agony,
> And wild remorse to rage succeeding.
> Oh, Mariamme! Where art thou?"

The Talmud records a weird tale about Herod in that he had her embalmed and used to have carnal intercourse with her corpse. Herod must have indeed become mad to have fallen victim to necrophilia, an insane determination to bend her to his will. *Talmud Baba-Batrab*, 3b.

[5]   Klausner, Joseph. *Jesus of Nazareth*. (Block Publishing Co.: New York: 1922), p. 151.

[6]   Josephus. *Antiquities of the Jews*, 15:1.

[7]   Zeitlin, Solomon. *Who Survived Jesus?* (Block Publishing Co.: New York: 1964), p. 42.

[8]   Josephus. *Antiquities of the Jews*, 15.8.

[9]   Josephus. *Antiquities of the Jews*, 15.11.5.

[10] Cornfeld, Gaalyah. *The Historical Jesus: A Scholarly View of the Man and His World*. (MacMillan Publishing Co.: New York: 1982), pgs. 142- 157.

[11] Eidersheim, Alfred. *The Life and Times of Jesus the Messiah*. (E. R. Herrick & Co.: New York: 1886), I, p. 217.

[12] Josephus.. *The Jewish War*, 1, 33, 1–4.

[13] *Meg. Taanith*, Section 9.

[14] Sanders, E. P. *The Historical Figure of Jesus*, (Penguin Books: London: 1993), p. 19.

[15] Sanders, E. P. *The Historical Figure of Jesus*, (Penguin Books: London: 1993), p. 21.

[16] He also feared his preaching would lead to revolt, as he proclaimed the coming judgment.

[17] Josephus. *Antiquities of the Jews*, 18.5:1–2, 109-119.

[18] Josephus. *The Antiquities of the Jews*, 18.5:114, 116, 119.

[19] Overstreet, R. Larry. "Roman Law and the Trial of Christ," *Bibliothecasacra*, Vol. 135, No. 540, Dec. 1978, p. 324.

[20] Greenridge, A. H. J. *The Legal Procedure of Cicero's Time*. (Oxford University Press: London: 1901), p. 410.

[21] Kunkel, Wolfgang. *An Introduction to Roman Legal and Constitutional History*. (Oxford University Press: London: 1975), p. 42.

[22] Josephus. *Antiquities of the Jews*, 18. 3. 1.

[23] Josephus. *The Jewish Wars*, 2, 9, 4.

[24] Walaskay, Paul W. "The Trial and Death of Jesus in Luke," *Journal of Biblical Literature*, Vol. 94, No. 1, March 1975, p. 86.

[25] Eusebius, *Ecclesiastical History*, II, 5, 7.

[26] Richards, John E. *The Illegality of the Trial of Jesus*. (Platt & Peck Co.: New York: 1915), p. 39.

[27] Christian legend puts the finishing touch to the story by having Pilate commit suicide or suffer death at the hands of the Emperor, or die as a penitent Christian.

[28] Blinzler, Josef. *Zum Prozess Jesu*, pgs. 35-36.

[29] Josephus. *Antiquities of the Jews*, 18, 4, 3.

[30] Sharman, H. B. *The Teaching of Jesus About the Future*. (Chicago: 1909) p. 103.

[31] Philo, *Leg Ad Gaium*, 38.

[32] Brandon, S.G.F. *Jesus and the Zealots*, (Manchester: 1967), p. 77; Benchorin, Bruder, *Jesus-Der Nazarener In Juedisher Cicht*, p. 195.

[33] Batey, Richard A. *Jesus and the Forgotten City*. (Baker Book House: Grand Rapids, MI: 1991), p. 180.

[34] Maier, Paul L. *Pontius Pilate*. (Doubleday & Co.: New York: 1968), p. 104.

[35] Bammell, Ernest. "The Poor and the Zealots," *Jesus and the Politics of His Day*. (Cambridge University Press: London: 1984), p. 109.

[36] Torrey, Charles C. *The Four Gospels*. (Harper & Brothers: New York: 1933). According to Torrey, each of the four Gospels was originally composed in Aramaic and later translated into Greek.

[37] Goldstein, Joseph & Katz, Jay. *The Family and the Law*. (The Free Press: New York: 1965), pgs. 9-11.

[38] Dollinger, John J., Vol. 2, pgs. 267-269, quoting Dionysius, the first Roman to ever obtain a divorce was Carbius Ruga.

[39] Plutarch, *Life of Cicero*.

[40] Gibbon, Edward. *The Decline and Fall of the Roman Empire*, Vol. 1. (The Heritage Press: NY: 1946), p. 1.

[41] Julius Caesar did this on one occasion. *Letters of Cicero*.

[42] Dollinger, John J. *The Gentile and the Law*. (Gibbings & Co.: London: 1906).

[43] Almost all states still have some felony or misdemeanor laws condemning homosexuality.

[44] Chandler, Walter M. *The Trial of Jesus from A Trial Lawyer's Standpoint*. (The Harrison Co.: Norcross, GA: 1976).

[45] Pliny, *Ep. X, 38*.

[46] Suetonius, *Caligula*, Ch. 5.

[47] Yamauchi, Edwin. *Harper's World of the New Testament*. (San Francisco: Harper: 1981), citing Rabbi Meir in *Idolatrous Worship*, p. 121-122.

[48] Josephus.*The Jewish Wars*, 7:203.

[49] Hengel, Martin. *Crucifixion*. (Philadelphia: Fortress Press: 1977), p. 37.

[50] Zugibe, Frederick T. *The Cross and the Shroud*. (New York: Paragon: 1988), p. 14.

[51] Marrow, James H. *Passion Ichnography in Northern European Art in the Late Middle Ages and Early Renaissance*. (Van Ghemmert Publishing Co.: Brussels, Belgium; 1979), p. 137.

[52] Walaskay, Paul W. "The Trial and Death of Jesus in Luke," *Journal of Biblical Literature*, Vol. 94, No. 1, March 1975, p. 90.

[53] Tacitus, *Histories*. 5.3.11.

[54] Philo. *Against Flaccus*, 72, 84.

[55] Josephus.*Antiquities of the Jews*, 12.256.

[56] Josephus.*The Jewish Wars*, 5.446-451.

[57] Zugibe, Frederick T. *The Cross and the Shroud*. (New York: Paragon: 1988), p. 37.

[58] Zias, Joseph and Sekeles, E. "The Crucified Man from Giv'at ha-Mivtar: A Reappraisal." *Israel Exploration Journal* 35 (1985), p. 26.

[59] *Acts of Andrew: The Passion of Andrew*, 51.1; 54.4.

[60] Keim, Theodore. *Jesus of Nazara*, Vol. XI, p. 250. (Williams & Norgate: London: 1883).

[61] This entire section relies heavily on *The Trial of Christ*, Walter M. Chandler, (Harrison Co.: Norcross, GA: 1976).

[62] Dollinger, John J. *The Gentile and the Law*. (Gibbings & Co.: London: 1906).

[63] Sherwin-White, A. N. *The Roman Citizenship*. (Oxford Press: 1939).

[64] Burris, Eli E. "The Religion of the Caesars," *The Biblical Review*, Jan. 1929, Vol. XII. (Biblical Seminary, New York, NY), p. 75.

[65] Stephen, James F. *Liberty, Equality, Fraternity*. (Henry Holden Co.: New York: 1873).

[66] Cohen, Jay Simcha. *How Does Jewish Law Work?* (Jason Aronson, Inc.: London: 1993), p. XI.

[67] Perkins, Pheme. *Reading the New Testament*. (Paulist Press: New York), pgs. 46-49.

[68] Perkins, Pheme. *Reading the New Testament*. (Paulist Press: New York: 1978), p. 28.

[69] Today "mens rea" (evil intent) or motive is required. To be convicted it must be proved you knew or should have known your act was illegal.

[70] Josephus.*Antiquities of the Jews*, 13.10.6.

[71] Larrson, Goran. *Annual of the Swedish Theological Institute*, Vol. 12. (Brill: Leiden, the Netherlands: 1983).

[72] Innes, Alexander Taylor and Powell, Frank John. *The Trial of Christ*. (Klock & Klock: Minneapolis, MN: 1899), p. 18; Salvador, M. *Historie Des Institutions De Moise*. (1822), p. 365.

[73] Daniel-Rops, Henri. *Daily Life in the Time of Jesus*. (Hawthorne Books, Inc.: New York: 1962), p. 309.

[74] Today the western wall of Herod the Great's expanded temple mount is the site most revered by Jews. An open-air prayer area visible today is the only portion of the western retaining wall of the Temple platform. This "wailing wall" is the nearest point to the Temple's Holy of Holies where observant Jews are permitted to go.

Archeological remains recently revealed a first century stairway, perhaps the very same stairway upon which Jesus had walked, taught, and ministered. In the temple courtyard, Jesus was separated from his parents on a Passover pilgrimage. Joseph and Mary later found him in one of the temple chambers "sitting among the teachers, listening to them and asking them questions; and all who heard him were amazed at his understanding and at his answers" (Lk. 2:46-47). Years later, Jesus "walked in the temple" in Solomon's Porch (Jn. 10:23), performing miracles, healing the sick and lame, and giving sight to the blind.

Also unearthed was the Stairway of the Assent, leading up to the Hulda Gates of the Temple Mount. Pilgrims to Jerusalem, including Jesus, used these stairs to ascend to the Holy Temple of God.

After Jerusalem was reunited in 1967, ground level was lowered 10 feet to expose more of the grandeur. There is some 52 feet of wall below the ground level of this plaza that may one day be exposed.

Wilson's Arch, named after a British explorer in the 1860's, has provided detailed information regarding the temple mount, supported a bridge that led from the temple mount west across the central valley identified by Josephus as the Tyropoeon Valley (Valley of the cheese makers) to the western hill of the city. The purpose of the bridge was to convey water and not for human traffic.

[75] Josephus. *Antiquities of the Jews*, 20:200.

[76] Damascus, Dung, Lion, Eastern, Joffa.

[77] Devaux, R. *Ancient Israel*. (Darton, Longmann, Todd: London: 1965), pgs. 289-299, 415-432.

[78] Jeremias, J. *Jerusalem in the Time of Jesus*. (Fortress: Philadelphia: 1969), p. 84.

[79] Jeremias, Joachim. *Jesus' Promise to the Nations*, pgs. 48-49.

[80] O'Brian, Patrick. *Daily Life in the Time of Jesus*. (Hawthorn Books: New York, NY: 1962), p. 424.

[81] Ayway, Srinivasa S. "The Legality of the Trial of Jesus," *Madras Law Journal*, Mylapore, India. (Platt & Peck Co.: New York: 1915), pgs. 102-105.

[82] Moore, G. F. *Judaism in the First Centuries of the Christian Era*, Vol. 2 (Harvard University Press: Cambridge: 1927), 2:70-72.

[83] Josephus.*Antiquities of the Jews*, 16.6.2-7; Devaux, *Ancient Israel*, Ibid. p. 403. Not only did pilgrims need money changed into the local currency for the annual Temple tax, but the Mishnah (Mt. 15:2), required Tyrian currency for some offerings, i.e., the selling of doves (Lev. 12:6; Lk. 2:22-24). Nehemiah (Neh. 10:32), told the people to pay one-third of a shekel for their Temple tax, but the traditional Temple tithe was one-half of a shekel (Ex. 30:13-14; 2 Chron. 24:4-14). The reason Nehemiah lessened the tax may have been due to poor economic conditions.

[84] Josephus.*The Jewish Wars*, 5.5.6.; *Antiquities of the Jews*, 15.11.3.

[85] B. Ketub. 66b; M.Sab. 6:5; B. Yoma 39b; Evans, Craig A. "Jesus' Action in the Temple and Evidence of Corruption in the First-Century Temple," *Seminar Papers*, Society of Biblical Literature. (Scholars Press: Atlanta: 1989), p. 524.

[86] Horsley, R.A. *High Priests and the Politics of Roman Palestine*, JSJ 17 (1986), pgs. 27-31; *Jesus and the Spiral of Violence: Popular Jewish Resistance at Roman Palestine*. (Harper & Row: San Francisco: 1987), pgs. 9-15.

[87] Josephus.*Antiquities of the Jews*, 18.1.1.

[88] Horsley, R.A. and Hanson, J.S. "Bandits, Prophets, and Messiahs: Popular Movements at the Time of Jesus," *New Voices in Biblical Studies*. (Winston: Minneapolis: 1984), pgs. 178-179.

[89] Markus, R. A. *Christianity in the Roman World*. (Thames & Hudson, Ltd.: London: 1974), p. 24; Tertullian, *Scorpiace*, 10.

[90] Tacitus. *Annals*, 15.44.

[91] *Origen, Contra Celsum*, viii.2.

[92] Tacitus. *Annals*, XIII, 32.

[93] Suetonius. *Nero Claudius Caesar*, 16. (William Heinemann Ltd.: London: 1914).

[94] Marsh, Henry. *The Rebel King*. (Longman Canada Ltd.: Toronto: 1957), p. 207.

[95] Wagner, Clarence H. Jr. *Jerusalem Courier*, Vol. 10, No. 4, "The Split Between Judaism and Christianity," (David A. Lewis Ministries, 1992).

[96] *Correspondence Between Pliny and Trajan*, Letters XCVIII.

[97] Octavius, 8, *Minucius Felix*.

[98] Tertullian. *De carne Christi*, 5.

[99] Eusebius. *Ecclesiastical History*, x.1.8.

[100] Markus, R.A. *Christianity in the Roman World*. (Thames & Hudson, Ltd.: London: 1974), p. 87.

"But what about you?" he asked. "Who do you say I am?" Peter answered,
"You are the Christ." Jesus warned them not to tell anyone about him.

—MARK 8:29-30

CHAPTER FOUR

Politics

THAT A COUNTRY AS SMALL as Palestine could ever contain all the grief,
corruption, and strife that Jesus witnessed illustrates something tragic
about humanity.

By any measure, the problems of Palestine in Jesus' day were acute. In
part, those problems stand out from those of other areas by contrast to the
glories of ancient Israel; in part, the problems of Palestine in Jesus' day
stand out as soon as anyone merely glimpses the breadth and depth of
what ailed this once proud nation.

But perhaps the greatest source of Israel's strife reflected her religious
expectation: the arrival of the enigmatic Messiah (or "Christ").

There was a great and fervent current of hope that flowed toward this
mysterious figure, an immense hope that lifted the hearts of generation
after generation of believers.

The hope of salvation and relief from early suffering through the coming of a Divine Redeemer rings through nearly all of the Jewish literature of

Painting: Michael Pcher, "Flagellation of Christ," Vienna, 1409–1498

Osterreichische Gallery, Belvedere, Vienna

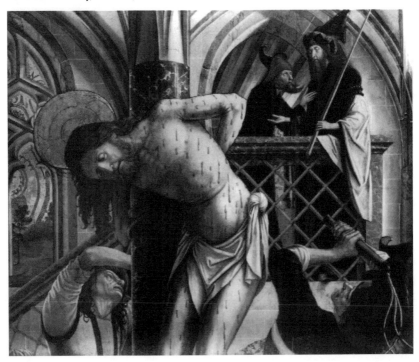

this age. Jewish literature from long before Christ was almost entirely religious. The book of Daniel caused the Jews to believe that Yahweh would not long let them remain under pagan domination. The book of Enoch, the work of several authors between 250 B.C.–60 A.D., took the form of visions of a patriarch who (Gen. 5:24) had *"walked with God,"* and the redemption of mankind by a Messiah and the coming of the kingdom of Heaven. At 150 B.C., Jewish writers published Sibylline oracles foretelling Jesus' final victory over their enemies.

The Messiah would be an earthly king who would be born of the royal house of David (Isa. 11:1). Enoch and Daniel called him the *Son of Man,* coming down from Heaven. All agreed in the end the Messiah would subdue the heathen and free Israel.

Energized by Messianic hope, armed resistance to Roman control began as early as the days of Herod the Great (38 B.C.).[1] Later it was under Pilate, whose rule the Jews suffered utter barbarity with many crucified due to seditious activities, that Jewish resistance first became a continual problem.[2]

Insurrection and zealotist activity intensified after the brief rule of Herod Agrippa I (A.D. 41-44). "The people were in a constant state of insurrection."[3] As many as 20,000 Jews died in an uprising precipitated by an indecent act of a Roman soldier at Passover and large scale revolt by the Jews was barely averted when a Roman soldier tore to shreds a copy of the Torah.

King Felix (A.D. 52-60) crucified a great many Zealots. In response, the Zealots stirred up the people and set fire to those villages which would not support their rebellion. Under the brief rule of Festus (A. D. 60-62) the country was under the grip of Zealots who plundered and burned villages and operated almost unchecked across Judea. This hostility erupted into full scale war from which the nation never recovered. Seventy years later, Bar Kochba was to lead a final revolt against the Romans.

It is hard to imagine a more intense record of political strife or clearer demonstration of the power of Israel's expectation to galvanize her people.

"Then Jesus declared, 'I who speak to you am he.'"

—John 4:26

There were a half dozen self-styled Messiahs between Christ's birth and the fall of Jerusalem. And he was not the most prominent of those Messiahs.

These pseudo-Messiahs were never persecuted by the Jewish authorities. Bar Kochba was the last of them, preceded by Simon Bar Giora, Menachem, and Eleazar Ben Dinseus. Other Messiah pretenders who were resistance fighters were Theudas, and Judas the Galilean (Acts 5:36-37). The Messiah was assumed to be a militant figure to drive the occupational power from the country:

> "Then the end will come, when he hands over the kingdom to God the Father after he has destroyed all dominion, authority and power. For he must reign until he has put all his enemies under his feet."
>
> 1 Cor. 15:24-25

Jesus scarcely had any chance to be acknowledged as the Messiah. The son of a Nazareth carpenter with no disposition for violence, Jesus did not conform to the stereotype of the Messiah. The immediate repercussions of Jesus' ministry were not extensive. Galilee, a remote northern province of Israel, was the main area of his early teaching.

Although his message had considerable influence, in the rest of Palestine its repercussions were limited. Jews outside Israel only heard of him casually from pilgrims returning from Jerusalem. The great mass of Jewish people probably were ignorant of his words. For a long time there was sympathy and enthusiasm among the people. *"All the people hung on his words"* (Luke 19:48).

Until the Sunday of his entry into Jerusalem, popular feeling was in favor of Jesus, but his Messianic character was unlike what was expected and caused a rapidly growing dissension. Other than the Samaritan woman, he revealed his Divinity only to his Apostles and required them to be silent.

The rich, the powerful, and Israel's ruling class were distrustful of him as they set traps and plotted against him. They wanted to avoid difficulties, detested agitators, and tried to keep on good terms with Roman authorities.

The small and powerful political elite did not represent the Jewish people, but governed domestic affairs and derived their power from the Romans. They were collaborators and their power depended upon maintaining order.

Jesus, like John the Baptizer, was a charismatic figure with a following and that alarmed them. He was not politically innocuous and had performed a provocative action in the temple. The elite perceived Jesus as a subversive figure who threatened the stability of the order over which they presided (John 11:47-53).[4] Jesus' social and religious vision imagined a world in which there were no elites and no domination.

A condemned man being led to the place of execution was not an uncommon spectacle as he stepped down the streets of Jerusalem from the Judgment Hall of the Antonio Fortress and climbed toward the Gates of Ephraim.

In the daily life of the Jewish people, the most important event in the history of the world may have passed unnoticed.[5]

From a picture of the state of things in Judea in A.D. 27, we have the Jewish people with their political independence gone, a network of unspiritual and burdensome observances imposed upon their daily life by priests, scribes, and rulers. Ground down by Roman taxes on the one hand and temple tithes and tributes on the other, they were dissatisfied with their hope of Messianic expectation who would restore the throne of David. The scribes and Pharisees, "blind leaders of the blind, proud, haughty, selfish, hypocritical sticklers for a ritual," and Sadducees, politicians in favor with the Roman rulers and in possession of temple offices and revenues, operated through a system of gigantic graft. Commingle these elements with hatred:

1. The Judeans hated the Galileans for their infusion of foreign blood, and being hated in turn for their arrogant pride by the Galileans.

2. The Jewish leaders hated each other, feuds reaching back for centuries with divergent views upon questions about religious faith and observance.

3. All these, Judeans, Galileans, and leaders hated in their heart the Roman rulers.

It was a poisonous compound in Palestine, especially in Jerusalem when Jesus of Nazareth appeared.

Despite the evangelists' strong inclination to ignore political issues, several issues made their way into the Gospels:

1. Jesus had at least one Jewish revolutionary and possibly more among his intimate followers (Luke 6:15; Acts 1:13).

2. Jesus' sayings reflect the current political tension and attest his attitude towards sedition.

3. Several sayings in the Sermon on the Mount have special relevance for the political situation: "Do not resist one who is evil," "Love your enemies and pray for those who persecute you," "Blessed are the peacemakers . . . "

4. Jesus cared about tax collectors and others who were held up to public scorn.

As the hope of the Messiah led to secular strife, so the presence of the Messiah led to religious strife. The chief priests and scribes were alarmed by his provocative but authoritative teachings. They resented his popularity and the way Christ "cleaned house" in the temple's Court of the Gentiles.

Jesus did four things in the "Court of the Gentiles": he began to drive out the merchants, he overturned the tables of the money changers and the seats of the pigeon sellers, he prohibited people from carrying anything through the temple and, he proclaimed the temple to be a house of prayer instead of a den of robbers.

Jesus sought to "make straight" the confusion of the Jewish sects and spent much of his time responding to the misguided ideas of these groups. He re-introduced Israel to the salvation and love of God. He countered the claims to righteousness which each group made, by declaring all of the sects to be sinners.

> "You snakes! You brood of vipers! How will you escape being condemned to hell?"   —MATT. 23:33

Jesus taught a person's righteousness should exceed that of the Pharisees (Matt. 5:20); warned his disciples to beware of the Pharisees and Sadducees (Matt. 16:6); denounced the Scribes and Pharisees for hypocrisy and self-righteousness (Matt. 23:1); and chided the Pharisees for their superficial methods (Mark 2:23). Over and over again Jesus challenged the religious authorities of the day.

At the time of Jesus' birth, Jews of Palestine were led by four groups: Pharisees, Zealots, Sadducees, and Essenes.

Pharisees

The Pharisees were separationists, from the word "perush" (means separate), a lay political-religious party which had arisen 200 years earlier to resist the threatening inroads of Hellenism.[6] Their aim was to defend and perpetuate the intensely religious and exclusive character of Judaism and to turn Israel into a kingdom of priests. They were the political opponents of the Sadducees who were disposed to cooperate with the Roman officials and who wished to take up the freer lifestyle of the Gentiles who surrounded them.

Pharisees were the law experts, master interpreters of the oral traditions of the rabbis. Most came from middle class families, tradesmen and artisans. Josephus said when important decisions were made, people relied upon the opinion of the Pharisees, rather than that of the king or the high priest.[7] Pharisees were chosen for high government positions because they were trusted by the people. Six thousand Pharisees lived in Palestine during the time of Jesus.

The Pharisees did not like Jesus because he did not fulfill their expectations of a Messiah who would support their intense national pride. He showed no disposition to free Israel. On the contrary, he insisted that their obligations to the Romans be fulfilled. The Pharisees criticized Jesus for eating with tax collectors and sinners (Luke 5:30). Generations of misinterpretation of the Old Testament prophecies led them astray. Their religious rules, forms, and ceremonies extended into a specific application to all phases of daily life—the individual was enmeshed in external religious performances. This mass of rules, known as "the tradition of the elders" (Mark 7:1-13), took precedence over all else. It robbed life of freedom, spontaneity and joy.

Most of the disagreements and controversies of the early Christian church arose with the Pharisees (Matt. 23:29-35). The Zealots and Essenes had been stamped out in the wars, the Sadducee nobility lost its possessions and influence, the Herodians had dissolved or become assimilated into the Romans. The only Jewish sect to have survived the catastrophe of A.D. 70 were the Pharisees.[8]

These men, loyal to the Mosaic Law, put up the greatest intellectual resistance to Christian missionary activity, being in a permanent state of hostility to Jesus.[9] This is not withstanding that their mentor Paul himself had been a Pharisee (Phil. 3:6; Acts 23:6), and the highly respected

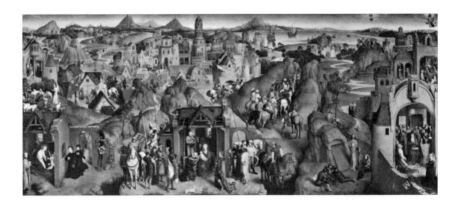

Above: "The Seven Joys of the Virgin," Hans Memling, 1478–1480, Alte Pinakothek, Munich

Below:
Crucifixion
Grunewald
Katlsruhe, Germany

Below Right: Pilate Showing Christ, Albrecht Duren

Pharisee leader Rabbi Gamiliel, whom Peter had to thank for being released after a two year arrest (Acts 5:34), and James, one of the brothers of Jesus, was an observant Pharisee.

Because of his closeness to them, it was natural for Jesus to engage in most of his discussions with them, which often led to violent arguments. Heated exchanges were typical of Jewish debate.[10]

There is no reference to Jesus ever viewing himself in a dangerous way. He praised the scribes when they sided with him (Mark 12:34), and violently attacked them when they did not (Mark 12:38-40). He "silenced the Sadducees" (Matt. 22:34), and it is curious that the Temple police issued an absolutely senseless search warrant: ". . . if anyone found out where Jesus was, he should report so that they might arrest him" (John 11:57), as huge crowds of people must have known that Jesus was staying in Bethany, a village on the outskirts of Jerusalem, where he had raised Lazarus from the dead (Matt. 21:17; John 12:1).

The Pharisees awaited the opportunity to destroy their Messiah.

Sadducees

The Sadducees were a wealthy elite social group of Jewish intellectuals who applied secular Greek techniques of logic to the problems of the day. They were the dominate group in the Sanhedrin before A.D. 70. The Sadducees rejected the oral tradition of the Pharisees and rabbis and accepted only the written law of Moses and condemned any teaching not based on the written word.[11] The Sadducees adopted the beliefs of the Greek philosopher Epicurus, who said that the soul dies with the body. They taught that every person is the master of his own fate. Their personal code was severe. Although they were hostile to Herod the Great, they were less hostile to subsequent Roman rule.

They felt the Pharisees were traitors and opposed Jesus when he agreed with the Pharisees (Matt. 22:31–33). They saw the sacrifice of Jesus Christ as a small price to pay for continuing peace.

Essenes

The Essenes were righteous radicals, seeing themselves as the guardians of mysterious truths that would govern the life of Israel when the Messiah appeared. They lived in remote desert areas and a tiny area of small towns and in Jerusalem near the very small Essenes' Gate. Their writings, *The Dead Sea Scrolls,* found in eleven caves at Qumran, show they were careful to avoid being corrupted by the society around them in the hope that God would honor their faithfulness.

The Bible does not tell of Jesus speaking directly to the Essenes, but it is certain he knew them.[12] Many of the Dead Sea Scrolls are nearly identical to Jesus' words.

Essene writings attacked Pharisaitic interpretation of the Law. They felt that people were being led astray by the "seekers of smooth things." Their goal was to find an application of the law which respected its importance, but which could be followed in the circumstances of ordinary life.

The Zealots

"Zealot" is a Greek word meaning, "the determined ones, the involved ones." Zealots were violent, single-minded revolutionaries. So complete was their hatred of all things non-Jewish, they opposed the use of Greek by Jews. Originating in 6 B.C., they were short lived, dying in a mass suicide at Masada in A.D. 73.

Some scholars cannot resist the temptation to explain Jesus himself as a zealotist resistance fighter.[13] The life of Jesus did show certain undeniably zealotistic characteristics. Neither the Essenes nor the Zealots are mentioned in the Gospels. Judas Iscariot was called a Zealot. Disciples James and John (sons of Zebedee) were nicknamed "Sons of Thunder," a pointed indication they were Zealots.

It is improbable Jesus was a Zealot, though words from his mouth that he came not to bring peace but rather fire and sword (Luke 12:49), and his direct order to the disciples to arm themselves with swords (Luke 22:36) could suggest a Zealot fellowship. But a Zealot uprising could hardly have been started with only two swords (Luke 22:38).

Characteristics connecting Jesus with the Zealots include: he proclaimed the Kingdom of God is at hand, was conscious of fulfilling a decisive divine mission in the establishment of a kingdom, was critical of Herod, and spoke ironically of kings who rule over the people and oppress them by the use of force (Luke 22:25).

Yet Jesus is presented as the "Prince of Peace" and the Jewish Christians did not participate in the Zealot uprising against Rome, but instead moved to Pella in East Jordan to establish a new community of their own.[14]

The Chief Priests

" . . . and laid plans to trap him in his words."

—MATT. 22:15

The high priest was appointed for life and was a symbol of Jewish national pride and Jewish religious superiority. Religious life centered in the temple where the high priest was exalted guardian and supreme commander. His only armed force was the Jewish Temple police who were officially tolerated. Roman governors introduced the innovation that *this appointment would be made (and unmade) by them at pleasure*. Many Jews believed the four families who held the priesthood did so illegitimately.

Prior to A.D. 70, the Romans ruled Judea through a prefect who appointed the high priest. The high priest was the *political liaison* between the Roman government and the people at large. He was to exercise a great deal of religious autonomy, provided he took responsibility for keeping the people loyal to Rome.

In *Antiquities of the Jews* Josephus describes events which occurred after the revolt against Rome:

> "Such was the impudence and boldness that had seized on the high priests, that they had the hardness to send their servants into the threshing floors, to take away those tithes that were due to the priests, insomuch that it so fell out that the poorer sort of the priests died for want . . ." (Ant.20.8.8)

Although rabbinic traditions were not written until much later, they provide reliable information about various facets of first century life. These traditions mention explicit bitter protests against the high priests and their families.[15]

There was a longing for a New Order whereby the corrupt would be punished for their sins and the poor and the meek would inherit the earth. This first century rage and political agitation against a corrupt aristocracy was proved by the elegance and wealth uncovered in the excavations of the House of Kathros in Jerusalem's upper city. In a lamentation against the corrupt temple priesthood, a passage in the Talmud reads:

> "Woe unto me because of the House of Kathros, woe unto me because of their reed pens . . . for they are high priests and their sons are

treasurers and their sons-in-law are Temple overseers, and their servants smite the people with sticks."

In *The Assumption of Moses*, a work written during the first century A. D., certain "unnamed rulers" were criticized as being "devourers of the goods of the poor," and being "filled with lawlessness and iniquity from sunrise to sunset."[16]

Aside from exploitive practices, the basic criticism was that these families had no authentic right to serve as high priests.

"Riches and power the new hierarchy had in plenty, but these could in no way make up for their lack of legitimacy."[17]

The priests were determined to have Jesus arrested to avoid tumult among the people (Mark 14:2) since "all will believe in him."

> "You know nothing at all! You do not realize that it is better for you that one man die for the people than that the whole nation perish."
>
> —JOHN 11:49b–50

That Caiaphas served eighteen years showed both his great understanding of Pilate and his close relationship to him. Caiaphas may have paid good money for his high priestly appointment which developed into a lucrative source of private income for the governors.

Jews despised the high priest as a Roman puppet but still recognized him as the lawful holder of the highest national and religious post.[18]

The Great Sanhedrin

The name "Sanhedrin" is from the Greek "sunedrion" meaning "sitting together." It was the top religious court of Israel and included Sadducees and Pharisees. During the rule of Maccabees, the Great Sanhedrin was the most august judicial tribunal the world had ever known. Its requisites of learning, courage, character and impartiality required for membership, the nature of jurisprudence and detail of its procedure surpassed any like assemblage which has ever administered the laws of any nation.

The origin of the Great Sanhedrin was in the wilderness, established by Moses under Divine commission:

> "Bring me seventy of Israel's elders who are known to you as leaders and officials among the people. Have them come to the Tent of Meeting, that they may stand there with you."
>
> —NUM. 11:16

The qualifications for a seat on the Sanhedrin were as follows:[19]

1. A Hebrew, and a lineal descendant of Hebrews;

2. Learned in the law, both written and unwritten;

3. Judicial experience beginning with one of the local courts and passed through two magistrates and Jerusalem;

4. Well grounded in astronomy, medicine, chemistry;

5. An accomplished linguist, familiar with all languages of the surrounding nations (thus, no interpreters were allowed in Hebrew courts);

6. Modest, popular, of good appearance and without haughty demeanor;

7. Pious, strong, and courageous;

8. A regular trade occupation or profession by which he gained his livelihood, otherwise he was absolutely disqualified;[20]

9. Although he must be a man of sufficient years, he was not to have infirmities that might render him harsh, obstinate, or unyielding;

10. Must have had children of his own;

11. Must not be a bastard.

The Sanhedrin was the representative body of great families and the chief judicial and political authority in Jewish society. The Romans gave it de facto official existence. It was made up in equal parts of representatives of the twenty-four priestly classes, scribes, doctors of the law, and elders of the people, including outstanding laymen chosen from heads of the chief families.

It was not just a court of law, but a pontifical college charged with the study of religious questions and political counsel. It had much the power of our current executive, judicial, and legislative branches of government.

It possessed none of the functions of a modern grand jury and had no power to originate prosecutions. It received accusations and tried accused persons impartially.

Some believe there were two Sanhedrins, a religious and a political one, existing during the time of Roman rule in Palestine. The political Sanhedrin was a tool in the hands of Roman rulers and consisted solely of adherents of Caiaphas. This political body was not bound by legal rules and could be called together at any time day or night, and at any place which seemed convenient. Their right to try Jesus as a dangerous rebel to the governor proclaiming the title of the king was, therefore, totally justified.[21]

The Sanhedrin could meet in threes (known as *Court of Three*), or twenty-three (the Minor Sanhedrin) (the size of many of our current grand juries) or all seventy-one (the Great Sanhedrin).

There was one fundamental issue on which there was a general consensus, that the Sanhedrin should be preserved to prevent further Roman encroachments. The Romans allowed them to exercise their religion and would not normally interfere with the manner of its exercise, including the temple police. There is no end to dispute among scholars, ancient and modern, as to whether the Sanhedrin had the power to try criminal cases and carry out capital punishment. Whether or not they had such power, it is clear the Romans had the power to withdraw that authority.[22] There is historical material available to warrant the conclusion the Sanhedrin had been deprived by the Roman authorities of a part of its jurisdiction under Jewish law.[23] The Talmud in its Palestinian and the Babylonian versions holds that forty years before the destruction of the temple capital punishment was taken away from Israel. They could not cope with the trial work due to the increase in the number of murders and not to be guilty of dereliction of duty had such jurisdiction taken from them. Thus, once again, historical research confirms that the Bible is correct.[24]

Josephus records the establishment of five small Sanhedrins in five different towns around 60 B.C., probably consisting of twenty-three judges.[25] It was, in essence, a legislative body preoccupied with political issues. The high priests were corrupt and would, upon occasion, break ordinances for the attainment of their purposes. If they could bribe Judas with thirty silver coins (Matt. 26:15), they could use any other illegal means to attain their goals or to get the Roman governor to do their bidding.

Jewish law never allowed trial by a single judge. The "Court of Three" was similar to our modern "justice of the peace" and used to try minor

Pilate Washes His Hands, The British Museum, London

The Death of Judas, The British Museum, London

cases. Every town of at least 120 families had a Minor Sanhedrin with general jurisdiction over all serious civil and criminal cases. It also served as the tax board, governing schools, highways, and sanitary regulations. As the largest city in Palestine, Jerusalem had two Minor Sanhedrins.

The Great Sanhedrin had general civil and criminal jurisdiction with twenty-three in the Chamber of Priests, twenty-three in the Chamber of Scribes, twenty-three in the Chamber of Elders, and two presiding officers.

In earlier times the Sanhedrin, established in Jerusalem in 170 B.C., had been composed entirely of the nation's leading priests.[26] By the time Judea had been made into a Roman province, Pharisees had made their way onto the council. They had an intense interest in religion and exercised great influence among the common people. The priests belonged to a smaller and more conservative religious party, the Sadducees.[27] Membership was for life and although we do not know the exact method of replacement, vacancies were probably filled either by the Sanhedrin itself or by nomination of the Roman governor.[28]

In the 107 years from the beginning of Herod's reign to the destruction of the temple, there were twenty-eight high priests. The Roman procurators liked to have plenty of changes because they exploited the appointment of a new holder of the office to obtain gifts from the successful candidate. This unedifying fact is actually recorded in the Talmud:

"And as the candidate paid money in order to become high priest, they (the procurators) were in the habit of depriving the high priest of office every 12 months."[29]

PROCEDURE OF THE SANHEDRIN

For a legal trial to take place, the accused appeared before the formally constituted Sanhedrin. In the Old Testament, justice was held "at the gate" of the city (Amos 5:15), and was administered by the elders, the leading citizens (Deut. 19:12) who might be called in at any time (Ruth 4:1-12) to arrest an offender (Deut. 19:12), determine his guilt, carry out the punishment themselves (Deut. 22:18), or command the witnesses of the crime to do so.

Lawful court hours began after the morning sacrifice and ended before the evening sacrifice. No part of any criminal case could be heard outside these hours. No session could be held on a feast day, especially the sacred Feast of Unleavened Bread.

Another distinction, which we take for granted, is the difference between the function of a witness and the function of a judge was much less clear in the Jewish system than in modern western practice.[30] The Jewish court was not much concerned or equipped to investigate facts. The main question it decided was the admissibility and competence of witnesses. If witnesses were competent and their evidence was clear and unambiguous, conviction would follow automatically.

In criminal cases, there were further checks to be made as opposed to civil cases. The witnesses must be reputable and respected people, and it must be clear their testimony was not the result of collusion or corruption was essential.[31]

Finally, it was important that the accused *has been informed* that his action was illegal. This would constitute *a formal warning*, and if the man did not observe it he would be committing a "presumptuous sin." In our modern day law, "ignorance of the law is no excuse," but in Jerusalem it had to be proved the accused acted intentionally in violation of the law.

To be a witness was a risky procedure. If they fail to make exactly certain of the facts they might be in grave personal danger.

If witnesses had heard Jesus speak blasphemy, it was their duty to testify against him. The judges had to make sure that certain conditions were fulfilled with no inconsistencies in their evidence that Jesus had spoken the incriminating words. There must be certainty about the exact words.

The next morning they were to return, to *give their answers separately*, commencing *with the youngest members*, to insure that they would be voting their own honest views and were not influenced by the vote of their seniors. Judges favoring acquittal always spoke first.

Around the judges swarmed an army of secretaries, ushers, and men charged with carrying out the court's orders. These people would act as ushers, clerks of the court or official scourgers. Often inquiries were required to be held before the day of trial, the results gathered together and given to two secretaries.

The law specified a certain diet for the judges so they would be healthy and energetic and might be able to carry on the trial with a clear mind and a calm mood. They were to go off in pairs and discuss the case informally, eating little, drinking no wine, and spend the night discussing the facts and searching for mitigating evidence for the defendant.

It was later when the Jews began to realize the Jewish religion was not something static, that it could be transformed from one place to another and adapt itself to new conditions. The Sanhedrin deteriorated rapidly and by A.D. 425 it became completely extinct.[32]

Sanhedrin members sat in a semi-circle, similar to an amphitheater. In the center sat the Chairman (Nasi), next to him on the right the chief justice. At two ends of the semi-circle were two secretaries. One took down the arguments in favor of the accused, and the other the arguments against him. Roman and Hebrew custom called for shorthand court reporters.[33] Unquestionably, a record was kept of the trial, but has long since been destroyed. The sessions were public and anyone had the right to enter and express an opinion.

Court procedure was as follows: The judges sat while the litigants stood. The prosecutor was the first to present his case. Witnesses were taken to a separate chamber and sworn to tell nothing but the truth. Then all but one were let out of the chamber.[34] The latter would be asked what evidence he had that the accused was guilty. If the witness stated the accused had told him one thing or that someone else had told something else, his testimony was not accepted.

Hearsay and conjecture were allowed from a trustworthy person, but had to be thoroughly cross-examined. In the criminal law, unlike civil law, responsibility for the life of an innocent person rested squarely upon the witnesses. It meant not merely one life, but the life of whole generations.

" . . . and they shall judge the people fairly. Do not pervert justice or show partiality. Do not accept a bribe, for a bribe blinds the eyes of the wise and twists the words of the righteous. Follow justice and justice alone, . . ."
—Deut. 16:18-20

The cross-examination of witnesses was done in a most thorough manner. The year, month, week, day, hour, and place was inquired into. Even if the testimony of the witnesses agreed, extenuating circumstances on behalf of the defendant were sought. If there were sufficient mitigating circumstances, he was freed immediately. If not, the trial was postponed to the next day.

On the second afternoon each judge must vote and give his reasons again. If his reasons differed from those he had used on the first day, his vote could not be counted for conviction. A conviction by unanimous vote on first ballot was legally considered to be an acquittal because it was felt such a conviction must be the result of passion and prejudice. If the accused was acquitted, he was released at once.

On the next day they got to court early and immediately took up the case. A judge deeming the accused innocent could not change his mind. On the other hand, judges holding the accused culpable could change their minds. For a guilty verdict, a majority of at least two was necessary. To free him, a majority of one was sufficient.

The function of the judges was minimal, except to make certain of the facts. There were grave penalties for giving false evidence—a comparable penalty to that which would have been sustained by the accused if convicted.[35]

The Sanhedrin sat on Mondays or Thursdays—occasionally at night— but never to pass a death sentence.

A curious point of Jewish procedure was that circumstantial evidence, however strong, was inadmissible. Two eyewitnesses were required. "A single witness is never to be believed." A witness' responsibility was exceedingly heavy. For this reason witnesses were chosen with the greatest care; women, minors, slaves, the deaf, the dumb, and the blind were all set aside as people who lied too easily.

After the witnesses had been heard, there were not true advocates in Israel as there were in Rome. The accused made his own defense. The court deliberated and pronounced its sentence, but great legal precautions were taken so that the verdict should be entirely just.

Roman governors had custody of the high priests' official vestments. This made sure the high priest who presided over the Great Sanhedrin would not exercise his authority without being strongly reminded of Rome's military presence. The insignia of the hierarch was kept in a stone chamber at the Fortress Antonia under a triple seal, affixed jointly by priests, temple officials, and the Roman military commander. They were handed over to him when he was required to wear formal dress and other insignia of his office (such as the annual three high festivals: Passover, Pentecost, and the Feast of Booths).

Crimes and Misdemeanors

The difference between crimes and misdemeanors was not very well defined. Misdeeds were roughly classified:

1. *Killing*. There was an exact distinction between murder and manslaughter.

2. *Physical violence*. There was a careful listing in order of the seriousness of the various wounds and blows.

3. Conduct prejudicial to the *family or morality* which ranged from marriage within prohibited degrees, rape, public cursing of a father by his own son, willful removal of landmarks, the use of false weights.

The biblical precepts and decisions of the rabbis show a great deal of thoughtfulness, judicial sense, and justice. It was not murder, for example, to kill a thief who had broken in by night, but killing him by daylight was illegal since he might have been seized alive.

But of all the kinds of wickedness, the worst in the eyes of the law and the least pardonable were crimes against religion.[36] Punishment was harsh and there was only one penalty for all crimes against religion, and that was death (which was the indictment that Jesus was condemned).[37]

A great legal system was thus in place, with detailed laws, procedures, checks and balances, history, precedent and common sense. Sanhedrin members were about to abandon them all and commit the most famous judicial murder in the history of the world.

Jewish Sects

Pharisees:
Traced to the B.C. second century Hasidim.

1. *Accepted the Torah as equally inspired and authoritative and all material contained within the oral tradition.*

2. *They held to a mediating view that made it possible for either freewill or the sovereignty of God to cancel out the other.*

3. *Had a hierarchy of angels and demons.*

4. *Taught that there was a future for the dead.*

5. *Believed in the immortality of the soul and in reward and retribution after death.*

6. *Champions of human equality.*

7. *Emphasis of teaching was ethical rather than theological.*

Sadducees
Probably began during the Hasmonean period (B.C. 166-63). Their demise occurred A.D. 70 with the fall of Jerusalem.

1. *Denied the oral law was authoritative and binding.*

2. *Interpreted Mosaic law more literally than the Pharisees.*

3. *Very exacting in Levitical purity.*

4. *Attributed all to free will.*

5. *Argued there is neither resurrection of the dead nor a future life.*

6. *Rejected a belief in angels and demons.*

7. *Rejected the idea of a spiritual world.*

8. *Only the books of Moses were canonical Scripture.*

Essenes

Probably originated among the Hasidim, along with the Pharisees, from whom they later separated (1 Maccabees 2:42; 7:13).

They were very strict and zealous Jews who took part with the Maccabeans in a revolt against the Syrians, 165-155 B.C.

1. Followed strict observance of purity laws of the Torah.

2. Notable for their communal ownership of property.

3. A strong sense of mutual responsibility.

4. Daily worship was important, along with daily study of scriptures.

5. Solemn oaths of piety and obedience had to be taken.

6. Sacrifices offered on holy days and sacred seasons.

7. Marriage was not condemned but avoided.

8. They attributed all that happened to fate.

Zealots

Originated during the reign of Herod the Great (6 B.C.) and ceased to exist at Masada.

1. Opposed payment of tribute for taxes to a pagan emperor, saying that allegiance was due only to God.

2. Held fierce loyalty to Jewish traditions.

3. Opposed to the use of Greek language in Palestine.

4. Prophesied the coming of the time of salvation.

Staalliche Kunsthalle Karlsruhe
Hans-Thoma-Stra Bez

One Solitary Life

He was born in an obscure village, the child of a peasant woman. He grew up in another village, where He worked in a carpenter's shop until He was thirty. Then for three years He was an itinerant preacher. He never wrote a book. He never held an office. He never had a family or owned a home. He didn't go to college. He never visited a big city. He never traveled 200 miles from the place where He was born. He did none of the things that usually accompany greatness. He had no credentials but Himself.

He was only thirty-three when the tide of public opinion turned against Him. His friends ran away. One of them denied Him. He was turned over to His enemies and went through the mockery of a trial. He was nailed to a cross between two thieves.

While He was dying, His executioners gambled for His garments, the only property He had on earth. When He was dead, He was laid in a borrowed grave through the pity of a friend. Nineteen centuries have come and gone, and today He is the central figure of the human race.

All the armies that ever marched, all the navies that ever sailed, all the parliaments that ever sat, all the kings that ever reigned, put together, have not affected the life of man on this earth as much as that one solitary life.[38]

Endnotes

[1] It is impossible to give an exact date to the rise of Zealotism which was a "spirit of resistance," found in the Maccabaen period. Kohler, C. K. "Zealots," *Jewish Encyclopedia* by C. Adler. (New York: 1907), Vol. XII, p. 639.

[2] Jensen, E. E. *The First Century Controversy Over Jesus as a Revolutionary Figure.* (JBL 60: 1941), pgs. 261-272.

[3] Brandon, S. G. F. *Jesus and the Zealots.* (Manchester: 1967).

[4] Wink, Walter. *Engaging the Powers.* (Philadelphia: Fortress Press: 1992), pgs. 109-137.

[5] O'Brian, Patrick. *Daily Life in the Time of Jesus.* (Hawthorne Books: New York: 1962), p. 495.

[6] Fallows, Rev. S. Samuel. *The Popular and Critical Bible Encyclopedia.* (Howard-Severance Co.: Chicago: 1902).

[7] Josephus. *Antiquities of the Jews*, 13.10.5

[8] Mommsen, T. *Das Weltreich der Romer.* (Stuttgart: (Undated), p. 348.

[9] There are seven type of Pharisees to be distinguished. Six are bad. Only the seventh, the "charitable Pharisee" who obeys God out of love is the true Pharisee.

[10] Frickey, Weddig. *The Court-Martial of Jesus.* (Grove Weidenfeld: New York: 1987), p. 145.

[11] Josephus. *Antiquities of the Jews*, 17.6.2.

[12] They lived at the same time as Jesus, in the same places (on the outskirts of cities), both had a passionate relationship to God, and knew the Kingdom of God was approaching.

[13] Cullmann, Oscar. *Jesus and the Revolutionaries.* (Harper & Row: New York: 1970), p. 5.

[14] Frickey, Weddig. *The Court-Martial of Jesus.* (Grove Weidenfeld: New York: 1987), p. 196.

[15] Farrer, F. *The Herods.* (Herrick: NY: 1898), p. 117.

[16] *The Assumption of Moses.* (Black: London: 1897), 7:3-10.

[17] Jeremias, Joachim. *Jerusalem at the Time of Jesus.* (Fortress Press: Philadelphia: 1969), p. 198.

[18] It is much like many modern politicians today—we may scoff at their opinions or qualifications, but respect the high office they represent.

[19] Ayway, Srinivasa S. "The Legality of the Trial of Jesus," *Madras Law Journal*, Mylapore, India. (Platt & Peck Co.: New York: 1915), pgs. 97-99.

[20] Aren't such qualifications glorious compared to our own U.S. Congress? Wouldn't our Congress be more responsive to voters if they were required to be skilled in a business, knowing the meaning of overhead, keeping expenses down, showing a profit at the end of the year, and strictly accounting for all monies!

[21] Zeitlin, Solomon, *Who Crucified Jesus?*, 2nd Ed. (1947), p. 172.

[22] Branscomb, B. Harvey. *The Gospel of Mark.* (Harper & Brothers: 1937), pgs. 271-277.

[23] Schneider, *Novum Testamentum*, Vol. 12 (1970), p. 24; see the amount of conflicting authority in *The Trial and Death of Jesus*, by Haim Cohn, pgs. 345-349; J. Talmud, Sanhedrin, 18(a); 24(b); B. Talmud, Sanhedrin, 41(a); Wilson, William R. *The Execution of Jesus.* (Charles Scribners Sons: New York: 1970); p. 14.

[24] Jeremias, S. J. *The Eucharistic Words of Jesus.* (Oxford Press: 1955), p. 66, n. 1. A marble block was found with the following Greek inscription: "Foreigners are forbidden to enter the sanctuary: violators will be punished by death." This warning was placed in front of the Temple, and confirmed by Josephus Flavius and Titus, the Roman commander. *Jesus in Selbstzeugnissen und Bildokumentationen.* (Reinbeck: 1978), p. 107; Josephus, Flavius. *The Jewish Wars*, 6.2.4.

[25] Gabinius divided the territory into five Sanhedrins, three allotted to Jerusalem, Gazara and Jericho. Schurer, Emil. *A History of the Jewish People in the Time of Christ*, Vol. 2. (T&T Clark: Edinburgh: 1893), p. 166.

[26] Mantel, H. *Studies in the History of the Sanhedrin.* (Cambridge, MA: 1961).

[27] Mishnah Sanhedrin, 1:6.

[28] Schurer, E. *The Jewish People in the Time of Jesus Christ*, Div. 2, Part 1. (Edinburgh: 1901:) p. 175.

[29] *Talmud, Joma*, 8b; Blinzler, Professor Doctor Josef. *The Trial of Jesus.* (The Newman Press: 1959), p. 92. The Talmud contains the rule the high priest must excel the rest of the priesthood in riches.

[30] Harvey, A. E. *Jesus On Trial: A Study of the Fourth Gospel.* (John Knox Press: Atlanta: 1976), p. 47.

[31] Derett, J.D.M. *Law in the New Testament.* (1970), p. 165.

[32] Schurer, E. *The Jewish People in the Time of Jesus Christ*, Div. 2, Part 1. (Edinburgh: 1901:), p. 191.

[33] Breed, David K. *The Trial of Christ from a Legal and Scriptural Viewpoint.* (Thomas Law Book Co.: St. Louis: 1948), p. 15; Eidersheim, Rev. Alfred. *The Life and Times of Jesus the Messiah*, 27th Ed., Vol. 2, p. 555.

[34] This procedure is similar to our modern "Rule on Witnesses," that all witnesses are to remain outside the courtroom so they cannot hear or be influenced by the testimony of the other witnesses.

[35] Josephus. *Antiquities of the Jews*, 4.8.15; Mishnah Sanhedrin, 11.6.

[36] O'Brian, Patrick. *Daily Life in the Time of Jesus.* (Hawthorn Books: New York: 1962), p. 200.

[37] Death was by stoning. Even though historians agree that Jews did not crucify, Josephus reports of Alexander Jannaeus (104-78 B.C.) crucified 800 Jewish allies of Demetrius, III, King of Syria. Confirmed by a recently deciphered temple scroll, Nahum 2:12-14 from Cave 4 at Qumran.

[38] Some have attributed this to Phillips Brooks, author of *O Little Town of Bethlehem*.

On hearing his words, some of the people said, "Surely this man is the
Prophet." Others said, "He is the Christ." Still others asked, "How can the
Christ come from Galilee? Does not the Scripture say that the Christ will
come from David's family and from Bethlehem, the town where David
lived?" Thus the people were divided because of Jesus.

—JOHN 7:40-43

CHAPTER FIVE

The Accused

JESUS OF NAZARETH,[1] born in 4 B.C., was a Galilean Jew, a religious visionary, and for a short time a preacher. The elementary biographical facts
about Jesus are either unknown or the object for scholarly controversy.
Even what he looked like is unknown.

He is an infinitely more mysterious figure than other founders of world
religions such as Buddha or Mohammed, whose biographies are known to
a fair degree of certainty. Some theologians use four distinctions: The "real
Jesus" (the man who did and said certain things in life), the "historical
Jesus" (a modern, hypothetical reconstruction of his career), the "earthly
Jesus" (Jesus during his life on earth), and the "risen Jesus," (the Jesus known
in faith, the presently reigning Lord of the church).[2]

The obscurity of Jesus' personality and life have encouraged his following. People of different civilizations have put Jesus into what they wanted
from him with little obstruction from facts.

Above:
Pieta, Van Der Wegdon, Capilla Real,
Grenada

Right: Kaisheimer Altar Ecce Homo

Pilate Washes His Hands
unknown, (c. 1250)
Namburg Cathedral
Germany

It takes a strong writer to do justice to Jesus since his mark is on all of our lives, believers and unbelievers alike. We are trapped between a sparse record from his own time and a flood of images from each generation between his and ours.

Jesus became such an important man in world history that it is sometimes hard to believe how unimportant he was during his lifetime.

First century literature that survives was written by a very small elite class of the Roman Empire. To them, Jesus (if they heard of him at all), was merely a troublesome rabble-rouser and magician in a small, backward part of the world. His trial did not make the headlines in Rome. If there were archives in Rome, there was no record of it. And if they were kept in Jerusalem, they were surely destroyed when revolt broke out in A.D. 66 or during the subsequent war. When he was executed, Jesus was no more important to the outside world than the two insurgents executed with him— one whose name we do not know.

But within ten years of Jesus' death, Romans knew someone named *Chrestus* was causing tumult among the Jews in Rome.

Jesus is the founder of the largest religion in the world (twice as large as its closest competitor). Although little is known about his youth, we know of his background. The year of Jesus' birth is not entirely certain. Matthew dates Jesus' birth at about the time Herod the Great died in the year 4 B.C., but some scholars prefer 5 to 7 B.C.

The lack of direct biblical information about Jesus' childhood, youth, and early manhood has intrigued Bible scholars for centuries in the eighteen years between his appearance in the temple in Jerusalem at A.D. 7-8 and his emergence as itinerant rabbi with a national agenda (Luke 2:41-52) known as "silent" or "hidden" years.

There were many traveling rabbis accompanied by small Yeshivas (learners or disciples) circulating throughout the land. Jesus was 30 years old (Luke 3:23) and his ministry followed his baptism at Bethany beyond Jordan, and the forty day Judean wilderness experience.

Virtually all of Jesus' active ministry, except the last few weeks, was in Antipas' Galilee, and his mission was directed to the Jews in the villages and small towns of Galilee, principally in villages such as Capernaum,[3] Sepphoris,[4] Caesarea,[5] and Bethsaida,[6] and Beth Shean.[7] He was a carpenter. Carpentry was a noble trade in the Holy Land. Respected biblical scholars considered it unseemly to make money off their studies so they engaged in a trade for their living. Joseph taught Jesus God's Word as well as a trade to earn a livelihood. Jesus was automatically apprenticed to his father (Mark

6:3) and neighbors recognized him as a small boy asking, " . . . is not this the carpenter's son?" (Matt. 13:55). Fishing and agriculture images were his frequent teachings. Some of his followers were fisherman.

He was acquainted with royal life (Luke 7:25) and his female followers included Joanna, the wife of Cuza, the manager of Herod Antipas' household; Susanna, and many others (Luke 8:3).

He would have been familiar with theater and the profession of acting, frequently used a Greek word "hupokrisis," meaning, one who plays a part, a stage actor (Matt. 7:5).

Jesus possibly spent years with one of the outstanding sages in Galilee. The Rabbi Shammai School was prominent in Jerusalem, as well as Rabbi Akiba. It was believed Jesus was a rabbi of Ben Hillel, a Galilean. He had friends among the Pharisees, especially those who followed Hillel. Simon the Pharisee invited Jesus to a meal in his home. Rabbi Nicodemus also came from Galilee and one night had a profound theological conversation with Jesus.

Jesus devoted himself to ministry as an itinerant rabbi, traveling the length of Galilee's 240 villages, Judea, Perea, Gaulinitis, and other portions of Israel.

Such rabbis were common in Jesus' day, traveling to the smallest villages and most remote parts of the country, and in some instances conducting classes in a home.[8] Often classes would be held in the village square, under a tree, in a field, along the seashore or in the synagogue, moving from place to place accompanied by crowds (Mark 3:7), only staying in a community for a few days or a few months. Jesus taught and practiced that itinerant rabbis were worthy of the support of their hosts (1 Cor. 9:14; Luke 10:7).

Jesus' profession as a craftsman and artisan (Mark 6:3) implied many skills including construction, masonry, and woodwork. While not traveling, rabbis were expected to provide their own living through their occupations.

The more contemporary views hold that Jesus did not emerge from obscurity totally unknown. Many knowledgeable scholars believe Jesus had achieved some of his ability and recognition, was highly educated, and was in touch with a much wider world than Israel, sophisticated, conversant with contemporary theater, sports, business, and commerce. He is viewed as a leading intellectual of his day, possibly the most learned rabbi of Torah and Talmudic studies, fluent in Greek, Hebrew and Aramaic. "Our idea that Jesus was just a country boy is no longer viable."[9]

Many believe Jesus was in touch with the urban world and had an immediate perspective of the urban environment and city life. Some archeologists believe Jesus was the product of Sepphoris. Sepphoris was built by some of Rome's leading architects and builders who had participated in Herod the Great's world renowned massive building projects. Some believe this was the "city set on a hill" (Matt. 5:14) as it is on a six hundred foot high elevation.

When Jesus' ministry began, Tiberias had become the developing capital of Galilee. But there is no indication that Tiberias ever achieved the magnificence or stature of Sepphoris.

Though exposed to this sophisticated urban city, with annual visits to Jerusalem, Jesus spent more time in Nazareth, more than any other single place following the return of the family from Egypt, until he launched his ministry.

A father was bound to teach his son, teaching the Torah and modeling the dignity, value and beauty of work.[10] Religious instruction began through prayer, scripture and blessings through daily prayer routines. It was common for young men to memorize virtually the entire Torah.

In the fifth year, a Jewish child was sent to school with the compulsory education of all children above the ages of six.[11] Appointments, arrangements of the schools, methods of teaching, subjects of study were quite well defined during Jesus' time. Until the age of ten, Torah was exclusively the textbook. From the ages ten to fifteen, traditional oral law was the principle educational focus. At age fifteen, a child entered an academy where he began intensive studies in the Genera or Talmud.

From the time of the Maccabees, all the schools were greatly aided by synagogues and the home. A school for Bible study was attached to every academy. Doubtless there was such a school in Nazareth in Jesus' time.

When Jesus was thirty he proclaimed the urgent need to repent in view of the coming judgment and heard John the Baptizer and felt called to accept his baptism. Jesus "saw heaven being torn open and the Spirit descending on him like a dove," and heard a voice saying, "You are my beloved Son" (Mark 1:9–11).

Jesus went from village to village, usually preaching in synagogues on the Sabbath. He developed a reputation, people thronged to see him, and he preached in open areas because of the crowds.

Jesus lived in a religious society which centered around the Torah and the temple. The temple was at the center of Jerusalem and was the symbolic and cosmological center of the Jewish universe. It was the religious, economic, and political activity of the Jews.

He lived in a colonial society. Palestine was a colony of the Roman Empire and had been since B.C. 63. Palestine was important to Roman imperial policy for two reasons; it was a land bridge to Egypt, the bread basket of the Empire; and it was a buffer against the Parthinian Empire to the east.

He lived in a cosmopolitan society that was in contact with other cultures, especially Hellenism, perhaps more urbanized that many commonly imagine. The use of Greek was widespread, and possibly Jesus was trilingual.

He lived in a rural peasant society (pre-industrial agrarian, 90% of the population).[12] Their social boundaries were patriarchal.

Jesus was probably conscious of the revolt of Judas of Galilee in Rome (Acts 5:37) and its subsequent suppression when he would have been nine years old, and about the nature of the high priesthood during the governorship of Gratus for he would have been twenty-one years of age.

Jesus visited Jerusalem annually, but was mostly brought up in the provincial environment of the small village of Nazareth.

Imported goods were expensive not only because they were dutiable, but because merchants had to pay 2.5% of their value to each city where they kept them overnight on the way to a point of sale. Of the money collected, Antipas was personally authorized to receive 200 talents ($1.30 per head of population).

We have little information as to what proportion of a family's annual income went in taxation; one scholarly guess is that the amount may have been between 40% and 50%.[13]

We know next to nothing about Nazareth in Jesus' time from either documents or archeology, nor are we in a position to know exactly what was implied in Nathaniel's contemptuous remark, "Nazareth! Can anything good come from there?" (John 1:46).

As to living quarters, houses were extremely small, made of basalt blocks, and strong enough to support an upper story.

When Jesus was teaching and four men brought a paralyzed man to see him, the house was too crowded with listeners for them to come near him, so they "Made an opening in the roof above Jesus and, after digging through it, lowered the mat the paralyzed man was lying on" (Mark 2:3-4).

Even in bright sunshine, we can imagine a woman (parable of Luke 15:8) searching for a lost coin in a house with small windows. No wonder she had to use a lamp.

Jesus was working with groups, which explained why Jesus when he wanted to be alone, often had to go into the countryside or the wilderness.

Public Ministry

"The Word became flesh and made his dwelling among us. We have seen his glory."

—John 1:14

"He then began to teach them that the Son of Man must suffer many things and be rejected by the elders, chief priests and teachers of the law, and that he must be killed and after three days rise again. He spoke plainly about this, and Peter took him aside and began to rebuke him."

—Mark 8:31-32

"When Jesus had finished saying these things, the crowds were amazed at his teaching . . ."
—Matt. 7:28

Jesus' public ministry began in the "fifteenth year of the reign of Tiberius Caesar" (Luke 3:1), (A.D. 26 or A.D. 28), halfway through the immensely long reign of Augustus Caesar and just before the death of Herod the Great. The first year of his ministry was a year of *seclusion*, the second a year of *popularity*, and the last one the year of *opposition*.

Every day he was teaching at the temple (Luke 19:47), thus assuming the rights of a prophet. When people listened to his teaching, they began to suspect he might be the Messiah. The Pharisees sent for the temple police, Levites who were specially appointed, to arrest him (John 7:32), but they could not bring themselves to do it (John 7:45).

In another equally embarrassing story "the chief priests, and scribes, and elders" tried to arrest him but "were afraid of the crowd" (Mark 12:12). When Jesus taught in the temple he attracted many to come and hear him.

When Jesus began his ministry, his message had an urgency and an authority about it, and that urgency and authority never diminished. The heart of his message was summarized one day when he preached on a mountainside (Matt. 5:1–11). This Sermon on the Mount, a radical interpretation of the Mosaic covenant, is respected for its moral significance even by non-Christians. Jesus demanded sheer perfection (Matt. 5:48), but also demanded dependance on God's grace (Matt. 6:12-14, 25-34).

His numerous parables were a call to decision, designed to provoke a crisis and force listeners to evaluate their lives and destinies. The parables gave challenges and aroused hostility. One characteristic that antagonized religious leaders was his unique use of the word "Amen," customarily used to affirm another's words or ratify a prayer or an oath. He used "Amen" solely to strengthen his own words.[14]

Jesus' public ministry offended the scribes and lawyers of Israel. They were official interpreters of the law. From the very beginning, tensions built between these men and Jesus. He was not ordained to the office, yet they called him "Rabbi" because he taught with greater authority than the scribes.

Jesus went from the law to the meaning behind the law. He went to the root of the issue, the cause, and reason the law had to be instituted.

> "Do not think that I have come to abolish the Law or the Prophets; I have not come to abolish them but to fulfill them."   —MATT. 5:17

He spoke against Herod Antipas (Luke 13:32) and personally challenged the king's evil rather than simply making a revolutionary statement against secular power. He denounced worldly rulers who lorded over others.

In Galilee there were Jewish plots to silence his voice. Other such schemes originated farther south in Jerusalem and the surrounding country of Judea (John 7:1).

As soon as he came to Jerusalem, it was to the temple that he made his way. Jesus' violent cleansing of the temple, comments about the den of thieves, and prediction that no trader would again be seen in the House of the Lord of Hosts, were aimed against unspiritual commercialism. He did not want anyone to carry merchandise through the temple courts (Mark 11:16). It was a direct insult to the Jewish aristocracy, an implied assertion the Kingdom of God was coming into force which negated the Sadducees claim to direct the Jews.[15]

The attitude of the common people toward Jesus and his public ministry was of another sort. The Pharisees were strong in Judea, but held far less sway in Galilee and it was from this environment that Jesus himself arose as one of the Galilean common people. Galileans regarded him as a great prophet and teacher, and it was from this class of Jewish people that Jesus drew his twelve Apostles. People eagerly awaited and welcomed him as he began his public ministry and "multitudes came to hear him" as he taught and healed them.

They hoped Jesus would proclaim himself the national Messiah of their expectations and looked anxiously to the day he would set up a visible kingdom. They waited until their patience failed. Many followers were disappointed and withdrew.

The healing of the lame man at the Pool of Bethesda raised the question of who Jesus is (John 5:12), and Jesus revealed himself as the Son who works closely with his Father to raise the dead and give life.

No where does Jesus witness openly to being the Messiah and Son of God until the solemn interrogation by the high priest makes his answer unavoidable in this hour of truth (Matt. 26:63–64). The disciples' lack of understanding (Mark 6:51; 8:17–21), shows how incomprehensible Jesus' mighty work was even to his closest companions. He presents himself as "I AM" to the disciples but also to the unbelieving Jews with whom he meets with strong opposition (John 6:41–51; 8:16–17).[16]

Jesus attracted the crowds by his words and miracles. He took great pains to gather them. He called people to follow him not only for their individual salvation but to make them "fishers of men" (Mark 1:17). He sent disciples out with a message of the imminent kingdom of God and with the command to heal (Mark 6:7–13).

Sadducees took small interest in anything but the politics and amenities of life, but now they were aroused to strenuous opposition. They were the Jewish officeholders and if an anti-Roman insurrection took place it would threaten their ability to preserve the peace (John 11:47-50). The Sanhedrin was united in its purpose to put Jesus to death (John 11:47–53), but "not during the feast, for fear that there would be a riot among the people" (Matt. 26:5).

Jesus' triumphal entry into Jerusalem was arranged. Throngs of Galilean celebrants of the Passover gathered and hailed him as the Messiah. Jesus accepted their worship and entered Jerusalem in their company. The demonstrations were like those given a king returning to his city in peace and victory. The strength of the popular following was so great that both Pharisees and Sadducees became alarmed. His appearance led to a "crisis" between believers and non-believers. Some accepted him. Some rejected him and a division occurred.

There were two separate feasts: Passover (one day) and Unleavened Bread (seven days). It was one long pilgrimage festival, one of three festivals that all male Jews were supposed to attend each year (Exod. 23:14).

In response to this commandment, whole towns emptied as people streamed to Jerusalem. Josephus states that one year 256,500 lambs had been slain, and at another Passover he estimated three million were present.[17] But this was an exaggeration, and probably the Temple area could accommodate 300,000 to 400,000 pilgrims as a more reasonable figure. Some people stayed or lodged with householders in Jerusalem, some in nearby villages (Mark 11:12), but many pitched tents outside the city walls.

Many pilgrims came a week early to get rid of corpse impurity. Taking care of the dead, and comforting those who had lost loved ones was a religious duty, taken very seriously and often even strangers mourned with the bereaved family. The removal of this impurity required one week (Num. 19).

Lazarus

Jesus' public ministry was punctuated by intensive personal crisis. Lazarus, whom Jesus loved, falls ill and his two sisters Martha and Mary appeal for help to Jesus who is some distance away, east of the Jordan. Jesus delays for more than two days and finally sets out for Bethany. Martha intercepts Jesus on the way and Jesus assures her, "Your brother will rise again," stating, "I am the resurrection and the life. He who believes in me will live, even though he dies; and whoever lives and believes in me will never die" (John 11:25).

Jesus arrives and finds Lazarus dead and in his tomb with a stone blocking the cave opening. Jesus orders, "Take away the stone," and "Lazarus, come out!"

Lazarus emerges to the amazement of on-looking sisters, disciples, and other witnesses, with "his hands and feet wrapped with strips of linen, and a cloth around his face" (John 11:44). Some witnesses to the miracle report to the Pharisees who are fearful that the Romans will destroy the Jews if belief in Jesus' miracles becomes widespread.

Lazarus' resurrection is the climax of Jesus' public ministry and provides the culminating sign and proof of Jesus' authority and power, symbolizes triumph over death, and establishes Jesus as the Son of God.[18] Caiaphas' prophecy that Jesus would die for the nation to avoid the nation's destruction by the Romans went further in that, Jesus was about to die for the nation and not for the nation only, but to gather into one the dispersed children of God (John 11:49-52).

Irenaeus and Tertullian, both second century writers, and fourth century writers Augustine and Ambrose all verify the story.

The Cleansing of the Temple

Jesus spent little time in the temple during his public ministry, except to teach. He was never pictured as going there to pray. Instead he went to the desert, sea, and mountain, to the fresh world of quiet nature for communion with God and relief for his overburdened soul.[19] That may have been because of his objections to some temple rituals (John 2:14). He was not a strict follower of the orthodox extra-biblical rigid rules of rabbinical Judaism.[20]

The temple had become a public marketplace. The temple treasury and banking facilities contributed to the wealth and power of the priestly aristocracy. The right to sell doves at artificially inflated prices, and exchange foreign coins *was a vested interest reserved to relatives of the high priests* and other persons drawn from the ranks of hierarchy families.

Jesus did four things in The Court of the Gentiles: he began to drive out the merchants, "those who sold" (Luke 19:45-46); he overturned the tables of the money changers and the seats of the pigeon sellers, (Mark 11:15; Matt 21:12; John 2:15); he prohibited people from carrying anything through the temple and; he proclaimed the temple should be a house of prayer instead of a den of robbers.

The cleansing of the temple was one of the most crucial actions of Jesus and the major reason for his death.[21] It was a protest against commercial activities, limited in area, intent and duration.[22] It was a deliberate public act, much as is a modern staged political demonstration.

There may have been two acts of cleansing, the first was early in Jesus' ministry (John 2:14-17), and during the first of the three Passover, and the second in the closing days of Jesus' ministry.[23]

Jesus' criticism and cleaning of the temple was not leveled at dishonest traders. Dishonesty was not unknown. If this had been Jesus' meaning, he would hardly have prevented people from carrying wares through the temple (Mark 11:16), for this is a regulation concerning reverence, not honesty:

"A man may not enter the temple with his staff or sandal or his wallet, or with the dust upon his feet; nor may he make a shortcut of it."[24]

Trade, even honest trade, was not the purpose—Jesus called into question the immense financial and economic power of the temple.

Jesus' own disciples continued to worship in the temple after his death (Acts 2:46; 3:1; 5:12, 42). Jesus gives explicit teachings on how a Christian should sacrifice at the altar (Matt. 5:23-24). He may have continued to preach in the temple compound as Passover approached (Mark 11:27-13:37).[25]

The Crown of Thorns
F. Fabbi

In a stroke, Jesus increased the circle of his audience from local Palestinian followers to international since hundreds of thousands of Jews, together with interested Gentiles, gathered at Jerusalem for the feast and would have come from everywhere. It provoked comment.

It probably gained the approval and sentiment of many people present, but the high priests were enraged.[26]

It has come to be interpreted as a "cleansing" in order to tone down its militancy which began to embarrass the early church. Jesus intended his contemporaries to understand the temple was "made with hands" and was about to be replaced with a temple "not made with hands."

The money changers were not priests, but persons approved or licensed to provide the service. This money did not actually support the priesthood which was provided for in other ways, but to pay temple overhead and support community sacrifices.[27] The Tyrian sheckel, selected amid controversy, paid by all Jewish males over the age of twenty is strange since, "the Tyrians (along with the Egyptians) are our bitterest enemies."[28] The decision was derived from the requirements to have temple dues paid in silver, coupled with the fact local mints were restricted to producing bronze and copper coins. Silver coins were minted only at imperial mints, and the precise reason may lie in the pre-Maccabean period when Jews might well have preferred Tyrian coins to those from Syria or Egypt.

The temporary interruption of business had little effect on the aristocracy but may have victimized lesser folk who suffered financial losses from the violent upsetting of their goods and place of business. *The action in the temple had been far more serious than is represented in the Gospels.*

Exposed as a public figure to misunderstandings and pressure of public opinion that naturally followed, Jesus did not allow himself to be carried away completely by it. He accepted the notoriety that the temple affair brought, but at the same time kept his distance from the role people wanted him to play. He was Messiah—but in his own way; associated with the Zealots but differing from them by his behavior and inspiration.[29] Jesus was an instigator and an inciter.

Jesus' driving out the merchants from the temple is regarded by some critics as fictional.[30] Some critics turn the temple incident into a large scale military operation, almost assuming Jesus acted as a leader of a secret army. It is impossible to find support for this theory.[31]

Jesus the Politician

Jesus was a carpenter, and son of Joseph also a carpenter. He had four brothers, James, Simon, Joses, and Judas, and more than one sister (Mark 6:3).

Eusebius of Caesaria, in his *Ecclesiastical History*, speaks of the grandchildren of another brother, Judas, who was living in Galilee during the reign of the Roman Emperor Domitian (A.D. 81-96).

Jesus was of the tribe of Judah and a descendant of David. He left his family to go to Palestine, but they soon followed and later met him while standing outside waiting for him to finish a public address (Matt. 12:47; Mark 3:31; Luke 8:20). He started preaching at the age of thirty (Luke 3:23).

Jesus did not baptize anyone, but his disciples did. He was more concerned with preaching.[32] He threw caution to the wind, and was heedless of the concern his itinerant mission was arousing among people in political and religious circles:

> "Do not suppose that I have come to bring peace to the earth. I did not come to bring peace, but a sword. For I have come to turn 'a man against his father, a daughter against her mother, a daughter-in-law against her mother-in-law—a man's enemies will be the members of his own household.'"
> —Matt 10:34–36

He took liberties with the Sabbath which the Law did not permit. He flouted religious convention in spite of the negative reactions of the "religious crowd." When he was reminded that he and his disciples were not keeping the Sabbath as they should, his answers varied:

1. He responded plainly it was his special privilege to disregard stricter aspects of the law when there was good reason to do so, exactly as his ancestor David had done;

2. Priests in the temple actually break the rules of the Sabbath by special dispensation (Matt. 12:5);

3. With an added hint of his own status as Messiah being "something greater than the temple" (Matt. 12:6), described the Sabbath was made for the good of man, not man for the Sabbath, and that the "Son of Man is Lord of the Sabbath" (Matt. 12:8).

Signs of danger began to appear. His preaching attracted considerable support which spelled trouble for Herod. John the Baptist's criticisms of Herod on ethical grounds was embarrassing enough, but Jesus was doing something more serious. He avoided open criticism of people in power and even recommended due obedience to them.

When Jesus learned John the Baptist had been beheaded, he left the masses to grieve (Matt. 14:13). He had already become such a public figure he was followed by crowds and could not keep his movements secret.

The tetrarch tried to "see" him (Luke 9:9), perhaps to convince him to abandon his Palestinian mission. Jesus continued to elude Herod until he was warned Herod had decided to kill him (Luke 13:31). Jesus knew this was the beginning of the end.

> "Go tell that fox: 'I will drive out demons and heal people today and tomorrow, and on the third day I will reach my goal.' In any case, I must keep going today and tomorrow and the next day—for surely no prophet can die outside Jerusalem! O Jerusalem, Jerusalem, . . . how often I have longed to gather your children together, as a hen gathers her chicks under her wings, but you were not willing!" —Lk. 13:32–34

If a Messiah failed to become a king, he either had to forfeit his credibility by fleeing for personal safety or else he had to die.

> "My kingdom is not of this world. If it were, my servants would fight to prevent my arrest by the Jews. But now my kingdom is from another place."
> —John 18:36

In our limited world, it is hard to imagine the conflict that must have existed during Jesus' day. When we strip the Gospels of the prefabricated image of the "Sweet Jesus of Nazareth" we encounter a conscious, voluntary conflict between very concrete, definite, well-defined groups that led to his execution.

Even the non-Christian historical witnesses of the time insist that Jesus died after having been condemned by Roman authorities as a political agitator.[33] But Jesus never had any conflict with the Roman authorities. Indeed the documents prove just the opposite.

Jesus' Predictions

"I am the good shepherd. The good shepherd lays down his life for the
sheep."   —JOHN 10:11

Long before his cleansing of the temple, Jesus knew he would be rejected and put to death (Luke 13:31). Jesus predicted with complete certainty to his disciples:

1. That suffering and a violent death awaited him; ". . . the Son of
    Man must suffer many things and be rejected by the elders, chief
    priests and teachers of the law, and that he must be killed and after
    three days rise again" (Mark 8:31).

2. Jerusalem would be the place of his passion.

3. It would occur during the approaching Passover.

4. Persons from whom he would suffer would be the Chief Priest,
    scribes, and Gentiles (Mark 10:33; Luke 13:31).

5. Crucifixion would follow a judicial session.

6. He would be scourged, reviled, and spit upon; "We are going up
    to Jerusalem," he said, "and the Son of Man will be betrayed to the
    chief priests and teachers of the law. They will condemn him to
    death and will hand him over to the Gentiles, who will mock him
    and spit on him, flog him and kill him . . ." (Mark 10:33–34).[34]

7. "The Son of Man is going to be betrayed into the hands of men.
    They will kill him" (Mark 9:31);

8. He would suffer a violent and shameful death (the Parable of the
    Wicked Vine Dressers, Mark 12:1–12).

Jewish leaders opposed Jesus from the beginning:

1. In his early ministry Jesus spoke to a paralyzed man, forgiving him of his sins. Religious leaders heard this and flew into a rage calling it blasphemy, that only God could forgive sins (Mark 2:7).

2. Jesus drove a demon out of a man. The religious leaders protested (Matt. 12:24).

3. The leaders criticized Jesus because his disciples did not practice the religious rite of washing hands before they ate. The leaders said it should be followed rigidly even though it was not prescribed by Scripture.

4. Jesus called leaders "hypocrites" and "blind guides" (Matt. 23:23-27).

Whatever was the cause of Jesus' death and whatever its significance for him and others, his submission to it was a voluntary act. He made no attempt to resist or escape from his enemies.

The rank and file of the people was, for a long time and to a large extent, friendly: they saw at close range his wonderful deeds of healing; they heard him speak "as never man spoke;" they felt something of his personal spell.[35] But the people were not prepared to accept his universalism, his abandonment of exclusive nationalism.

However Jesus may have foreseen his approaching death, it is not likely that he knew in advance the details of the fatal process.[36] He may have expected to suffer death by the characteristically Jewish method of stoning.In the midmost heart of grief, his passion clasped a secret joy.

Devious Questioning

The Pharisees conferred with the Herodians, a remarkable alliance because of their vast differences. The Essenes and Sadducees pooled their resources in their attempts to destroy his cause. One tactic used by these alliances was to ask a continuing barrage of questions with the intention of bringing forth incriminating answers.

The day after the temple incident, when Jesus was back in the temple, priests and scribes tried to trick him into criminal conduct by asking him questions:

1. In the case of a *woman caught committing adultery*, Jesus' response was to stoop down without saying a word and write, "If any one of you is without sin, let him be the first to throw a stone at her." Jesus said to her, *"Then neither do I condemn you. Go now and leave your life of sin."*

2. The Scribe asked, *"And who is my neighbor?"* Jesus answered with the parable about a neighbor who had fallen among thieves. Teaching about the Samaritan, Christ answered, *"He that showed mercy on him you should go and do likewise."*

3. Two men went to a temple to pray, one a Pharisee and one a Publican. *The Pharisees* stood and *prayed out loud* but the Publican did not lift his eyes unto heaven and prayed for God to be merciful to him, a sinner. Christ said everyone who exalts himself is wrong and people who humble themselves shall be exalted.

4. The disciples of the Pharisees sought to entangle him with honeyed words as a cover for their well laid legal trap: "Teacher," they said, "we know you are a man of integrity and that you teach the way of God in accordance with the truth. You aren't swayed by men, because you pay no attention to who they are" (Matt. 22:16).

5. The Pharisees used the legal precedents that Jesus was guilty of breaking the Sabbath and should be sentenced to death for *gathering grain on the Sabbath* as he picked ears of corn. He reminded his accusers that even David had taken the holy bread to satisfy his hunger (I Sam. 21) and that priests worked on the Sabbath (Num. 28:9–10). "The Son of Man is Lord even of the Sabbath" (Mark 2:28).

6. "The Sabbath was made for . . ." applies for the harvesting of grain to eat that day. For the withered hand he replied: "Which is lawful on the Sabbath: to do good, or to do evil, to save a life or to kill?" (Mark 3:1–6).

7. Scribes and Pharisees urged, *"Show us a sign from heaven"* (Matt. 16:1), trying to trap Jesus into sorcery or false prophecy (Matt. 12:38).

"Le Calvaire" by Andrea Mategna, 1431–1506, Musees Nationarex, Louvre, Paris

Crucifixion with Magdeline, Agnolo Gaddi, 1350, Uffizi, Florence

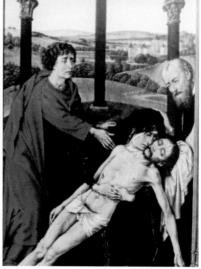

Top: The Crucifixion, Fra Angelico

Middle: The Deposition
by Angelo Brozino
Museum les Beaux-Arts
Besancon France

Bottom: Pilate Washes His Hands
by Jan Leivens
Stedelijk Museum
Amsterdam

Bottom: "Pieta"
Van der Wegden
Caysilla Real
Granada

Bottom Right: Pieta Giovanni Bellini, Vatican, Rome

Middle Left: The Dead Christ (1480–1490)
Andrea Mantegna (1431–1506)
Milan Pinacoteca di Brena

Bottom Left: The Descent from the Cross
Master of the Saint Bartholomew Altarpiece
1480-1510 Wood
Louvre Paris

Above: Entombment by Caravaggio
Vatican Museum Rome Italy

Above: The Descent from the Cross
Rosso Fiorention 1521
oil on wood, panel
Pinacotecca Comunale Volteria

Below: The Passion of Christ
by Hans Memling
Galleria Sabuda Italy

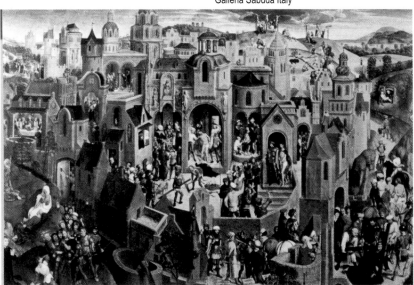

"Pieta"
Michelangelo
Vatican Rome

Top: Artist M.J. Ford
Kailua, Hawaii

Above: Crucifixion
Oil on canvas
Spain, 17th Cent

Above: Ecce Homo, Philippe de Champaigne, Museum des Beaux Arts, France

Above: The Despoiling of Christ, El Greco,
Toledo, Spain

Below: Blind Folding by Grunwald

Below: Flagellation of Christ, 15th Century
Musee Goya
Hotel Deville, France

The Crucifixion by Fra Angelico

Pieta c.1530-1535
Rosso Fiorentino 1496-1540

Crucifixion
Unknown
Spain, 12th Century

Above: Christ's Arrest
Antony Van Dyck 1599-1641
Louvre Paris

Above: The Baptism of Christ c.1475
Andrea Verrocchio 1435-1488 and Leonardo Davinci 1452-1519
Uffizi Florence

Christ Driving the Money Changers from the Temple
by El Greco
The William Hood Dunwoody Fund.

The Flogging
by Bruce Herman
Gloucester Massachusetts

Cristo Partacroce
by Tiziano Vecellio
Scruolo Giande
De San Rocco

Calvary Triptych
by Van Der Wegden

Above: Christ to People

Below: Giotto, Giotto di Bondone, Padua

Below: The Descent from the Cross
(oakwood, polychromed & gilded)
South Netherlands, early 16th Century

The Transfiguration by Raphael

Cross and Sunset
by Dana Bodnar
East Orange, N. J.

Ordet Wood Polychromed
Torsten Renquist (1971)
Sweden

Mocked
Unknown

Below: "Crucifixion Altarpiece"
by Roger Van Der Weyden
Kunsthistorisches Museum, Vienna

Agony in Garden/Kiss

Artist M.J. Ford
Kailua, Hawaii

Right: Tizian Crown with Thorns

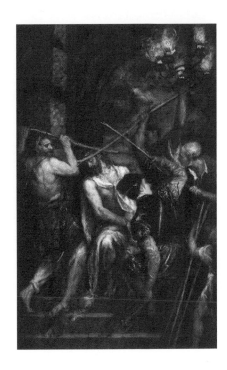

Germanches National Museum
Nurnberg

Germanches National Museum
Nurnberg

Germanches National Museum
Nurnberg

Germanches National Museum
Nurnberg

Germanches National Museum
Nurnberg

Below: The Gethsemane events probably occurred in this cave. Gethsemane (oil press) and evidence of an ancient oil pressing plant was discovered inside the cave, the largest on the eastern slope of the Mount of Olives. It is here Jesus probably spent the night before his arrest and that Judas betrayed him with a kiss.

The "place" called Gethsemane (Mk. 14:32, Matt. 25:6–36) indicates the events of Gethsemane took place in a spacious cave that can now be reached by a long corridor to the right of the courtyard leading to the traditional Tomb of the Virgin. The cave would have been an excellent place to spend the night—warm, dry and roomy. The nights were cold and the dew heavy (Jn. 18:18), and it is improbable Jesus and his disciples would have spent the night out in the open sleeping amid olive trees in the spring.

Above: Images of the "Garden Tomb", in "Gordon's Calvary."

Below: The Convent of the Sisters of Zion. The pavement, named Lithostrotos, was the scene of the public trial of Jesus.

Christ Blessing
Andrea Solario
New York Metropolitan Museum of Art
New York, NY

The Agony in the Garden
Raphael
New York Metropolitan Museum of Art
New York, NY

Christ Before Pilate
Rembrandt
New York Metropolitan Museum of Art
New York, NY

Pilate Washing His Hands
Mattia Preti
New York Metropolitan Museum of Art
New York, NY

The Road to Calvary
Martin Schöngauer
New York Metropolitan Museum of Art
New York, NY

The Entombment
Moretto da Brescia
New York Metropolitan Museum of Art
New York, NY

8. *"Is it lawful for a man to divorce his wife for any and every reason?"* (Matt. 19:3) Jesus told the Pharisees, *It was not so from the beginning.* They had not made out a legitimate charge of heresy nor had they discredited him as a teacher.

9. *"By what authority are you doing these things?"* He turned the question back to them: *"I will also ask you one question. If you answer me, I will tell you by what authority I am doing these things. John's baptism—where did it come from? Was it from heaven, or from men?"* (Matt. 21:23–24).

His inquisitors had no answer. If they said it was from heaven, Jesus could have then asked, "Why did you not believe him?" If they said it was of men, then they need fear the multitudes that followed Jesus. They responded, "We don't know." Jesus answered them: *"Neither will I tell you by what authority I am doing these things."*

10. "Tell us then, what is your opinion? *Is it right to pay taxes to Caesar or not?"* (Matt. 22:17) was a trick question with which a skillful cross-examiner would be familiar. If he said, "Yes, it is lawful," it would lead to suspicion and distrust among those who followed him and believed him to be their king. If he said it was unlawful (Matt. 17:24-27), he could have been charged with treason by the Romans. The tax was based on a census taken in the provinces every four years. Numbering the people was bitterly resented as an infringement of Jewish law and was reviewed as a method of enslavement. It was a census year and tax was due for payment. He separated legal and spiritual obligations as he declared, *"Give to Caesar what is Caesar's, and to God what is God's"* (Matt. 22:21).

11. The Sadducees attempted to trick Jesus with *a question about seven men*, who in turn performed the duties of a husband to their dead brother's widow (Matt. 22:24–28; Mark 12:20–23). Jesus showed that they were wrong in their interpretation of the Scriptures. In fact, the brother was not to marry his deceased brother's wife, but was to act toward her as that deceased brother would have done, enabling her to produce a son who would take his brother's name. In this way the name would be perpetuated and not die out.

12. The question about David's son is another story that portrays conflict between Jesus and the Pharisees (Matt. 22:41-46). "What do you think about the Christ? Whose son is he?" The Pharisees answered, "The son of David." Jesus then raises the question as to how the Messiah can be the son of David in light of Psalm 110: *"And no one was able to answer him a word, nor from that day did anyone dare to ask him anymore questions."*

13. Conflicts with Jesus' teachings in relationship to the Jewish law include the question of *associating with tax collectors and sinners* (Mark 2:13-17), "Those who are well have no need for a physician, but those who are sick." On the question of *plucking ears of grain on the Sabbath* (Mark 2:23-28), "The Sabbath was made for man, not man for the Sabbath." On the question of *eating with unwashed hands* (Mark 7:1-8); the question of *divorce* (Mark 10:2-9), "Therefore what God has joined together, let man not separate."

14. Jesus cured a paralytic by saying, "Your sins are forgiven." Scribes murmured that he arrogated to himself the authority to forgive sins, terming it blasphemy (Mark 2:1-12).

15. Jesus called a tax collector to follow him and dined with tax collectors. He defended his right to call sinners (Mark 2:13-17).

16. Jesus defended his disciples in not fasting by saying that as long as the bridegroom was with them, the wedding guests should not fast (Mark 2:18-22).

17. A lawyer posed a question: *"Which is the greatest of the Law?"* He answered, *"men should love the Lord their God with their heart and with all their mind . . . the second commandment is like it: men should love their neighbor as themselves"* (Matt. 22:36).

Jesus criticized the Scribes and Pharisees for their passion for ceremony and ritual: *"Woe unto you, Scribes and Pharisees, hypocrites!"*

The violence of the charges Jesus brought destroyed any hope of reconciliation. The determination of the temple officials to destroy Jesus grew more and more intense. Every attempt to trap and discredit him had failed. Their only recourse was action and the action had to be swift.[37]

Jesus' opponents gathered at the house of Caiaphas with the deliberate intention of arresting Him. The tactic of trapping him into self-incrimination had been put aside. The high priestly family recognized the challenge to their authority and wealth. Ironically, priests were supposed to intercede for a man before God, but now the chief priests were desperately searching for a way to ensure his condemnation.

1. We have no way of knowing exactly what took place in the authority's private chambers.

2. The plot of the conspirators was said to be that of the chief priests and scribes (and in Matt. 26:3, the elders), and the plot is laid in the court of the high priest.

3. The Pharisees alone are not named.

4. The details of the conspiracy are not important, but their motives to act against him are clear: they considered him a threat to the delicate balance of political order in the city and they did not want him to ignite an insurrection.

Political Crisis

To grasp the depth of the priests' fears, more focus should be directed to the revolutionary background of the ministry of Jesus. The Gospels themselves divorce Jesus almost completely from the national crisis and from political affairs.

Jesus was not interested in supporting one of the parties at the expense of the others, but he seems to have seen dangers in the reigning Jewish establishment of the day as they did in him, and to have made no secret of his views. His attitude to the temple and that of his followers was ambiguous. They remained faithful in attending the temple for teaching and worship, but they also remained critical of those who controlled it.

The temple authorities kept an eye on his activities while criticizing Jesus for neglecting the laws of purification.

The Gospels were not concerned about political issues and are not records of Jewish life in Jesus' day. They are documents designed to show Jesus was the spiritual Messiah and Son of God, and they included only the material useful to the church in illustrating his divine mission. There was no reason to describe the political scene amidst which Jesus had worked, and they had no interest in the political problems of Jewish national life.[38]

Reading Josephus, it is hard to imagine a more intense record of political strife. Undoubtedly, there were many acts of resistance crowded from Josephus' pages which were written in other records that have been destroyed. Thousands gave their lives in battle or were crucified because of open sedition or their actions threatened the civil order. Not only were people crucified on political charges but also those politically innocuous lost their lives because of the nervous apprehension of the procurators. The list of those accused of political crimes and sent to their deaths is long, particularly during the reign of Pilate who crucified "countless" Jews.[39]

Still, it is clear the political life in Judea had a direct bearing on his career, and he faced the political question wherever he went, especially in Galilee where Zealots were particularly active. Whenever he attracted a crowd it was necessary for him to set forth clearly the nature of his mission. John records that on one occasion a crowd sought to make him a king which reflects how easily the people misunderstood his intent. Listeners were eager for hints to interpret his career in terms of the national crisis:

1. Several of Jesus' sayings reflect the current political tension and attest to his attitude towards resistance and sedition. The problem of submission to Rome as to whether taxes should be paid shows the pressure Jesus encountered to declare himself on the central political question.

2. His words concerning the attempt to establish the Kingdom of God by violence is best explained as a direct condemnation of the zealotic cause (Matt. 11:12).

3. The Sermon on the Mount has special relevance for the political situation. Not resisting "one who is evil, loving your enemies, praying for those who persecute you.." and "blessed are the peacemakers . . ." are rejections of political violence.

Jesus entirely excluded political affairs from his orbit, claiming no political program and enunciating no political principles.[40]

Jesus never took part in governmental activities, whether local or national. It is hard to find in any of his recorded sayings, apart from the tribute to Caesar, bearing directly on any specific political practice. Why should one who came to speak "the words of eternal life" have anything to do with petty political questions of only temporary and local importance?

We must be careful not to exaggerate the political discontent felt by the Jews of Palestine because they were under the rule of Roman governors. The Sadducees had no complaints to make and they opposed any manifestation of any ill-will towards the ruling powers as dangerous to the settled order of things (John 11:47-50). For different reasons, the Essenes would be equally adverse from any overt enmity. In regard to the Romans, the Jews as a people had in 4 B.C. actually sent a deputation to Augustus begging that they might be placed under an imperial governor rather than under the sons of Herod the Great.[41] Some Pharisees even appreciated the political suzerainty of the foreigners because it left them freer for the study of the law.[42]

There were also a large number of Jews who believed it was Israel's duty not to revolt against the government, but to await redress at the hands of God.

Still, the national mind on the whole was in a state of most profound disquiet at the condition of things as they were. Politically, Israel was in chains. Instead of having a Jewish monarch of David's blood righteously and mightily reigning over them at Jerusalem, one half of the country (Judea and Samaria) was administered by a Roman Procurator, and the other half (Galilee, Peraea, and lands north and east of the Sea of Galilee) under the two sons of the hated Herod.

No serious minded Jew, unless he was Sadducee or Essene, could do other than regard the whole situation with profound disgust.[43]

Jesus shows himself to be in favor of the Jews dutifully paying the taxes demanded of the Roman government while he takes the opportunity to remind them that at the same time they must be no less careful to comply with the demands made upon them by God.[44]

Jesus wanted to prevail upon Israel as a people to give up the old yearning for vengeance on Rome, to submit meekly for the time being to servitude and injustice and trust wholly to deeds of love and words of truth. He wanted to outmaneuver political domination, convert enemies to friends, and stand "as a light to them that are in darkness."

The title "Messiah" could imply a revolutionary political leader, but there was no clear-cut consistent usage of the term in Jesus' day. Jesus avoided the title during his lifetime.[45] He never called the whole people to follow him, nor did he make them all disciples, although he did expect them all to repent.

This is true despite a lack of unanimity among Jews about Rome. Sadducean leaders were sympathetic to the Roman governor in Judea. Pharisees reflected the temper of the populace as a whole. They ardently wished the Romans gone, but there seemed little to do about the problem. It was not until some forty years after Jesus' time that their caution was finally overridden by patriotism, hatred, and religious fervor.

Was Jesus Dangerous to the Empire?

"Every day he was teaching at the temple. But the chief priests, the teachers of the law and the leaders among the people were trying to kill him. Yet they could not find any way to do it, because all the people hung on his words."   —LUKE 19:47-48

"Keeping a close watch on him, they sent spies, who pretended to be honest. They hoped to catch Jesus in something he said so that they might hand him over to the power and authority of the governor."
                                                                    —LUKE 20:20

Certain teachings of Jesus were truly potentially disruptive:[46]

1. He opposed surplus possessions and traveled with women not related to him, a variance with prevailing social patterns.

2. He insisted that social relationships be governed by service and humility, seriously challenging the existing social order.

3. He rejected the use of violence, criticized gentile kings for the domination of their subjects, emphasized humility and urged service to others be performed in everyday living.

4. He discouraged disciples from seeking prominent places at banquets or competing with one another in seeking honors.

5. As to the payment of taxes, he did not believe the Empire was privileged but rather was to be evaluated how it adhered to the Law of God.

The Romans were not the only force politically hostile with which Jesus had to reckon with in the city. It was the Roman practice to make important native offices available "only to men who stood to lose most heavily by wars or revolutions and whose position in the community was analogous to that of the nobles in Roman society."[47] The best example of this was the unusually successful rapprochement between the Annas family and Pilate.

The Plot to Kill Jesus From Three Perspectives[48]

Why did the leaders want Jesus killed? What was their motivation in seeking his death?

1. The Point of View of the Religious Leaders

They wanted Jesus killed because he claimed to have authority from God. They said he was guilty of blasphemy (Matt. 9:3), responded negatively to his demonstrations of divine authority (Matt. 9:34; 12:24), and questioned his source of authority, claiming that it came from Satan (Matt. 9:34).

Their plot to kill Jesus is linked to spiritual blindness. They did not know how to read the signs of the times or discern the implication of God's power for the future. Jesus frequently accused them of not understanding Scripture. He used such phrases as "haven't you read" (Matt. 12:3; 19:4; 22:31), "have you never read" (Matt. 21:16), or similar expressions.

As they were unable to perceive who Jesus was, they regarded his actions as presumptuous, his claims blasphemous, and him an imposter. This gave their threat to kill him an ostensibly noble motive. They believed that by putting him to death, they were serving God. They precipitated disputes to entangle (Matt. 22:15), test (Matt. 19:3), or accuse (Matt. 12:10). His claim to possess divine authority (Matt. 12:8) prompted the leaders to look for a way to accuse him, monitor him, and find an occasion to sentence him to death.

Jesus' apparent challenge to the law threatened the leaders because it constituted a claim to divine authority. They never accused him of heresy or false teachings, but as a blasphemer and imposter. They did not seek to kill him because they disagreed with him, but because he claimed to be God.

2. The Point of View of Pilate

Pilate perceived it was "out of envy" (Matt. 27:18) of Jesus that they wanted to kill him because he claimed divine authority. Crowds were astonished at Jesus' teaching because he "taught them as one who had authority and not as their teachers of the Law" (Matt. 7:29) and the crowds moved from being astonished to glorifying him (Matt. 9:8). "Nothing like this has ever been seen in Israel" (Matt. 9:33). Pilate believed that Jewish temple officials wanted Jesus killed out of envy. The religious leaders were hypocritical and insincere in their dealings with Jesus, pretentious in their piety and inconsistent in their speech and actions.

Because they were hypocritical, religious leaders greatly prized the opinions of the people and often attempted to hide vain motives with pious pretense. Pilate's perception then makes sense. The Jewish leaders of the day envied Christ as one who was regarded by others as possessing authority which the leaders themselves lacked.

3. The Point of View of Jesus

Jesus' perspective of the leaders' plot to take his life may have been different; not that they sought to kill him because he claimed to have divine authority or because others responded to him as if he had such authority, but because he did have such authority and because the leaders were, in fact, enemies of God.

In his parable of the two sons (Matt. 21:28), and of the wicked tenants (Matt. 21:33), the leaders are depicted as disobedient children knowingly disregarding their father's wishes or being described as rebels who killed their master's son and heir knowing full well who he was. In fact, they killed him because of who he was!

Jesus does not regard the religious leaders as people who "know not what they do," but considered them to be murderers who will be held accountable for fighting God (Matt. 23:29-36). They would not be forgiven and would be sentenced to hell (Matt. 23:33). They were "thinking evil" in their hearts (Matt. 9:4); he called them "a brood of vipers" and "children of hell".

All three perspectives show that Jesus was killed because of his "divine authority". The religious leaders thought they wanted to kill Jesus because he claimed to be God. Pilate thought they wanted to kill him because others responded to him as God. But Jesus knew they wanted to kill him because he really was the long-promised God-man, Immanuel, the divine Messiah of Israel.

Ironically, no one believed that Jesus was to be killed because he advocated treason, ministered to Gentiles, advocated paying taxes to Caesar or took a hard line stance on the issue of divorce. As important as such legal issues were, they did not represent the heart of the conflict between Jesus and his enemies. It is inconceivable Jesus would have been handed over to the Romans for execution for any other reason than the fact that he was King of the Jews.

Yet, he was executed for dissent, convicted simultaneously for dissent against the temple establishment and against the Roman Empire. What an accomplishment was that dissent—to be capitally executed at the same time by both temple and state![49]

The Great Pacifist was crucified as a criminal insurrectionist.[50]

ENDNOTES

[1] Nazareth was a lovely village nestled in the Zebulon Mountains south of Zippori and north of the Megiddo Valley. It was not known to be the residence of anyone important and the common expression, "Can any good thing come out of Nazareth?" was true except for Jesus. Jesus left to go up to the Jordan River, later returned to Nazareth, but because of their unbelief moved on to other sites. He preached in the synagogue and walked unharmed through the angry mob that tried to throw him headlong over the cliff to his death.

[2] Meier, John P. *A Marginal Jew: Rethinking the Historical Jesus*, Vol. 1, (Doubleday: New York: 1991), pgs. 21-40.

[3] Capernaum, located on the northern slopes of the Sea of Galilee was a central city for Jesus' public ministry in the north. It was the home of one of Jesus's closest companions and disciples, Simon Peter. He lived in the home of Simon Peter and healed Simon's mother-in-law (Mk. 1:29-34). He cured a paralytic who was lowered from the roof (Mk. 2:1-4), and preached to the multitudes (Mt. 12:46-50). He healed the woman with an issue of blood and brought the daughter of Jairus back to life. The courtyard on some of the houses leading into the courtyard provides for an open area which would have allowed space for a large number of people to "gather at the door," of Peter's home to hear Jesus' preaching (Mk. 1:33; 2:1-2).

[4] Tradition says that Sepphoris was the seat of the Roman governors and a major Jewish center of upwards of 30,000 inhabitants where the Sanhedrin officiated after the destruction of the Temple in Jerusalem.

Sepphoris was the home of Anna and Joachim, the parents of Mary, where she was born, lived, and blessed. Josephus described the city as an "ornament of all of Galilee," and the Roman Christian Pilgrim Antonius Martyr adored the countryside "with reverence for the blessed Mary."

It may have been the peaceful and charming fields surrounded by vineyards and bursting with purplish harvest and wild flowers inspired Jesus to compose the beautiful parables: the parables of sowing and harvesting, of the wheat, of the lilies of the field.

[5] Caesarea, built by Herod out of white stone, was the scene of some of the most significant events in the book of Acts. The Apostle Paul made at least three recorded visits to Caesarea, "Entering the house of Philip the Evangelist...and stayed with him" (Acts 21:8). This was his last visit. It was to Caesarea that Paul was finally taken as a prisoner to be tried by Felix, the governor.

Herod build a hippodrome outside the city walls, and in the year A.D. 6 the city became the seat of the Roman governors of Judea.

The auditorium was the scene of Paul's enthusiastic witness about Jesus of Nazareth. Today you can physically stand in the very auditorium where Paul faced Agrippa.

Throughout the centuries, Caesarea was the site of battles between the Crusaders and Moslem regimes.

Caesarea-Philippi was the headquarters for the Tetrarchy of Herod's son, Herod Philip. The ruins of that site can be seen today with its towering walls. On the slopes from this city, Jesus gathered his disciples and taught them an important lesson regarding his authority and their duty. Perhaps it was on the spur of Mount Hermon nearby on whose site the Crusader fortress of Minrud was built that Simon Peter made his great confession and where Jesus was transfigured in their presence (Mt. 16:13; 17:1-9).

[6] Bethsaida was a fisherman's village located on the slopes of the east side of the Jordan where it empties into the Sea of Galilee. It was the original home of Peter and Andrew and the site of the great battle between Jews and Romans in A.D. 66. This is where the Jewish priest from Jotapata, in charge of the Jewish forces in Galilee was taken prisoner, capitulated to the Romans, and tried to get the other Jews to lay down their arms and surrender. He was scurrilously labeled "Josephus of the Flavians," simply known today as Flavius Josephus (Jn. 1:44; 12:21; Mk. 6:45; Mt. 11:21).

[7] Beth Shean was the largest and most majestic Roman city currently being excavated, one of the most magnificent cities built in the region.

Following General Pompey's conquest of Beth Shean in 63 B.C., the city grew quickly, becoming the capital of the magnificent Roman cities of the Decapolis.

Jesus visited this region (Mk. 7:31) which stood astride the main road between Jerusalem and the Galilee. Josephus records that Vespian "sent away his son Titus to Cesarea, that he might bring the army that lay there to Beth Shean, which is the largest city of the Decapolis."

8 Rabbinic documents specify different type of rabbis. The term used for those who had a semikkah (ordination) which required the presence of at least three ordained persons. When asked if he had the rabbinic authority to cast out miscreants from the temple, he declined to answer (Matt. 21:23; Mark 11:29; Luke 20:1-8). The offices of rabbi, elder, and judge were combined into one function. There was the *rabbe*—an intern rabbi, licensed to teach the law; rebbi—a recognized leader of rabbis; and a *rav*-the chief rabbi of Israel; for a sage of Israel called *Rabboni*, a teacher rabbi who had heard designation through some particular speciality or achievement.

9 Batey, Dr. Richard A. *Jesus and the Forgotten City*. (Baker: Grand Rapids: 1989).

10 *Sanhedrin*, 99b.

11 Josephus. *Antiquities of the Jews*, 17.6.2.

12 Lenski, Gerhard. *Power and Privilege: A Theory of Social Stratification*. (McGraw-Hill: New York: 1966).

13 *Jerusalem as Jesus Knew It*. (Thames & Hudson, Ltd.: London: 1978), p. 25.

14 Tambasco, Anthony J. *In the Days of Jesus*. (Paulist Press: New York: 1970), p. 85.

15 Grant, Michael. *Jesus, An Historian's Review of the Gospels*. (Collier Books: New York: 1977), p. 151.

16 Schnackenburg, Rudolf. *Jesus and the Gospels*. (Westminster John Knox Press: Louisville, KY: 1914), translated into English 1993.

17 Josephus. *The Jewish Wars*, 6.420-27; 2.280

18 Kee, Howard Clark. *Medicine, Miracle, and Magic in the New Testament Times*. (University Press: Cambridge: 1986), pgs. 86-94.

19 Foster, R. C. *Studies in the Life of Christ*. (Baker Book House: Grand Rapids, MI: 1979), p. 364.

20 Cornfeld, Gaaylah. *The Historical Jesus*. (MacMillan Publishing Co.: NY: 1982), p. 157.

21 Betz, Thus D. *What Do We Know About Jesus?* (SCM Press: 1968), p. 86.

22 Borg, Marcus J. *Conflict, Holiness, and Politics in the Teachings of Jesus*. (Edwin Mellen Press: Queenston, Ontario: 1984), p. 171.

23 Kiehl, Erich H. *The Passion of Our Lord*. (Baker Book House: Grand Rapids, MI: 1990), p. 33. Debate continues over whether this was only one event, or whether there were in fact two events. All three synoptic writers mention a cleansing of the temple at the end of the Jesus' ministry and only John has one at the beginning (John 2:14-17).

24 Berakhoth 9:5.

25 Fredriksen, Paula. "Jesus and the Temple, Mark and the War," *Seminar Papers*, Society of Biblical Literature, (Scholars Press: Atlanta: 1990), p. 293.

26 Klausner, Joseph. *From Jesus to Paul*. (MacMillan: 1943); Zeitlin, Irving M. *Jesus and the Judaism of His Time*. (Polity Press: Oxford: 1988), p. 150.

27 Sanders, E.P. *Jews and Judaism*. (Fortress Press: Philadelphia: 1983), pgs. 84-87.

28 Richardson, Peter. "Why Turn the Tables? Jesus' Protest in the Temple Precincts," *Seminar Papers*, Society of Biblical Literature. (Scholars Press: Atlanta: 1992), p. 514.

29 Procmee, Etienne. *Jesus as Seen by His Contemporaries*. (Westminster Press: Philadelphia), Ch. 8, pgs. 110-120.

30 Goguel, M. *The Life of Jesus*. (Allen and Unwin: 1933), pgs. 4-12.

31 Procmee, Etienne. *Jesus as Seen by His Contemporaries*. (Westminster Press: Philadelphia: 1973), p. 112.

32 Saliba, Kamal. *Conspiracy in Jerusalem: The Hidden Origins of Jesus*. (Tauris and Co., Ltd.: London: 1988), p. 110.

33 Segundo, Juan Luis. *The Historical Jesus of the Synoptics*. (Orbis Books: Mary Knoll, NY: 1985), p. 72.

34 Dodd, Dr. C. H. *Neotestamentieca*. (London: 1962), p. 563.

35 Cadox, Cecil John. *The Historic Mission of Jesus*. (Harper & Brothers: New York), p. 252.

36 Bacon, Benjamin W. *Studies in Matthew*. (London: 1930).

37 Connick, C. Milo. *Jesus: The Man, the Mission, and the Message*. (Prentice Hall: Englewood Cliffs, NJ: 1963), p. 360.

[38] Sharman, H. B. *The Teaching of Jesus About the Future*. (Chicago: 1909), p. 103. "To the men who produced the synoptic Gospels, it did not seem important to sketch the political background. They were not influenced by a purpose to make the acts and words of Jesus more vivid and vital by the portrayal of the events and movements of the day."

[39] Wilson, William Riley. *The Execution of Jesus*. (Charles Scribners Sons: New York: 1970), p. 90.

[40] Cadox, Cecil John. *The Historic Mission of Jesus*. (Harper & Brothers: New York), p. 163.

[41] Josephus. *Jewish Wars*, 2.6; *Antiquities of the Jews*, 17.11.1.

[42] Bousset. *Die Religion des Judentumsmim spathellenistischen Zeitalter*, (1926); Cadox, Cecil John. *The Historic Mission of Jesus*. (Harper & Brothers: New York), p. 167.

[43] Simkhovitch, Vladimir G. *Toward the Understanding of Jesus*. (New York: 1923).

[44] Cadox, Cecil John. *The Historic Mission of Jesus*. (Harper & Brothers: New York), p. 172.

[45] Kealy, Sean P. *Jesus in Politics*. (The Liturgical Press: Collegeville, MN: 1990), p. 59.

[46] Schmid, J. *Das Evangelium Nach Lukas*, 4th Ed. (Regensburg: Pustet: 1960), pgs. 315-19.

[47] Jackson, F. and Lake. *The Roman Provincial System in "The Beginnings of Christianity"*, Part 1, Vol. 1, p. 186.

[48] *Seminar Papers of the Society of Biblical Literature*. (Scholars Press: Atlanta, GA: 1990), pgs. 603-11.

[49] O'Meara, Thomas F. "The Trial of Jesus in an Age of Trials," *Theology Today*, Vol. 28, No. 4, Jan. 1972, p. 454.

[50] Fosdick, Henry Emerson. *The Man from Nazareth*. (Harper & Brothers: New York: 1949), pgs. 188-213.

" . . . The hour has come. Look, the Son of Man is betrayed into the hands of sinners."

—MARK 14:41

CHAPTER SIX

The Trial

MILLIONS HAVE READ of the "trial" of Jesus Christ as set forth in the four Gospels and Book of Acts. The discrepancies in the story of the trial as told by the evangelists have been the theme of many books.[1]

In even the most controversial trials in world history, the accused had guaranteed rights, and proof of guilt was first established by competent evidence from reliable witnesses.

The treatment of Jesus was brutal and spiteful. The victim of mob rule, his persecutors determined to intensify his suffering and humiliation. I have never seen a more deliberate disregard for the laws and rules of procedure, or a trial more filled with conspiracy, animosity, and corruption.[2]

In Matthew, the trial of Jesus is one great big proceeding with everyone there; Pilate, Herod, and the Jewish judges. In Mark there are two separate trials; before the high priest, and before Pontius Pilate (15:1-20). In Luke

189

there are three trials; before the high priests (22:54-71), Pilate (23:1-5), and before Herod Antipas (23:6-12).

The Gospel accounts of the proceedings have undergone much scrutiny and cannot exactly be harmonized:

> "The moment we begin to criticize or harmonize these different forms of the proceedings, or attempt to revise or restate what happened, or prefer one of the Gospel's evidence to the detriment of the others, we are in the realm of mere conjecture, and any conclusions arrived at must be put to a marked extent subjective and precarious. We can only be guided by probabilities."[3]

It makes little difference. The Messiah is tried before the nations and the king (Ps. 2:1–2). And the story of Jesus must start with his arrest.

JUDAS AND THE ARREST

> "Then one of the Twelve—the one called Judas Iscariot—went to the chief priests and asked, 'What are you willing to give me if I hand him over to you?' So they counted out for him thirty silver coins. From then on Judas watched for an opportunity to hand him over."   —MATT. 26:14-15

> ". . . I tell you the truth, one of you will betray me."
> —MARK 14:18

> "Am I leading a rebellion, that you have come with swords and clubs? Every day I was with you in the temple courts, and you did not lay a hand on me. But this is your hour—when darkness reigns."
> —LUKE 22:52–53

As an informant, Judas was paid thirty pieces of silver—referred to as "blood money"—the price of a slave. Judas was a thief, taking funds for himself from the common purse. As the group's treasurer he had access to those funds, and sometimes used them to his own advantage (John 12:6).

Judas chose nighttime to betray Jesus because the crowds were not present. Gethsemane was reasonably close to the city and the high priest's house, so a mob rescue attempt was unlikely to succeed and Jesus could easily be held prisoner.[4]

GETHSEMANE

Gethsemane was a habitual rendezvous (Luke 22:39), a place (Mark 14:32) or orchard (John 18:1), and Jesus often met there with his disciples (John 18:2).

The New Testament does not mention a "Garden" of Gethsemane. A Cave at Gethsemane on the other hand, is a possible Biblical site.[5]

After the chief priests, chief officers, and priests came in person (Luke 22:52) and Jesus is arrested, there was no fear or hesitation on his part:

"Shall I not drink the cup the Father has given me?"

—JOHN 18:11

The "multitude who heard him gladly" (Mark 12:37) would have been outraged, and the only chance of arresting him was to choose a time when he would not be accompanied by a crowd.

Jesus crossed the Kidron Valley, and climbed up the Mount of Olives to a *place* called Gethsemane (Matt. 26:36). There is no mention of a garden in Mark, Matthew, or Luke. The Gospel of John mentions a *kepos* or *garden*, a general term translated as *cultivated tract of land*. Today, there is a cave located in this cultivated area. John says Jesus "went out" (of something) to meet the soldiers (John 18:4). Peter is questioned by a witness who asked him, "Didn't I see you in the garden?" (John 18:26)[6] Gethsemane, which means oil press, was once used for olive oil pressing.[7]

Jesus often frequented Gethsemane. He liked the gardens and hills surrounding the city and it was a favorite walk. His eye turned to meet the rising of this last sun. Dawn was coming.

The arrest took place sometime later than 11:00 P.M. The breaking up of the passover sader in a house in the upper city and the arrival of the armed band at the foot of Olivet, are several things that point irresistibly to the hour being late: The disciples were manifestly tired and even Peter, the fisherman accustomed to lonely vigils on the deep, could not keep awake; Matthew and Mark refer to three separate periods of slumber, broken up by the periodic return of Christ.

Judas guided the group (John 18:2), which consisted of a detachment of temple police dispatched by the chief priests.[8] The Sanhedrin officers were pleased when Judas chose to cooperate. They needed his help to show precisely where Jesus could be located.

> "Now the betrayer had arranged a signal with them: 'The one I kiss is the man; arrest him and lead him away under guard.'"   —MARK 14:44

During April, sunset comes to Jerusalem at 6 P.M. The walk across the Kidron Valley to Gethsemane would take at least 15 minutes.

The Sanhedrin had to work fast since Pilate, though he was available to the public from dawn, would like other Roman officials, retire into his private life at about 11 A.M.

Caiaphas had to collect a quorum by daybreak (first light 4:30 A.M. or sunrise 5:30 A.M.). The prefect must not be given the opportunity to adjourn the hearing; it should start in his Praetorium not later than about 10 A.M., or in the parlance of the period, halfway through the fifth hour. If everything went according to plan, Jesus would be executed soon after 11 A.M.

Some scholars place the time frame as follows: Arrest at 12 midnight; 3 A.M. to 6 A.M. taken before Caiaphas; 4 A.M. to 7 A.M. further mocking and beating and trial before Sanhedrin; 7 A.M. to 10 A.M. taken before Pilate, then to Herod; and the final appearance before Pilate with formal order for execution. After six hours on the cross, Jesus cries out in intolerable pain at 3 P.M.

Jesus addressed the Jewish members of the arresting crowd, pointedly asking why they came out to arrest him as a common criminal.

> "Friend, do what you came for."   —MATT 26:50

Judas' historic kiss of Jesus was a sign of betrayal.[9] From the moment of the kiss, Judas vanishes from the scene, not to reappear again until his suicide. He does not appear as a witness at the trial. Judas led the large band armed with lanterns, torches and weapons, then realized he had miscalculated and staggered away into the night.

Wholly desperate, Judas returned to the elders who paid him the silver coins, throwing the money into the sanctuary. The elders retrieved the money, but hesitated to put it in their temple treasury because it was blood money. Ever worshipfully attentive to the letter of the law, they decided the appropriate thing to do was to buy land for a cemetery for foreigners. To this day, it is called the "Field of Blood (Hakeldama)."[10]

The Jewish participants in Jesus' arrest, the captains of the temple (Luke 22:52), and a band or speira (John 18:3-12), were military commanders and their subordinates as well as some elders and chief priests. The temple police may have turned to the general public for help in catching a dangerous fugitive from justice. They may or may not have known their quarry. Only a few days earlier a "very great multitude" welcomed Jesus into Jerusalem and "all the city was moved" (Matt. 21:8). The priests were careful "lest there be an uproar of the people" (Mark 14:2) if they did him any harm. It may be the chief priests mobilized a mob of ruffians, but Jesus saw the men who came to arrest him as the same as those who sat daily with him as he taught in the temple and who needed no identification of him.

The arresting party "laid hands on him and seized him" (Mark 14:46; Matt. 26:50). Jesus may have remained unshackled throughout the arrest. There were police "officials" guarding Jesus and one slapped him for speaking arrogantly (John 18:22). The arrest order was against Jesus alone and not the disciples. Though to be effective, the action should have been taken simultaneously against his disciples. Indeed, years later Peter was brought to trial and Stephen and other apostles were charged and tried (Acts 5:18).

Surprising is the disciple who drew his *machaira* (a dagger-sword) and struck the ear of Malchus, a servant of the high priest. He was not seized by the temple police. Peter was allowed to go free and no one detained him. The Roman soldiers who witnessed violence towards a Jewish policeman were not moved to action. Whether they enjoyed this sort of domestic fracas or believed it was a matter for the Jewish police, they may have been impressed and satisfied with Jesus' reprimand that "all they that take the sword, shall perish with the sword" (Matt. 26:52).

Jesus looked back for his friends as they disappeared into the night. It is inconceivable the disciples were not concerned about what happened after the arrest. There is no Christian claim they were present during the legal proceedings, Jewish or Roman; but surely some information was available to them as to why Jesus was crucified.

His short, intense public career had taken its toll as he had thought and studied, preached and worked, planned and executed, without haste, without rest. The end came quickly.

Death overtook him as he had just begun to develop his public ministry. His success was modest. Fame was out of the question. In his home region, he was laughed at, repudiated, and even pronounced crazy (Luke 4:28; Mark 3:21). The occasional approval he achieved was constantly countered by doubts among his fellow men, strife and quarrels with those around him, and controversies with the disciples (John 6:60-67). An air of resignation and loneliness hovers over the entire biblical narrative.

Gethsemane was behind him now.

The transition is clearly delineated. Up to this time Christ was permitted to move about freely. He could go where he pleased. He could enter Jerusalem, or he could stay out of it. Now the Man of Sorrows enters upon a new phase.

ANNAS

"(They) brought him first to Annas, who was the father-in-law of Caiaphas, the high priest that year."   —JOHN 18:13

Annas was appointed in 7 A.D. by the Roman Prefect Quirinius and was deposed in A.D. 15 by Valerius Gratus. He remained a powerful force for fifty years since five of his sons and sons-in-law became high priest, something that never happened before.

The propertied family of Annas was involved with the obscure moving of the Sanhedrin to the bazaars, and some would relate this hint of merchandising to Jesus' attack on the temple moneychangers. There was special animosity toward the house of Annas as greedy and repressive.[11]

Stephen (the first martyr), and James, (Jesus' brother), were all put to death during the tenure of priests of the House of Annas. Possibly James, the brother of John, (the first of the Twelve to be martyred) also perished under the House of Annas (Acts 12:1-3), which means that every famous Christian who died violently in Judea before the Jewish revolt in 66 A.D. suffered during the tenure of a priest related to Annas.

Annas managed to preserve an actual preeminence in public affairs, succeeded in keeping the sovereign priesthood in his family, and in the eyes of his countrymen always remained the only legitimate pontiff and the real power behind the throne. In the eyes of the high priest, the main object of rule was not so much to render justice as it was to discover and frustrate a plot. He viewed the "kingdom" of Jesus as a visionary movement agitating Judea which could continually involve the danger of a new uprising against Rome.

196 The Trial of Christ

The high priest asked Jesus about his "disciples and doctrine," apparently being concerned about the influence that his words might have and the success of his preaching.[12]

> "I have spoken openly to the world," Jesus replied. "I always taught in synagogues or at the temple, where all the Jews come together. I said nothing in secret. Why question me? Ask those who heard me. Surely they know what I said."   —JOHN 18:20-21

Officially, Annas had no right to demand a hearing of Jesus. It could never have the character of an official action. Annas had no legal authority and was a retired officer of the national church. He gained his personal wealth from the booths and tables the young fanatic had broken up.

Why was Jesus led before Annas first? Perhaps Annas was staying in the house of Caiaphas.[13] It may be the two shared the same home or it is possible that each lived in a separate apartment of the same palace. It may have been two different wings belonging to a single group of buildings sharing a common courtyard. The fact that litigation began with an "informal" action is an insult showing the kind of mentality that was to judge Christ.

Perhaps events simply drifted that way of their own accord. Gathering the seventy members of the Sanhedrin required time and those working behind the scenes may have taken advantage of the opportunity to make use of this interim by placing Jesus before Annas for a so-called preliminary hearing.

Annas undoubtedly took delight in seeing Jesus. It was a source of grim pleasure to the old aristocratic family to see before them the man who had almost started a revolution against the authority of the priesthood. Every disdainful speech that Christ directed against the high priests became personal insult to the honor of Annas' family.

The Gospels are divided about what exactly happened to Christ at the residence of Annas. He may have spent the whole night in the company of those who arrested, blindfolded, beat and mocked him.[14] He may have spent some hours in a cave type jail with a small circular opening in the ceiling through which he was lowered by rope.

Annas examined Jesus alone, perhaps in the presence of servants or some other hierarchs. Such interrogation was unknown in Jewish criminal trials. Historians believe he might have been present at one of two smaller courts existing in Jerusalem at the time to handle less serious criminal affairs, but when he realized the unusual importance of the case, then passed it along to the Great Sanhedrin.[15]

Jesus differed radically from the ordinary teachers. Instead of ordinary teaching, discussing and passing on matters learned, he announced God's will afresh with authority even greater than the prophets of the Old Testament, showing self-assertion and insistence on his own absolute authority. This free and fearless tone was unheard of in Jewish courts.

CAIAPHAS

Caiaphas was a designation of the entire family, belonged to the Sadducean party, and came from a village near Jerusalem (Acts 5:17). He was the most prominent Jewish personage of the Second Temple period who was deposed from office 36 C.E. This was the year that L. Vitellius, governor of Syria, intervened in the affairs of Judea, deposing Pilate upon the complaint of the Samaritans and "after he had bestowed these benefits upon the nation, he removed from his sacred office the high priest Joseph, surnamed Caiaphas."[16] Thus, in one year both principal actors in the tragedy of Jesus, the Sadducean high priest and the Roman prefect were removed by the Syrian governor.

Caiaphas was appointed about the year A.D. 18 by marrying the daughter of Annas (John 18:13). It is testimony to the staying power of Caiaphas that after such a revolving-door high priesthood between the years A.D. 15-18, he remained high priest not only during the last eight years of Valerius Gratus, but also eleven years of the rule of Pilate. He ruled by far the longest of the nineteen high priests in Jerusalem in the first century, rivaled only by the nine year tenure of Annas—a shrewd strategist and politician.

Josephus wrote that the entire family "are indeed more heartless than any other Jews when they sit in judgment."[17]

Caiaphas recognized the danger menacing him and his friends when Jesus' disciples preached the new faith:

> "The chief priests and the Pharisees gathered the council and said: 'What are we to do? For this man performs many signs. If we let him go on thus, everyone will believe in him, and the Romans will come and destroy both our holy place and our nation.' But one of them, Caiaphas, who was high priest that year said to them: *'You know nothing at all; you do not understand that it is expedient for you that one man should die for the people,*

and that the whole nation should not perish.' He did not say this on his own accord, but being high priest that year he prophesied that Jesus should die for the nation."   —JOHN 11:47-51

The high priest was responsible for good order in Judea. To keep his job, he had to remain in control. The high priest cared about the Jewish populous, and his counselors had the task of preventing trouble and clashes with Roman troops.

Both Caiaphas and Pilate, who also wanted to maintain domestic tranquility (and collect tribute) misunderstood that Jesus had in mind a kingdom not *of this world.* They mistakenly executed him as a rebel (John 18:33-38) after a long discussion about what kind of "king" Jesus claimed to be. If they thought he was planning a military takeover, surely they would have had Jesus' lieutenants arrested, too.

The execution of the leader shows they feared Jesus would rouse the mob, not that he had a secret army. In other words, they understood Jesus and his followers very well.

Their civic responsibilities were to stop riots, which Roman troops would put down with great loss of life, hence Caiaphas' entirely appropriate statement:

"It is better for you that one man die for the people, than that the whole nation perish . . . ."
                                                         —JOHN 11:50

It is clear Jesus alarmed some people by his attack on the temple and his statement about its destruction.

The decision to put Jesus to death is fixed before his entry into Jerusalem. The Sanhedrin publicized openly and issued a demand to inform on Jesus.

Many historians believe there was a three-way conspiracy between Antipas, Pilate, and the Sanhedrin to entrap Jesus, knowing in advance Jesus would be arrested, tried before the Sanhedrin and taken before Pilate. Both Roman rulers might be using Herod's palace in the western quarter or the Antonio Fortress northeast of the temple, or Pilate might be in one and Antipas the other.[18]

It seems certain that before the fateful word was given to the arrest party to proceed to Gethsemane, that some communication must have taken place between the Jewish leaders and Pilate.[19] Such a serious case like this would never have been thrust upon Pilate early on Friday morning without his knowledge and first ascertaining his readiness to take it. But no Gospel writer refers to a prior consultation with Pilate.[20]

It would be absurd in the ordinary course of events to hold judicial proceedings on a day when the principal officers and witnesses could not be present. That Pilate did sit at that day or hour and proceeded to hear the case points to an understanding of a very definite kind.

There must have been some kind of calendar for the trial of Jewish prisoners whose cases necessitated review by the prefect, and in the preparation of the calendar Pilate's personal convenience would invariably be consulted.

There was only one man in Jerusalem who could seek an audience with Pilate at an hour ordinarily devoted to his private pleasure. That man was Caiaphas, the high priest. It was Caiaphas, in all probability, who sought an audience with Pilate. He alone could present with the full authority of his supreme office the high reasons of state behind the prosecution.

One thing is absolutely clear: The removal of Jesus—to save the people from perishing. *Jesus must die for the whole nation.* The high priest's words were acutely significant. His comment was couched in the terms, implying that the original hearers were only being reminded of what they already knew.[21]

Caiaphas justified his fateful decision by arguing for expediency. There is the sense that people favorably disposed Jesus' teachings and would come to his aid.[22]

Although Caiaphas decided to act because he feared the possible success of the Jesus movement and its possible success would cause violent Roman intervention, his anxiety was not unfounded though perhaps exaggerated. Roman military forces not only fought against Jewish rebels, but also crushed any enthusiastic Jewish prophetic movement that aimed to free Israel.[23]

Caiaphas could have reasonably feared that Jesus' activity would lead to a similar end and the catastrophic destruction of the temple.[24]

The Romans discovered the Sanhedrin as an effective vehicle for translating their own general objectives into the specifics of daily living, including the use of capital punishment. A feature of Roman policy was to utilize leaders and existing institutions wherever possible.[25]

The opposition of the House of Annas was based on power and politics.[26]

NIGHT PROCEEDINGS OF THE COUNCIL

The Sanhedrin was more concerned with Pilate than with Jesus. The place was a tinder box. Everybody knew that. If Jesus incited rebellion, Rome would crush Judea like a flea. Jesus arrived at the time of Passover, at the height of pilgrim and tourist season. With a whip, he interrupted the commerce and economy while suggesting a better idea, another way, a new system.

A quorum of twenty-three was needed before the proceedings could commence in a lawful manner.[27] They entered the hall in numbers. From the synagogues of Gadara, Tishbe, and Gerasa in the Decapolis, members and the families of Saul, Jehoshaphat, and Isaac from Israel.

Eventually all or most of the seventy-one members would enter and pass the clerk at the door.[28] The Gospels chronicle a race against time, Jesus arrested late on the evening of Thursday, and the high priest attempted to summon the rest of the seventy members of the Sanhedrin. Would they willingly appear at a late night session—and just before a feast, taking into account their alcohol consumption? "All the chief priests, and the elders and the scribes," were present (Mk. 14:53).

Those present possibly included: Caiaphas, Annas, the four sons of Annas, Eleazer, Theophiluous, Mattias, Ananus; the three sons of the ex-high priest Simon Ben Boethus, Rabbi Jonathan Ben Uziel, Joazer (author of a famous Targum), Rabbi Onkelos, Ishmael Ben Phabi, Simon Ben Cantharu; John, a former high priest; Alexander, a priestly partner of the sons of Annas; and Ananias Ben Nebedeus, noted for his excessive gluttony; Helcias, keeper of the temple treasury who gave Judas the thirty pieces of silver; Sceva, an ex-high priest and the father of those seven sons who gave themselves up to witchcraft (Acts 19:13-14); Isachar Ben Keifer Barchi; Rabbi Gamaliel; Rabbi Helias; Hezron; Jehoshaphat; Jehoram; Daniel; Saul; and Isaac.[29]

Chambers of Elders members included: Ben Kalba Sehmia (one of the richest men in Jerusalem); Ben Tzitzith Hacksab; Simon (bold and courageous); Doras (influential and cruel); John Ben John; Dorotheas Ben Nathaniel; Tryphon Ben Theudion; Cornelius Ben Ceron; and Nicodemus.

Chamber of Scribes members included: Onkelos; Samuel Hakaton (Samuel "the less, a bitter anti-Christian); Rabbi Zadok; and Jonathan Ben Zakai.

Herod the Great, offended at the attitude of a large proportion of the Sanhedrin towards his schemes to rise into power, put to death forty-six of the seventy-one members and filled its ranks with sychophants of his own choosing, headed by high priests of his own selection. From that time the Sanhedrin became the instrument of whatever cabal was in power at Jerusalem.[30]

We thus have Scribes and Pharisees "blind leaders of the blind," proud, haughty, selfish, hypocritical sticklers for ritual held and *operated through a system of gigantic graft* under the control of the few high priestly families of which the house of Annas was the head.

The priesthood was hereditary; the Jewish priests traced their lineage to Aaron, Moses' brother the first priest (Ex. 28:1), the family of Zadok the priest who anointed Solomon (1 Kings 1:28-45). The previously ruling Zadokite family was deposed when Simon the Hasmonean ascended to the high priesthood (1 Macc. 14:41-9). When Rome deposed Archulaus and sent a prefect to govern Judea, it also began to appoint the high priest. It granted the right to name the high priest to a member of Herod's family, but sometimes it was retained by the prefect or procurator of Palestine, or by the legate of Syria. During A.D. 6-66, the priests were always chosen from one of four families of aristocratic priests.[31]

The populous disliked some of the individuals who served as high priests. The mob hunted down and killed one former high priest when the revolt against Rome broke out in A.D. 66. First Herod, and then Rome, took control of the high priests' vestments and released them only on special occasions.

Joseph Caiaphas was a success, served eighteen years, longer than any other high priest under Roman rule, and for ten of those years Pilate was prefect. They cooperated well.

Members did not rise to the level of excellence that was required, and had fallen from its high estate. They bowed to nepotism, money, and personal interest. The Talmud speaks sorrowfully of the sacrilege:

"What a plague is the family of Simon Boethus; cursed be their lances! What a plague is the family of Ananos; cursed be their hissing vipers! What a plague is the family of Cantharus; cursed be their pens! What a plague is the family of Ismael Ben Phabi; cursed be their fists! They are high priests themselves, their sons are treasurers, their sons in law are commanders, and their servants strike the people with staves!"[32]

The council was divided between Pharisees and Sadducees who were represented by the chief priests. The elders were heads of the leading families.[33] The Pharisaic members of the council were scribes, the professional Bible scholars, experts in the Torah and its interpretation.

Although Caiaphas presided, the function rightfully belonged to Rabbi Gamaliel who held the presidency since the death of his father Simon and grandfather Hillel. He was a man of broader mind and sincerely attached to the doctrine of Hillel (a great lawyer of his time and stickler for legal form and procedure). Jesus should have been defended by his friend Gamaliel or perhaps a scribe such as Narada, a priest, son of Hacksab.[34]

Since the exile of Archelaus and the final subjugation of Judea, the Sanhedrin no longer had power to punish its prisoners with death.[35]

There was a change of law that points to Roman control of the death penalty. The right of pronouncing sentences of life and death were taken from Israel forty years before the destruction of the temple (thus, A.D. 30).[36]

An early Jewish Fasting Scroll reports that in September A.D. 66, Roman soldiers were driven out of Jerusalem and five days later "they (the Jews) began again to execute evil doers." This means Jewish authorities regained the right to punish by death, and that the first executions according to Jewish justice took place.[37]

Legal scholars conclude the Romans may have permitted Jews to execute for certain clear religious offenses, i.e., violating prohibitions yet circulating in certain quarters of the temple and perhaps for adultery. Notices were posted in the temple, both in Greek and Latin, warning Gentiles to enter no further than a given point. Anyone who transgressed, even a Roman citizen, was subject to immediate execution without the need to send the culprit to the prefect. Apart from this, the prefect's right to execute was exclusive and absolute.

The Jews did have capital punishment (jus gladii)[38] until 70 A.D. After that time they introduced strangulation as a method of secret execution. Isolated examples of capital punishment include:

1. The warning inscription on the Balustrade in the Temple, reading:

"Let no foreigner enter within the screen and enclosure surrounding the sanctuary. Whosoever is taken so doing will be the cause that death overtaketh him."

2. The stoning of Stephen (Acts 7).

3. The stoning of James, the brother of Jesus in A.D. 62 recorded by Josephus and Eusebius.

4. The plan to stone the adulterous woman (John 7:53–8:11).

The view that the death sentence was a privilege withheld from the Jews under Roman occupation is disputed by some scholars.[39]

Jesus was brought to the Sanhedrin down the broad streets of the Street of David, across the Xystos, which was a kind of square flanked by the Herodian Palaces, and across a bridge which connected the upper town with the Temple Esplanades. The British archeologist Robinson has uncovered the colossal foundations of this bridge which as a giant arch spanned the Valley of the Tyropeo.[40]

There are four possible meeting places of the Sanhedrin. Josephus calls the meeting place the Town Hall, which must have stood where the oldest city wall led from the Xystos Square in the upper town to the western portico of the temple square.[41] The buildings were burned by the Romans after they destroyed the temple. It must have been a rather low lying area because there is mention of "going down" to the meeting place of the Sanhedrin (Acts 22:30; 23:10). According to the Mishnah, the Sanhedrin met in the inner hall of the temple (known as the Hewn Stone Hall), as the hall was roofed with one single dressed stone. The Talmud states the Sanhedrin left this area forty years before the destruction of the temple, and moved from the Hewn Stone Hall into the Hall of Annas situated on the Temple Mount. Others believe it was located on the Mount of Olives, and still others believe they were connected by a bridge. Most scholars accept the House of Caiaphas as the usual meeting place in A.D. 30.[42]

THE MIDNIGHT SEARCH FOR WITNESSES

The chief priests searched for two witnesses who could totally agree on the crime of blasphemy.

The Pentateuch stipulated that "at the mouth of two or three witnesses, shall the matter be established" (Deut. 19:15-18). Only eyewitnesses were competent to testify in criminal cases as Hebrew law did not permit the use of circumstantial evidence. Unlike modern law, the Pentateuch and Talmudic law required the testimony of each witness to cover *the entire case*. Proof could not be made by one testifying to partial facts which constituted a *link in the chain* of evidence. No oath was required, as all were expected to tell the truth without swearing to it, given the solemn sanction of the Ninth Commandment: "Thou shall not bear false witness against thy neighbor." As each witness testified, the presiding officer of the court administered a solemn warning:

> "Forget not, oh witness, that it is one thing to give evidence in the trial as to money and another in a trial for life. In a money suit, if thy witness-bearing shall do wrong, money may repair that wrong. But in this trial for life, if thou sinnest the blood of the accused and the blood of his seed to the end of time shall be imputed unto thee . . . therefore was Adam created one man and alone, to teach thee that if any witness shall destroy one soul out of Israel, he is held by the Scripture to be as if he had destroyed the world . . . wherefore, let us think and believe that the whole world is created for a man such as he whose life hangs on thy words. But these ideas must not deter thee from testifying to what thou actually knowest. Scripture declares:
>
> The witness who hath seen or known, and doth not tell, shall bear his iniquity."
>
> "It's not conjecture, or whatever public rumor has brought to thee, that we ask; consider the great responsibility that rests upon thee; that we are not occupied by an affair, like the case of pecuniary interest, in which the injury may be repaired. If thou causest the condemnation of a person unjustly accused, his blood, and the blood of all the posterity of him, of whom thou wilt have deprived the earth, will fall upon thee. God will demand a fee and account, as he demanded of Cain an account of the blood of Abel. Speak."

The accused was never compelled to testify against himself, yet if he did confess it was accepted into evidence and considered in connection with the case.

There were no lawyers or advocates in ancient Hebrew law, no prosecutors, as this part was played by the accusers. The judges were the defenders. Any verdict which showed a unanimous vote of guilty indicated the prisoner had no friend or defender, and to the Jewish mind this was a conspiracy against the accused.

One of the unanswered questions of history is whether Joseph of Arimathea and Nicodemus had yet arrived to answer to the midnight summons. Apparently not one member was courageous enough to stand against the scheming of Caiaphas.[43]

No effort was made to bring forward any of those who had been healed. Lazarus lived little more than the proverbial "stone's throw" away at Bethany, but no witnesses relating to the word or works of Jesus were brought by Jesus.

THE JEWISH PROCEEDINGS AGAINST JESUS

"Why do we need any more testimony?"

—LUKE 22:71

The Sanhedrin's proceedings were flagrantly illegal, violating most of the Jewish judicial regulations described in the Mishnah. It cannot be assumed *all* the Mishnaic regulations were enforced during Jesus' lifetime, particularly those relating to the handling of capital cases but it is probable *some* of the rules were applicable during the first century.

Jesus was condemned for one crime (blasphemy) and later executed for another (treason).

Did Jesus blaspheme by claiming power which alone belonged to God, of forgiving sins and exercising a supernatural power? Incriminating expressions of Jesus included:

1. Before Abraham was born, I AM (John 8:58).

2. My father works until now, and I work (John 5:17).

3. His reasons for healing on the Sabbath (Mark 3:4; Lk. 13:15–16).

4. His trial confession that the Son of Man would sit at God's right hand (Luke 22:69; Mark 14:62; Matt. 26:64; Acts 7:55).

5. He made Himself God (John 10:33).

6. I and the Father are one (John 10:30).

7. He presumed to say he was the Son when the Father alone knew who the Son was (Matt. 11:27; Luke 10:22).

Jewish officials changed the charges to *treason* after they had convicted him of *blasphemy*, for three reasons:[44]

1. They had to get Pilate to execute him, and for this they needed *political charges* since the Jews lacked the authority to execute Jesus.

2. They did not want to assume the public blame for Jesus' death, but wanted Pilate to appear the culprit. They duped him into believing Jesus was a political offender.

3. The Jews did not take Jesus to Pilate for a trial at all. They only sought to ratify their own conviction.

We are wrestling with *two* trials, on *two* entirely different charges, in *two* courts, before *two* sets of magistrates. Jewish officials simply built a case against Jesus for use before the governor.[45]

The political issue of "kingship" was central when Jesus was accused before Pilate. To Romans, the title "Messiah" (Christos) would have been equivalent to "king" (basileus).

What was Jesus' reply to these questions about Messiahship? A verbatim record would be of vital interest to us and give insight into one of the most perplexing questions: "What concept did Jesus have of his own ministry?" In reconstructing his trial, we have many missing witnesses.

No one reported on the trial before the Sanhedrin, all the potential witnesses, the disciples, fled as Jesus was arrested. One of the disciples actually fled naked (Mark 14:52). They returned to Jerusalem after the terrible events of Golgotha, when the city resumed its daily routine the Passover Feast was over, the pilgrims departed and the Romans retired to the Antonia Fortress.

Even at the crucifixion, few of those close to Jesus were present except Mary Magdalene. Jesus' mother stood at the foot of the cross and another Mary was presented as Jesus' mother's sister (John 19:25). Thus, three women all named Mary stood under the cross, among them two sisters with the same first names. Only Galilean women were present. If others were present, they were unknown in Jesus' life and work.

Above:
Beweinung Christi
Botticelli
Staatsgemä

Below Left:
What is Truth?
Nikolai Ge, The State Gallery
Moscow

Below Right:
The Crucifixion
Michelangelo (1475 - 1564) Ivory
Private Collection (Guaidon)

Truly this man was the Son of God

LEGAL TESTIMONY

The Prisoner was conducted into the court and the trial began. He was tired and hungry, the effect of a sleepless night and previous days of fasting was manifest upon his face.

The witnesses were called. They were selected, instructed to testify against him in *exact agreement*, but they failed and the law tilted in favor of the accused.

> "We heard him say, 'I will destroy this man-made temple and in three days will build another, not made by man.'"
>
> —MARK 14:58

"I *will* destroy," is far different from "I *have power* to destroy." This was a travesty of justice; a pre-arranged scheme to do away with Jesus. Long established practices were blatantly ignored.

There were three kinds of legal evidence:

1. *Vain testimony* meant it was rejected. Earlier witnesses who disagreed among themselves were in this category.

2. *Standing testimony* could be admitted temporarily but would not be held as established until other witnesses had confirmed it.

3. Equal, or *adequate testimony*, the "testimony of those agree together," had failed.

Even if the witnesses had agreed, their testimony still did not constitute a capital charge. *Jesus never intended his words in the literal sense applying to the structure of a building*. He was referring to his own body, the Temple of God incarnate. He was to be destroyed, raised, and resurrected within three days of his death.

The prediction that the temple would be destroyed was considered by his accusers at trial that he threatened to destroy the temple (Mark 14:58; Matt. 26:61). Indeed, as he hung on the cross onlookers taunted: "Aha! You who would destroy the temple . . . save yourself and come down from the cross!" (Mk. 15:29; Mt.27:40). Later, Stephen was accused of saying that, "Jesus of Nazareth will destroy this place," that is, the temple (Acts 6:14).

Jesus thought the trade in the temple area was dishonest, and he foresaw that the nation would one day revolt against Rome. Whatever it was, the priests took it as some kind of threat and his enemies decided to say that he had threatened it. Although they neglected to agree on what their testimony would be, it is clear the people thought that he was threatening it.[46]

If Jesus said anything at all about the coming destruction of the temple, he meant that God would destroy it.

It has been argued that it is admissible for the Sanhedrin to make Jesus' testimony the sole basis of the death sentence.[47] Although Jewish courts adhered to legal forms in the use of evidence of witnesses, the spirit of law in passing a sentence may have been quite a different matter, especially on his own admission of a capital crime where both law and custom left free scope for the definition of this crime. Blasphemy was a very elastic concept.

But Jesus was not threatening a Jewish institution. His words were not a malicious threat to a holy place—but a spiritual statement with spiritual significance.

On both counts relating to the temple and the Mosaic law, the rulers found Jesus was guilty of blasphemously *opposing God.*

The question was asked of him, "Do you answer nothing? What is it which these witness have against you?" Jesus did not answer, " . . . He held his peace, and answered nothing" (Mark 14:61). The high priest's tactics were unlawful and Jesus knew that. He knew there was no intention to hold a fair trial. He had already made the point that they should ask the witnesses.

Jesus acted with great dignity. To try a man without stating what his crime was, especially when his life was on trial, was an outrage.

The professional ethics expected of a Sanhedrin judge were not at all different from those required of a judge in our time and place.[48] The judges were enjoined to unearth every conceivable argument in favor of the accused.

TRIAL ERRORS

The Mosaic Law espoused the principle that there should be one law alike for Israelite and alien, and that the accused must be *kindly treated.*

It was the function of the court to save and not to destroy human life. Their criminal code was explicit, humane, and embodied much of what we now consider essential elements of enlightened jurisprudence.

Every presumption was indulged in favor of a defendants innocence until a final guilty verdict was pronounced. The trial had to be conducted in public, and no evidence could be produced in his absence.[49]

The prosecution produced not one scintilla of evidence to show that Jesus had ever impiously or irreverently used the name of the Supreme Being, or had claimed for himself super human power without an express acknowledgment of God as its author. He had wrought many miracles, but always disclaimed that his works were of a supernatural order. He admitted that the powers were from God and not of his own:

> "The words I say to you are not just my own. Rather, it is the Father, living in me, who is doing his work."   —JOHN 14:10

The Mishnah, later codified at end of the second century, proves massive violations of established law occurred:

1. *Annas' interrogation.* It was improper for Annas to interrogate Jesus alone, without other judges present.[50]

2. *Leniency.* The procedures of the Sanhedrin encourage an actual bias in favor of the accused. The Mishnah stated: "The Sanhedrin that executes more than one man in seven years is a slaughterhouse."

3. *Sabbath.* It was forbidden to hold trials on Sabbath holidays or preparation days. The proceedings against Jesus took place on the Seder night.

4. *Public trial.* Trial proceedings had to be conducted in open session and in the temple courtyard Beth Din (*Sanh.* 11:2). The proceedings against Jesus probably took place in the private residence of Caiaphas, not their regular meeting place.

5. *Delay.* Only acquittals could be announced immediately following trial proceedings. A guilty verdict had to be postponed until the following day, until one was sure the verdict corresponded to God's

will (Num. 9:8; 15:34), specifically in the case of blasphemy (Lev. 24:11-12).

6. *Prosecutors.* The facts on which a sentence is based must be contained either in the deposition of the injured party (Deut. 21:18), or from testimony of at least two witnesses (Deut. 19:15). The evidence against Jesus was introduced by the presiding official of the court during the session.

7. *Cross-Examination.* The accused must be given an opportunity to cross-examine and confront his accusers, divided into two modes of examination the *hakiroth* and *bedikoth*.[51] The hakiroth is related to the modern defense called alibi (if the accused can prove he was at a different place at the time of the crime then he cannot have committed the crime). The bedikoth is a broader scope of examination allowing the accused to inquire as to all relevant facts supporting the accuser's story.

8. *Caiaphas prejudiced.* It was error for Caiaphas to have acted as judge after having publicly declared that Christ deserved death.[52]

9. *Presumed guilty.* The Sanhedrin erred in not taking into consideration the innocence of Jesus.[53]

10. *Sequestration of Witnesses.* According to law, witnesses were sequestered. The practice of separating witnesses is still used today in criminal cases which helps prevent conspiracies to defraud the court. It was required that judges take proper precautions to prevent witness tampering. Witnesses were not allowed to hear each other testify as their testimony might be influenced by others' testimony.

11. *Reverse Seniority.* The high priest speaks first in finding Jesus guilty and urging the other judges to find him guilty with the immediate result that "they all judged against him as being guilty, punishable by death" (Mark 14:64). Judges with less seniority voted before those who had more seniority (to prevent undue influence). One judge is forbidden to say to the others, "Adopt my view."[54]

12. *Unanimous vote.* A unanimity of judges voting for condemnation nullifies the conviction in capital cases (in order to prevent collusion or railroading).[55] In capital cases a verdict of acquittal could be reached by a majority of *one*, but a verdict of conviction had to be reached by a majority of *two*. In capital cases, a conviction could be reversed to an acquittal.

13. *Confession.* A confession of the accused was not sufficient in contrast to Roman criminal procedure. But Jesus was sentenced on the basis of his confession alone. It was error to have sought words without first establishing a prima facie case.

14. *Prejudice of Sanhedrin.* If Jesus committed blasphemy in the Sanhedrin, the judges would be eye-witnesses and witnesses to a crime were prohibited from being a judge. In Jesus' case all the members of the council participated in the verdict.[56]

15. *Sobriety.* The participants in a trial were required to be in a state of mental sobriety and clarity. This court supposedly sat in judgment not only after having been rudely awakened from sleep, but only a few hours after all the members had drunk quantities of wine at a Seder.[57]

16. *Daytime.* In capital cases, trials must occur during the daytime and the verdict must be reached during the daytime and occur over at least two days. Since the Jewish day started with sundown, Jesus was tried, convicted, and sentenced all in one day.

17. *Judgment seat.* If Caiaphas left his seat and went over to the table of the members sitting in the courtroom (Mark 14:60), it was a violation of the law because one who "sits" in judgment must indeed remain seated to demonstrate his exalted position over those summoned before the court.

18. *Agreed testimony.* The two witnesses' testimonies must be consistent with each other from start to finish and agree on every detail. If they contradicted each other, their evidence was invalid (Num. 35:30; Deut. 17:6).

19. *Failure to warn*. No person may be convicted of blasphemy unless two lawfully qualified witnesses testify they had first warned him of the criminality of the act and the penalty prescribed for it.[58]

20. *Elements of the crime*. The capital offense of blasphemy consisted in pronouncing the name of God, which may be uttered only once a year by the high priest in the sanctuary of the temple. Since the divine name was not enunciated, there was *no corpus delicti*.

21. *Mob violence*. It was error to have left Jesus unguarded to the unrestrained license of the mob in the gallery of Caiaphas' palace or court for an hour or more.

22. *Oath*. Witnesses were to be solemnly warned and carefully examined regarding their testimony. The Gospels do not report such procedure or that the witnesses were in any way held accountable for their false testimony.

23. *Double jeopardy*. Pilate should have released Jesus when he "found no fault in him" (Matt. 27:24), and should not have subjected him to subsequent trials before Herod and Pilate.

24. *Presumption of innocence*. Capital cases must begin with *reasons for acquittal* and may not begin with reason for conviction (Sanh. 4:1). The trial begins with false testimony against Jesus but there are no witnesses for the defense.

25. *Allocution*. Everything had to be done to insure the possibility of a stay of execution, if at the last minute evidence in favor of the accused turned up. A person stood with a towel at the door of the court and another mounted on a horse situated halfway to place of execution where he could see the execution as well as the person at the door. If the court said they had something to argue in favor of acquittal, the man at the door waved the towel and the man on the horse then rushed to stay the execution. This procedure could occur up to five times. A herald had to cry out, announcing the offense, who the witnesses were, and to request that if someone knew anything that would favor acquittal, such a person should come forward and plead the case of the convicted person.[59]

The Charges

Jesus was accused of a threefold crime:[60]

1. *"We have found this fellow perverting the nation,"* (that he was a revo-　　　lutionary);

2. He was *"forbidding to give tribute to Caesar,"* (that he excited people not to pay their taxes);

3. That he said of himself that *he was Christ, a King.* (Luke 23:2)

But, more specifically, the underlying charges include:

Violations of the Sabbath: In the Mishnah, there were thirty-nine separate types of prohibited work or violations of the Sabbath including plucking ears of corn. The penalty for a certain type of offense was death if the offense was both deliberate and flagrant. There were lesser penalties for cases involving inadvertent transgressions.[61]

It was legal to do certain "acts" on the Sabbath so long as it was not actual "work." It was "legal" to do "good", such as rendering emergency aid.

> The Sabbath was made for man, not man for the Sabbath. So the Son of Man is Lord even of the Sabbath.　　　　　　　　　　—Mark 2:27-28

They said Jesus was responsible for minor violations of the Sabbath which brought him into conflict with the Jewish authorities (John 5:10-16; Mark 3:1-6; Matt. 12:9-14; Luke 6:1-11).

The type of work prohibited in the Mishnah involved acts of physical exertion, such as objects being carried from place to place, men traveling, or performing routine acts of physical work.[62] By this interpretation Jesus committed no indictable offense.

Purity. Jesus denied the purity regulations laid down in the Old Testament:

> Listen to me, everyone, and understand. Nothing that goes into a man from outside can make him unclean; it is the things that come out of a man that make him unclean.　　　　　　　　　　—Mark 7:14

According to this, all foods were considered clean. Jesus disavowed any difference between clean and unclean animals and foods. The contraventions of the purity regulations take up far less space in the Gospel accounts than those of the Sabbath but many scholars believe the rejection of the purity regulations was the more significant. An entire legislative code was cast to the winds and revolutionary new rules formulated (Mark 7:14-16).

The transgression of purity regulations cannot be linked to Jesus' condemnation. There is no known case of anyone being condemned to death for infringing food laws, and there is no evidence that violations of dietary laws were ever prosecuted.[63]

Jesus imagined a community shaped not by the politics of purity, but by the politics of compassion.[64] Jesus traveled, ate with the people he encountered, shared their table, and healed the sick, frequently through touch. Eating with the poor, the outcast, and sinners meant that Jesus did not attend to the niceties of purity; healing the leper, the demoniac, the hemorrhaging woman. He disregarded taboos and demonstrated his contempt for the prejudices of purity.

In Leviticus and Numbers, there is a forest of "purity codes" distinguishing between holy and common, *tahhor* (clean) and *tameh* (unclean).[65] Willful, deliberate transgression, of rules prohibiting contact or consumption of certain unclean animals including their blood, or eating the fat of permitted ones is sinful. Other purity rules focus on the human body. Discharges from the genital area, menstruation, miscarriage, or childbirth, and seminal emissions cause impurity, as does contact or even proximity to a corpse (Lev. 21:1-3).

For all these conditions, the Bible prescribes periods of separation, lustrations, and offerings after which the person can again "approach the Tent of Meeting" and enter the zone of holiness surrounding the altar. Scripture assumes that people will contact impurity as a matter of course.[66] Impurity is not prohibited, and being impure implies no moral censure. A person is not thereby a sinner, nor is a pure person necessarily righteous. The remedy is not forgiveness, but rather purification.

Inclining Revolt. The charge that Jesus "*stirred up people*," inciting the people to riot in rebellion against Roman power, was an effective bit of political demagoguery. Rebellion against Rome was just what some Jews wanted, but they knew this charge would catch the ear of Pilate and any false accusation was good enough to stick.

Jesus may have been perceived as a leader of a seditious or politically dangerous movement since they crucified him with "two robbers" (Matt. 27:38; Mark 15:27; Luke 23:32; John 19:18). The Gospels have, therefore, preserved the fact that "Jesus was arrested, accused, condemned and executed on a charge of rebellion."[67]

The charge was false, but like so many other things said about Jesus by his enemies, it was true in a deeper sense than they meant or knew. *Jesus did stir up the people*. He walked up and down Judea, the crossroads of the world, shattering old traditions and letting loose ideas destined to shake the whole world. Great crowds followed him, immense excitement often attended his work. But no charge should have been made of inciting political rebellion.

Blasphemy. There is disagreement among scholars over this[68] because it seems to conflict with the rabbinic requirement that for a capital offense to be established it was necessary for the blasphemer to *pronounce* the Divine Name (Lev. 24:15). It is true, Jesus unmistakably alluded to being the Messiah.

"If anyone hears my words and pays no regard to them . . . (he is judged because) I do not speak on my own authority, *but the Father who sent me has himself commanded me what to say*" (John 12:47-49).

The clearest sign of his messianic mission was the raising of Lazarus. Although Jesus need not have prayed aloud, he did so to show that he was acting as God's agent:

> I said this for the benefit of the people standing here, that they may believe that you sent me.   —JOHN 11:42

Jesus was enunciating no novel doctrine, but echoing teachings already known at the time that "sufferings wash away the sins of men," the same teaching which Josephus ascribed to the Essenes.

It has been argued that the definition of blasphemy underwent a change between 30 C.E. and 200 C.E., between the time of Jesus' death and the writing of the Mishnah. The scriptural term for blasphemy is "nakab" (Lev. 24:16), which means to "pronounce distinctly," "Cursing God" which Jesus did not do (Lev. 24:15-16).

The claim to be Messiah, without any of the ordinary qualifications of a messiah—a claim admitted by a solitary prisoner in the full power of his enemies—must have seemed a presumptuous insolence, a kind of taking God's holy promises in vain.[69]

"We have a law, and according to that law he must die, because he claimed to be the Son of God."[70]   —JOHN 19:7

The Jewish leaders sought to kill Jesus because he blasphemed, "making himself God" (John 10:33).

Plotting. The crime which Jesus was supposed to have "plotted against the temple" was unknown to Judaism. All he did was to promise a miracle: that "a" temple would be destroyed and rebuilt within three days.

False Prophet. Jesus was accused of seducing the people (Matt: 27:63; Luke 23:2; John 7:12;) by *false prophecy.* The charge of magic only turns up in an occasional utterance of the enemies of Jesus during his public life (Mark 3:22; Matt. 9:34), and not at all in the legal proceedings.[71] There is no indication in the Gospel accounts that Jesus was investigated or tried as a false prophet. No one asked him whether he claimed to be a prophet who had received a revelation from God.[72]

Predicting the temple would someday be utterly destroyed, (Mark 13:2; Matt. 24:1), was not an actionable offense. Jeremiah, Ezekiel, and others predicted the destruction of the first temple. Messianic claimants appeared before the time of Jesus as they were to do after him, and there is no record of their having been persecuted.[73] Such a prophecy would not have amounted to a punishable offense as Old Testament prophets before him had been given the same message by God. The trial of the prophet Jeremiah (Jer. 26:1-19) initially aroused great resentment and resulted in a capital charge against him. He was fully acquitted and rehabilitated once it was proved his prophecy was motivated by deep concern for Israel.

"If a prophet announces to you a miraculous sign or wonder, and if the sign or wonder of which he has spoken takes place, and he says, "Let us follow other gods" (gods you have not known) "and let us worship them," you must not listen to the words of that prophet or dreamer. The Lord your God is testing you to find out whether you love him with all your heart and with all your soul. It is the Lord your God you must follow, and him you must revere. Keep his commands and obey him; serve him and hold fast to him. That prophet or dreamer must be put to death, because he preached rebellion against the Lord your God, who brought you out of Egypt and redeemed you from the land of slavery; he has tried to turn you from the way the Lord your God commanded you to follow. You must purge the evil from among you."   —DEUT. 13:1-5

This passage makes Jesus a false prophet in the eyes of those who reject his message. The Pharisees believed that the people were being led astray by a false prophet working signs and "the Pharisees heard the crowd muttering this about him, and the chief priests and Pharisees sent officers to arrest him."

The Babylonian Talmud speaks of "Yeshu" being stoned "because he practiced sorcery and enticed Israel to apostasy." He was an "instigator and inciter."[74]

His general attitude is perfectly plausible in the history of time. The Jewish populace was attached to the temple. When Emperor Caligula wanted a statue of himself placed in the temple, farmers left their fields, even though it was seeding time, to protest.[75] The chief priests and scribes saw Jesus' actions as a critique of their administration of God's house.

Cleansing of the Temple. The meager indictment does not accuse Jesus of riotous behavior in the precinct of the temple, but for reasons advanced in this book, I believe it was this final economic challenge to the House of Annas, fueled by earlier fears of Jesus upsetting the temporary political peace, that caused the conspiracy against him.[76]

Tearing down the Temple. What was the historic utterance that lay behind the charge?

". . . I will destroy this manmade temple and in three days will build another, not made by man."   —MARK 14:58

"This fellow said, '*I am able* to destroy the temple of God and rebuild it in three days.'"   —MATT. 26:61

To think that a person could pull down the temple of Herod, and replace it by another within three days by some super normal or magical powers is beyond imagination, not really spoken by a sane person. That was a feat that no one would ever be called to justify.

Jesus hated shams, hypocrisies, and futile boasts, had a very sane and disciplined mind, and was a lover of truth, sincerity, and inner humility. There were no facts to justify the Sanhedrin's belief that Jesus had an unstable mind.

SUBVERTING THE NATION

"We have found this man subverting our nation. He opposes payment of taxes to Caesar and claims to be Christ, a king."

—LUKE 23:2

The phrase "subverting our nation" was used in a political sense that the people believed he could free them from the Roman yoke. It was his claim to be "Christ the King" that caused Pilate's concern.

Equal to God. Jesus was condemned as soon as he claimed to be the Son of Man, such as his bold pronouncement of forgiveness over the paralytic (Mark 2:7),[77] and explicit expressions where Jesus seems to claim divine status: "Before Abraham was born, I Am" (John 8:58) and, "I and the Father are one" (John 10:30). He had pronounced himself equal to God; but only to a select few, and thus, was the basis of a charge.

THE GREAT CONFESSION

There was a crucial moment in the trial where all the universe held its breath as it waited for the answer. This great confession lifted the whole scene. No longer were small men involved, but Jesus was bearing witness to himself. This confession reverberates throughout the ages. If Jesus had said, "No," the trial would have ended and he might have been acquitted. He would have walked out a free man and there would have been no way of entrapping him. If he said, "Yes," he signed his own death warrant, making the cross a virtual certainty.

Jesus knew what he was doing. The cry of blasphemy went up. Garments were torn in hysterical horror.

The externals of justice were soon forgotten. The spitting, the slapping of his face, the mockery and the hostility of the Jewish authorities broke. Instead of a court of justice, it was a frenzied circus of hatred in which there was no attempt to maintain the appearance of impartial justice.

Upon hearing the words, *only* the high priest "rent his robe."[78] The practice of rending one's garments in horror had progressed from King Hezekiah's time (2 Kings 18:37; 19:1) to the point where the practice is described as a stylized behavior of judges in the Talmud, a sign of resistance to impious utterance. Upon hearing the divine Name desecrated a priest must tear (rend) his garment.[79] The Sanhedrin required the courtroom to be cleared of the public. Each witness was asked exactly what he had heard, and when it had been repeated, all the judges stood and tore their garments.

Although we are constantly reminded in the Apostles' Creed that Jesus "suffered under Pontius Pilate," in truth, Caiaphas "had the greater sin." (John 19:11)

The summoning of false witnesses gained Caiaphas nothing. He was compelled to make use of the last resort, the oath. He made use of his official status as a high priest and legal authority and *demanded* that Jesus take an oath.[80] If (says the Mishnah) one shall say, "I adjure you by the Almighty, by Sabaoth, by the Gracious and Merciful, by the Long-Suffering, by the Compassionate," or by any of the divine titles, they are bound to answer. It placed the Nazarene in the 'presence of God' (I Sam. 14:39; Deut. 5:26).

> "The high priest said to him, 'I charge you under oath by the living God: Tell us if you are the Christ, the Son of God."[81]
>
> —Matt. 26:63

But in reality all the words which he spoke were oaths. He did not need the ritual of taking an oath and instructed his disciples to avoid them (John 5:33-37). Christ was continually adjuring himself.

In the Jewish manner, he put Jesus under oath (called upon in the name of God to bear testimony to the truth), unlike American courts wherein the witness places himself under oath.

Throughout his public ministry, Jesus was repeatedly challenged to tell if he were the promised Christ. He never denied it but never overtly asserted it either. The reason was almost certainly Jesus' wish not to precipitate the crisis of persecution by the Jewish authorities and execution by Caesar's procurator prematurely. But now Jesus knew his hour had come.

The events in the temple court and the language Jesus used were not calculated to avoid any impression of insurrectionary vision. Both Jewish and Roman authorities were defending themselves against a perceived real threat.[82]

It is only Mark who says that Christ said unequivocally *"I Am"* (Mark 14:62). Matthew says, *"You have said so"* (Matt. 26:64). Luke says, *"If I tell you, you will not believe me, and if I asked you, you would not answer"* (Luke 22:67).

Right: The Descent from the Cross
Rembrandt
National Gallery of Art, Washington D.C.

Below Right: Christ Before Caiaphas
Giotto ca. 1305

The answer, "I Am" (ego eimi) is a Messianic claim that heretofore Mark has suppressed as secret lest Jesus be misunderstood. Jesus' answer is an open acceptance to such a vocation.[83] If Jesus replied "Su eipas" (Matt. 26:64) which means "you have said it," could be understood in the affirmative as "you have said so" or "I am he." Some experts in Aramaic translate it, "It is you who say it, not I!"[84]

Scholars disagree as to whether the Hebrew idiom carried merely an affirmation or a particularly emphatic affirmation.[85] It may be compared with the modern slang, "You said it!" Jesus was saying "the High Priest had said it."[86]

He sealed his fate with his reference to himself as the Messiah for the first time. In his lifetime only one of the disciples, on one occasion, was prepared to identify him as such—Simon Peter in Caesarea Philippi (Matt. 16:15; Luke 9:20):

> On the way he asked them, "Who do people say I am?" They replied, "Some say John the Baptist; others say Elijah; and still others, one of the prophets." "But what about you?" he asked. "Who do you say I am?" Peter answered, "You are the Christ." Jesus warned them not to tell anyone about him.
>
> —MARK 8:27-30

Jesus was very reserved regarding titles (John 16:15). For him, the worship of his own person was unthinkable. He allowed himself to be addressed as "Master," or "Rabbi," but found even "Good Master" an exaggeration, and promptly reprimanded anyone who addressed him thus:

> "Why do you call me good? . . . No one is good except God alone."
>
> —MARK 10:18

When Jesus was asked, "Are you the King of the Jews?" they meant are you a "leader of the Resistance?" Was he disturbing to the people, telling them not to pay tribute to Caesar or calling himself a king? The accusers alleged facts, the governor decided what to make of them and since there was no defense, Pilate had no option politically but to convict.[87]

"The voluminous annals of Talmudic lore are witness to the punctilious conduct of legal principle and practice throughout these ages and to the care taken by the Rabbis to avoid falling into possible pitfalls of illegality."[88]

When the case was transferred from the Sanhedrin to Pilate at the Praetorium, they did not ask their findings be confirmed, but laid a fresh charge of treason, namely that Jesus was a *political agitator* with pretensions of being the King of the Jews (Matt. 27:11; Mark 15:1; Luke 23:1).

Jesus was sentenced to death and executed by *Roman* authorities as a *rebel* against their suzerainty in Judea and by the Jewish authorities as a challenge to their money and status quo.

THE PLACE WHERE JESUS MET PILATE

Was it the Praetorium (Matt. 27:27; Mark 15:16; John 18:28), the Fortress Antonia (northwest of the temple), the Palace of Herod adjacent to the Citadel, or the Hasmonean Palace overlooking the Temple Mount from today's Jewish quarter? The Gospels give few details regarding the position of this building although we have some hints:

1. It must have been situated within the city walls in a high part of the city since Jesus is "led out" of Jerusalem to be crucified (Mark 15:20) and the crowd came "up" to Pilate (Mark 15:8).

2. The actual building in which Jesus was examined by Pilate (John 18:28) and mocked by soldiers (Mark 15:16) was the square with the Judgment Seat, a stone pavement indicating a place or square.

3. An eight century old tradition holds that the Fortress Antonia was the Praetorium of Pilate. From the description given by Josephus, it must have been a magnificent building making it look like a royal palace.[89]

4. Other scholars identify the Praetorium with the Palace of Herod on the west hill of Jerusalem south of the Jaffa Gate.

Over the centuries because of war, destruction, and building and rebuilding of homes and structures, current day Jerusalem is some fifteen to fifty feet higher than the topography of Jesus' time.

Before Pilate

"My kingdom is not of this world. If it were, my servants would fight to prevent my arrest by the Jews. But now my kingdom is from another place."   —John 18:36

At 6:00 a.m., April 3, A.D. 33, Nisan 14, of the year 3793 on the Jewish calendar, Pilate looked out over Jerusalem as the sun was starting to daub a hazy mist hovering over the summit of the Mount of Olives.

Caiaphas requested an interruption of his early morning schedule and ordered his ivory magistrate's chair could be moved outdoors to the regular afternoon location facing the Esplanade, to face the multitude as he ascended his elevated tribunal.

His *judgment seat* was in the outer courts of Herod's palace, located in front of the entrance and between the great marble wings of the palace upon an elevated spot called the "Gabbatha."[90] The tribunal was raised in conformity with a maxim of Roman law that all criminal trials should be conducted from a raised tribunal. The ivory chair was placed from which, under Roman law, the judge would ask, "What accusation bring ye against this man?"

We do not know precisely the palace where Jesus was tried by Pilate (Matt. 27:19), except that Pilate was sitting on a platform (bema) in the presence of the crowds (Luke 23:4). It was conducted outside since Jesus' accusers would not go inside "in order that they should not be made unclean, but could eat the . . ." (John 18:28).

Josephus tells of other prefects who addressed angry crowds in Jerusalem from a platform.

As Pilate looked down from his dais, he could see Jesus stationed directly in front of the tribunal with members of the Sanhedrin flanking him on both sides.

Pilate paused to review the charges that Jesus was an instigator of sedition, a resistance leader; that he opposed payment of the tribute; and that he claimed to be a king, (high treason was the most heinous crime known in Roman law).[91] The instant Pilate sees Jesus he asks, "Are you the King of the Jews?" (Matt. 27:11; Mark 15:2; Luke 23:3; John 18:33), yet no such phrase had been used by Jesus' accusers. Pilate pounces at once on the charge of kingship because someone coached him beforehand.

Jesus was aware of the conspiracy:

"Is this your own idea," Jesus asked, "or did others talk to you about me?"
—John 18:33

Pilate's quick question implies previous notice of the cause and of the man.[92] If Jesus had been arrested by Roman troops, he would have been taken into Roman custody since the Romans had places of detention in Jerusalem (Acts 23:10).

Pilate was *concerned with keeping order* in his province and the turbulent city of Jerusalem, particularly during the Passover Feast. The high priest and his clique of collaborating politicians were pleased the young troublemaker was going to be out of the way.[93] If Jewish opposition to Roman rule could be temporarily allayed by a crucifixion, the bargain was worthwhile.

To Pilate the internal squabbles of the Jews must have seemed incomprehensible. Riding into town on a donkey, disturbances in the temple, quarreling with scribes and Pharisees about rituals, and attracting crowds as a miracle worker, healer, and exorcist would have hardly interested Pilate. His only concern was to assert his authority while not inciting worse violence than he had quelled.

Pilate probably crucified thousands of men, not just hundreds. Thousands of innocent men stood before him and other inquisitors, procurators and interrogation officers. The powerful could torture, kill and destroy.

Philo, in his *Delegation to Gaius*, complains that Pilate was characterized by "venality, violence, robbery, ill treatment, insult, ceaseless executions without trial, and irrational and terrible cruelty."

Reports of Jesus' actions were confusing—that he had quarreled with the scribes and Pharisees about questions of ritual observance, attracted popularity as a miracle worker and healer, or had caused demonstrations. Even more disturbing, he upset the military by attracting large crowds. When a crowd gathers insurrection flourishes. Witnesses may have told Pilate that some of Jesus' followers were Zealots.[94]

It is possible Jesus may have been personally unknown to Pilate up until the moment he was ushered into the governor's presence.[95]

The question uppermost in the minds of the interrogators would have been *whether Jesus constituted a threat to public safety and order.* This was enough to arrest him and give him to the Romans as a scapegoat.

"What shall I do, then, with Jesus who is called Christ?"
—Matt. 27:22

1. The trial was public with the governor sitting on the judgment seat (John 19:13).

2. Two or three accusers serving as private prosecutors stood face to face with the accused and stated the charges (Acts 24:1).

3. The accused had the right to defend himself. If he remained silent, he was given three opportunities to change his mind and reply to the charges.

4. Under certain circumstances there could be conversation between the governor and the people.

5. The governor could seek counsel from a committee (Acts 25:12), but this committee was not a jury.

6. While sitting on the judgment seat, the governor formally pronounced the sentence (John 19:13–16).[96]

Because of their adherence to the laws, Jewish leaders would not come into the precincts of the Praetorium because there were altars to Roman gods. In this sacred week they could not enter such a place or they would be defiled (John 18:28).[97] Because of these scruples, Pilate moved his judgment seat outside the palace.

With all his faults, Pilate was a product of the Roman law system[98] and he would not affirm the conviction. He tried to evade the issue as he scornfully instructed the leaders, "Take him yourselves and judge him by your own law" (John 18:31). Pilate was no fool. He knew he was dealing with an unusual type of case since none of the trappings of armed rebellion or political power were present. Pilate tried to find a way out by ordering Jesus to be whipped and released. It was a play in a legal game.

A man tried before the governor could be found guilty and sentenced, could be found not guilty and acquitted, could be found that the case was not proven and further evidence could be required.

Two distinct elements in Pilate's character met and intensified each other: One was the sense of law and justice which as a Roman magistrate he possessed and which required him to demand respect for the law; the other was his scorn for the leaders of Judaism. Both these sentiments clamored for Jesus' acquittal.

"With this he went out again to the Jews and said, 'I find no basis for a
charge against him'."   —JOHN 18:38

THE ROMAN CONDEMNATION

Pilate arrived in Jerusalem shortly before the day of Jesus' trial. His residence was in the coastal city of Caesarea and like other procurators he made
the journey with a detachment of troops because of the threat of uprisings.

In the eastern provinces of the Empire, Greek was the language generally used in the administration of justice. The Evangelists make no mention
of interpreters, but it is possible that Galileans for the most part grew up
familiar with Greek. Jesus used Aramaic and his words were translated by
an interpreter, while the Greek words of the judge were translated into the
language of the country; for only in this way could the public follow the
proceedings. We know from Cicero and Josephus that governors conducted
their legal proceedings with natives through interpreters.[99]

We should not over-exaggerate the importance of the first meeting between Pilate and Jesus. The trial was surely conducted informally, quite unlike the processes which we associate with courtroom activity today. Judicial
administration in the provinces was less precise and technical than required
in Rome itself. For the governor it was nothing new to face accused criminals
from among the Jewish populous or to pronounce death sentences.

The usual crowd had assembled at Jerusalem for the Feast of Unleavened Bread, and the Roman cohort (Speira) had taken up its position on
the roof of the portico of the temple, for a body of men invariably mounts
guard at the feast to prevent disorders from such a concourse of people.[100]

The very means of execution shows that Jesus died as an offender against
Rome,[101] not against the Jewish nation. Crucifixion was exclusively a Roman means of execution, never a Jewish one.[102]

The conduct of Pilate is inexplicable as to why he was overwhelmed by
the Jews, confused, afraid, utterly unable to act on his own judgment, and
subject to the whims of the crowd. He even agreed under pressure to set
free an insurrectionist who was awaiting execution. This depiction is strange
in the case of any procurator and it is especially incredible for Pilate. Pilate's
unrelenting determination was the hallmark of his ten year rule. He continually showed contempt for any Jewish attempts to influence him, and
was eventually recalled because of his excessive cruelty and iron-handed-
ness. It is hard to find in any ancient literature more specific information
about a leader who was unswayed by the opinions of his subjects.

The Conviction

Of the many crimes listed in Justinian's *Digestes*, none corresponds exactly with the high treason crime with which Jesus was charged. Broadly speaking, there are several definitions of crimes that can be concocted of a claim to kingship:

1. Anyone who did anything aimed against the Roman people and their safety was regarded as infringing the law.

2. A private person who deliberately and maliciously exercised the functions of an official.

3. Anyone who maliciously caused friends of the Romans to become their enemies.[103]

Jesus was condemned because he gave an affirmative answer to questions about his claim to be a king:

1. The Jewish inquiry centered about the term "Messiah" and the Roman trial about the term "king".

2. At the end of the Roman trial, the soldiers made sport of Jesus by their taunts, "Hail, King of the Jews!" and by arraying him in a mock crown and robe.

3. The words placed on the cross are best explained as a summary of Jesus' own claim, or at least what Pilate understood that claim to be.[104]

Claudia Proculla

"Don't have anything to do with that innocent man, for I have suffered a great deal today in a dream because of him."   —Matt 27:19

Pilate was susceptible to mysterious signs which enjoyed so much credence among the Romans of his day. All Rome was sure that Julius Caesar would have escaped the dagger thrusts on the fatal Ides of March had he listened to Calpurnia who begged him not to go to the Senate because the night before in a dream she had seen him pierced by many wounds. Some say she was a convert to Judaism, which may explain Pilate's reluctance to condemn Jesus.

Convinced of Jesus' innocence, Pilate's wife Claudia Procula may have strengthened his thought that Jesus was innocent. Pilate probably thought one more Galilean didn't seem important.

Claudia's dream may have won her a Greek canonization in the Greek Orthodox church but does not appear to have made much of an impression upon her husband.[105] Poets and artists try to reproduce her dream.

Pilate was at his wits end. When he saw that nothing had worked, but rather that a riot was building up, he took water and washed his hands before the group saying:

"I am innocent of this man's blood. It is your responsibility!"

—MATT. 27:24

The ceremony of washing the hands as a protestation of innocence is a typically Jewish custom, nor was not unknown among pagans (Deut. 21:6). Pilate, having served a good four years in Judea, conformed to a Jewish custom to make himself clearly understood by the Jews, who, for the most part, did not understand his Greek language.

WHY DID PILATE HAND JESUS OVER TO HEROD?

Jesus came from the region of Herod's authority. Earlier, a trial was conducted in the province from which the accused came, but this practice was later changed so that a criminal was tried in the province in which the crime was committed.[106]

Pilate was not obliged to hand him over but wanted to do so as a compliment and to free himself from an awkward case. It was a diplomatic courtesy to improve his relations with Antipas which were strained at the time. Pilate did not act out of kindness. He saved face. He had nothing to lose and everything to gain. He and Antipas became friends from that day (Luke 23:12).

The enmity between Herod and Pilate may have had its origin in Herod's participation in the opposition to Pilate over his setting up votive tablets in Herod's former palace in Jerusalem. However much Pilate may have resented Herod's part in the matter, he had to do all he could to eliminate the bad feelings for it is an historical fact that Antipas was "persona gratissima" with Emperor Tiberius.[107]

Pilate tried to pass the buck and expected the Tetrarch to acquit Jesus. He declared that Herod did not find him guilty, "For he sent him back," (Luke 23:15) and concluded Herod must have considered him innocent, which confirms Pilate's decision and in the end absolved him from the responsibility of Jesus' death.

QUESTIONING BY HEROD ANTIPAS

"Go tell that fox, I will drive out demons. . . ."

—LUKE 13:32

Herod had heard many things about Jesus and hoped to see some miraculous sign or magic. The ruler thought of Jesus as a great magician. Herod "was a man utterly incapable of taking a serious view of anything and even overlooked the business about which the Jews were so eager, for he began to pour out a flood of rambling questions and remarks without pausing for any reply." Jesus did not answer Herod by so much as a word. During Jesus' last journey through Perea, Antipas' southern domain, he knew Antipas proposed to kill him (Luke 13:31). As far as Herod was concerned, this was simply an incident by which he could be entertained.

History's verdict is against Herod. He was more guilty than Pilate. Pilate was not an expert in Jewish law whereas Herod could make claim to such expertise. Herod ridiculed and mocked him, considered Jesus with contempt, arrayed him in a gaudy robe and sent him back to Pilate.

The appearance of Christ before Herod represents a remarkable moment in his suffering. Before the Sanhedrin Jesus had to battle against false testimony. In the presence of Pilate he stood against unbelief. Against Herod it was superstition.

A long history of suffering lies behind the question that is agitating the king. Herod Antipas had John the Baptist killed because he did not have the courage to refuse the favor that his daughter Salome had asked of him.

During the time the Baptist was being held captive, Herod secretly visited him more than once. Herod was happy to know Pilate had referred Jesus to him.

1.   Herod was glad because Pilate granted him the honor of a share in the procedure.

2. He was exuberant because the situation gave him an opportunity to put Jesus to death.

3. Herod's conscience would feel better because the depressing uncertainty over killing John the Baptist could now be relieved by an opportunity to see if Jesus were an ordinary man of flesh and blood.

Herod reveals himself as he truly is. He asks for a sign. It may be that faith first asks for the word, but superstition would rather have a sign, a miracle to be performed.[108]

This was a temptation for Christ, the third time in the legal process that he had been tempted. Had Jesus explained or shown his powers to the Sanhedrin, his death would have been postponed. Again he was tempted. How easy it would have been for Christ to have escaped his own fate.

The significance of the gorgeous robe placed on Christ was as a caricature. Persons dressed in a *toga candida* as they presented themselves as candidates for a particular political office. Herod was mocking Christ by ludicrously making him a candidate for the kingship, mocking Jesus as a pretender to the crown.

THE FINAL QUESTIONING BY PILATE

Pilate's determination to release Jesus caused the Jews to cry out:

If you let this man go, you are no friend of Caesar. Anyone who claims to be a king opposes Caesar.   —JOHN 19:12

The use of *friend* in a political context goes back to early Egypt. The term *"friend of Caesar "* was used in the latter period of the Roman republic when both Augustus and Tiberius used the term for those worthy of special political recognition and status. For Pilate these words challenging him as a "friend of Caesar" contained a fearsome threat. Pilate knew the suspicious nature of Emperor Tiberius. Tiberius had grave emotional problems. A recent study suggests that some of the Roman Emperors suffered from the effects of lead poisoning.[109] Tiberius regularly deprived suspended enemies of the right to make a will. This meant confiscation of property and loss of Roman citizenship as well.

There was never any *verdict* pronounced by Pilate in Matthew or Mark; except "I find no fault" (John 18:38). What is mentioned was his command to *scourge* Jesus. *Pilate did not order him to be crucified.* Jesus was *delivered* "unto them to be crucified" (John 19:15) "to their will" (Luke 23:25). Only Luke speaks of a sentence (Luke 23:24).

Pilate couched his sentence in a form which was bound to offend the Jews. Instead of saying, "he has made himself King of the Jews," he used the words, "Here is your king" (John 19:14). He pretended to recognize the kingly claim of Jesus and was finding a man guilty in effect saying: "This man, guilty of high treason is your king."

Legally, Jesus was tried and convicted for the violation of a specific Roman law enacted by Augustus in 8 B.C. which made it a capital offense for anyone to declare himself to be a king without the express consent of the Emperor. Little did Pilate know this trial and crucifixion would go down in history as among the most momentous events in the life of mankind:

"He would have been very much surprised if he had been told that the poor little Jew who appeared before him that day would cause his own name to be handed down in an immortal story."[110]

Pilate did nothing to deserve his fame. It was just another routine trial of a stubborn and foolish Jew. There was no court of appeal to set him right. He did not care that one less Jew was alive. He would make a routine report to the Emperor of the trial, probably as one item among many in a monthly return and that would be the end of the matter.

THE SCOURGING

Then Pilate took Jesus and had him flogged. The soldiers twisted together a crown of thorns and put it on his head. They clothed him in a purple robe and went up to him again and again, saying, "Hail, king of the Jews!" And they struck him in the face.   —JOHN 19:1-3

It is not in accordance with some Christian sentiment to dwell on the physical sufferings of Christ. But as an attorney, the cause and manner of death are factors in the case.

Jesus was exposed to many cruelties before the final horrors of the crucifixion. He was stripped and stretched against a pillar or bent over a low post, his hands tied so that he had no means of defending himself. Flogging was a legal preliminary to every Roman execution.[111]

The soldiers may not have had hatred in their hearts. They were not Jews and were probably conscripts who may have been from different countries. They indulged in rough horseplay, but acted in ignorance.

Jesus was in good physical condition before his walk to Gethsemane. He had traveled by foot throughout Palestine. Between the hours of 9:00 P.M. Thursday and 9:00 A.M. Friday he suffered great emotional stress, abandonment by his closest friends and a physical beating. After a traumatic and sleepless night he had been forced to walk more than 2.5 miles to and from the sites of the various trials.[112]

The leather thongs and sheep bones cut into the skin and tissues, into the underlying skeletal muscles and produced quivering ribbons of bleeding flesh.[113] Among the Jews it was customary to limit the strokes of the lash to thirty-nine for fear of infringing by mistake upon the letter of the law fixing the maximum at forty.[114] Such caution was unknown to the Roman law which prescribed no maximum number of strokes.[115] The whip made up of thongs of hardened leather studded with small pieces of bone and lead, sometimes with sharp points called "scorpions". The sufferer was bound by the hands to a low column, and was kept from moving out of the bending position so that all the strokes might reach their mark. At first the skin became livid and bloody, and soon it was torn to shreds, the flesh coming off in strips. We read in the passion stories of certain martyrs that the bloody anatomy of a body was exposed to the horror stricken gaze of the onlookers, and it was not infrequent that the condemned man succumbed during the torture.[116]

Josephus records that he himself had some of his opponents scourged until their entrails were visible.[117]

The soldiers tore off the robe of Jesus which reopened the scourging wounds.[118]

He was pierced for our transgressions . . . and by his wounds we are healed.

—ISA. 53:5

Why did Pilate order this terrible punishment for Jesus? The Roman decided upon this measure because he saw in it the last possibility of saving Jesus.

Scourging was intended for various purposes including an inquisitional torture (Acts 22:24); a death sentence; an independent chastisement;[119] and as an introductory stage to execution after sentence of death.[120] Scourging was usually carried out in the public square in front of the praetorium but it is certain Jesus was scourged inside the building (John19:1).[121]

Pilate's prime motive was to demonstrate the harmlessness of the alleged pretender to the throne. He expected the people to see his claim to kingship and the accusations based on it in a ridiculous light.[122]

THE RELEASE OF JESUS BARABBAS

There is Jewish documentation of a "paschal amnesty" in a passage in a Mishnah tractate.[123] Historical research indicates that the prisoners of whom the Mishnah speaks are persons in prison for political offenses and, therefore, prisoners that the king or governor alone could pardon. The custom came into being during the Hasmonean era when the number of political prisoners was continually increasing. The Jewish king would pardon and release a prisoner, this gesture being an indication that peace and harmony should reign during the time of festivals and that political strife should cease. The Hasmoneans were keenly interested in as many pilgrims as possible coming to Jerusalem because they were a great source of income for the temple and priesthood. In the course of time the people had come to regard the custom of "priviligum pasehale" more and more as their right. When the Romans took over Palestine the custom was already deeply rooted.

Some believe a parallel has been found in Roman law, namely, the custom of pardoning and acquitting individual prisoners in response to the shouts of the populace. Attempts have been made to explain it by certain known forms of Roman jurisdiction, but no exact parallel has been established. A papyrus in A.D. 86 shows that Septimius Vegetus, a prefect of Egypt, said to an accused man: "You deserve to be scourged for the following reasons: But I am pardoning you for the sake of the crowd and I shall be more humane than you have been. . . ." We do not know if this Egyptian crowd was appealing to some custom or some special occasion in demanding a pardon.

Barabbas was described as a "bandit"[124] who had instigated rebellion and committed murder in an insurrection. So, the Gospel story is full of dramatic irony. A presumed freedom fighter is released and one innocent of such activities is condemned.

Secondly, his name is curious since his name "Jesus" was removed from many manuscripts of Matthew. A further oddity is that Barabbas is the Greek form of Aramaic Bar-Abba and means "son of the father," precisely what Jesus claimed to be in John's gospel.

The crowd who clamored for Barabbas to be released was not the same crowd who had cried "Hosanna" a few days previously. The Jerusalem mob consisted of people over whom the ecclesiastical authorities would have a much greater influence. Priests and scribes were mingling with them, stirring them up, and using their influence to see that Barabbas was asked for instead of Jesus.

After being whipped and flogged, Jesus, who could now barely stand, was pushed across the threshold of the Praetorium and appeared "wearing the crown of thorns and the purple robe" (John19:5). Pointing to him, Pilate exclaimed to his screaming accusers:

"Behold the man!"

THE TITULUS

"As they led him away, they seized Simon from Cyrene, who was on his way in from the country, and put the cross on him and made him carry it behind Jesus. A large number of people followed him, including women who mourned and wailed for him."   —LUKE 23:26-27

A sign stating the crime was either carried in front of the prisoner or hung around the neck of the condemned man to be nailed finally to the tree of torture. It was traced on a wooden board coated with white lead or gypsum in black or red characters which stood out from the white background and were legible at a distance.

The titulus is the main evidendce for the trial before Pilate, a precise indication of what was occurring.[125] No doubt many onlookers saw the titulus because the place of crucifixion was near the town.

The wording slightly varies in the Gospels, and was written in three languages; Latin, the language of the masters of the world; Greek, the tongue spoken universally in the whole east; and Hebrew or Aramaic, the vernacular of the Jews of Palestine.[126] It was written: "IESUS NAZARENUS, REX IUDAEORUM," "Jesus of Nazareth, King of the Jews."[127]

THE ALLOCUTION

The Sanhedrin did not lightly put a man to death.

A sentry was placed at the door of the Judgment Hall with a towel in his hand. Another sentry was mounted on a horse at a place where he would be in reasonable proximity to the place of execution, but close enough to the Judgment Hall to be able to see the sentry with his towel. If there was any change, he would give a signal and halt the execution promptly.

The sentry with the towel would signal the horseman and the procession would be halted so the prisoner could be returned to the court.[128] He could be brought back four or five times to be heard. If one of the judges said: "I have something to say in favor of acquittal," the one at the door waves the flags and the horseman races off and stops the execution, even four or five times, so long as there was substance to what he had to say.

A herald with a crimson banner led the procession bearing the name of the condemned, his transgression, and the witnesses against him. The public was invited to come forward and speak on his behalf.

At several points the convicted felon is asked to confess his sin. This will secure for him his place in the world to come.[129]

The Via Dolorosa

The Via Dolorosa winding along the streets of the old city is the traditional route Jesus followed bearing his cross from Pilate's Judgment Hall in the Antonia, to Calvary Hill ("Golgotha").

The Latin title via dolorosa means "the Sorrowful Way" and was first used by the Franciscan Boniface of Ragusa in the second half of the sixteenth century, (also known as the Via Crucis, the "Way of the Cross"), divided into fourteen segments by a series of stops, or stations, where pilgrims pray. No gospel references are appended to five stations (Three, Four, Six, Seven, and Nine). Stations Three, Four, Six, Seven, and Nine have no basis in Scripture.

The historical Way of the Cross starts in the area of the modern citadel, just inside Jaffa Gate. Jesus would have been led across the upper forum into a street leading into the Gennath Gate.[130]

The quarry in which Jesus was crucified is today covered by the Church of Holy Sepulchre.[131] The present Via Dolorosa developed out of a circuit of holy places in Jerusalem the Franciscans developed for pilgrims in the fourteenth century. The Franciscans were made custodians of the Holy Land in 1335 and served as guides to the holy places. In the Fourteenth Century, pilgrims usually spent ten to fourteen days in Jerusalem, and in order to guarantee that they saw everything systematically, the Franciscans over the years developed a careful routine.

After leaving the Holy Sepulchre, pilgrims were shown a series of mementoes of Jesus near the flagstone in the courtyard of the Holy Sepulchre on which Jesus fell; the Judgment Gate to which the death notice had been affixed and by which Jesus left the city for Golgotha; the tavern where the soldier got the sour wine (Mark 15:36); the house of Veronica; the house of the rich man (Luke 16:19-31); the crossroads at which the cross was transferred from Jesus to Simon of Cyrene (Mark 15:21); the place where Jesus encountered the women of Jerusalem (Luke 23:27-31); the steps where Mary collapsed when she mounted to see her son; the arch where Jesus was condemned; the school Mary had attended as a girl; the house of Pilate (Mark 15:1); the house of Herod Antipas (Luke 23:6-12); the house of Simon the Pharisee, where Mary Magdalene was pardoned (Luke 7:36-50); the beautiful gate of the temple (Acts 3:2); the temple of the Lord (Luke 2:27); the house of Anne, where Mary was born; the pool of the sheep gate.

Even though there was a strong Christian presence in Jerusalem during the first three centuries, the Christianization of the city took place only in the fourth century.

In the eleventh century, the Fatimids forbad Christian processions in the streets, and when the Holy Sepulchre was restored by the Emperor Constantine Monomachus in 1048, a series of chapels were incorporated, dedicated to the passion of Christ.

Memory weakened by the twelfth century when Crusader control made it possible for Christians to again have public processions. Arabs changed the route in 1187 when they resumed control of the Temple Mount.[132]

The Via Dolorosa is defined not by history, but by faith, the achievement of generations of Christians who desired above all to be in contact with what was tangible in the life of Christ. This was the reason for their pilgrimage. They asked, "Where did this happen?" and as they stood, their imaginations brought them alive. They traveled in hope and found him in prayer.

There are fourteen "stations of the cross" that mark sacred events along Christendom's most hallowed road.[133]

1. Jesus is condemned—the Praetorium (Mark 15:16).

2. Jesus takes up the cross—the "Ecce Homo" arch (John 19:5).

3. Jesus falls "the first time."

4. Jesus meets his mother.

5. Simon the Cyrenian is forced to carry the cross (Mark 15:21).

6. Veronica wipes sweat from his face.

7. Jesus falls the second time.

8. Jesus consoles the women (Luke 23:28).

9. Jesus falls the third time.

10. Jesus is stripped of his garments.

11. Jesus nailed to the cross (John 19:18).

12. Jesus dies (Matt. 27:50).

13. Jesus is taken down (Luke 23:53).

14. Jesus is laid In the Tomb (Matt. 27:60).

From the scene of the trial to the site of execution is nearly one mile. It is possible Jesus may have had to travel as far or farther while an ever-increasing multitude of spectators gathered around the advancing procession.

Most cruel of all, however, was the shame.

GOLGOTHA AND THE CENTURION

When Solomon started building his temple around 950 B.C., he took stone from the northern site on Mt. Moriah near where the Dome of the Rock now stands. Workings under the wall are still known as Solomon's Quarry, which left a vast open space ideal for traders together with caravans of camels and donkeys. The area near Skull Hill acquired another name "the Place of Stoning," a place for executions.

> "They came to a place called Golgotha which means 'The Place of the Skull'."
>
> —MATT 27:33

For centuries, scholars and theologians have studied the important question about where Jesus' crucifixion actually took place:

1. The location of *Golgotha* or *Gordon's Calvary* is the best known since the 14th century, which is northwest of the old city on a small hill that features the eye sockets of a human skull.

2. Another location is the present site of the Church of the Holy Sepulcher, the oldest church still in existence has held position as the best known site since the 4th century.

The church fathers of the fourth and fifth centuries record that Hadrian built a temple to Aphrodite/Venus on the site where Jesus was crucified in a malicious desire to smother holy ground so that Christians were not able to worship there any longer and would lose their faith in Christ.

Socrates records:

"After the period of his passion, those who embraced the Christian faith greatly venerated the tomb, but those who hated Christianity, not caring for the memory of the place, covered the spot with a mound of earth, erected a temple to Venus, and put up her image there."[134]

Constantine's laborers managed to unearth the tomb of Christ, build a new mound of earth, and erect a Christian basilica. It was dedicated in September, A.D. 335. Eusebius writes that a small building which housed the supposed tomb of Christ was built on the western side of this church.[135]

Constantine's workmen did considerable digging and may have discovered the tomb in which Jesus' body rested. Very little would now remain of the tomb since it was hacked down by Caliph Hakim in 1009.

Hadrian's temple is now somewhere near that occupied by the Church of the Holy Sepulchre. Substructural walls built to support the Hadrianic structure have now been discovered in excavations in various parts of the church. Late in the second century after visiting Aelia Capitolina, Melito wrote of Christ being crucified, "in the middle of Jerusalem."[136]

When Pilate pronounced sentence, the execution lay only minutes away. There were none of the delays which in our own day normally separate the time of condemnation from the time of punishment.[137]

The crucifixion may have begun at the third hour (that is the third hour after dawn) or 9 A.M. The Hebrew day began at sunset. The night was divided into four *watches* of three hours each; the day, which began at about 6 A.M. at that time of the year, was divided into twelve hours, beginning at sunrise.

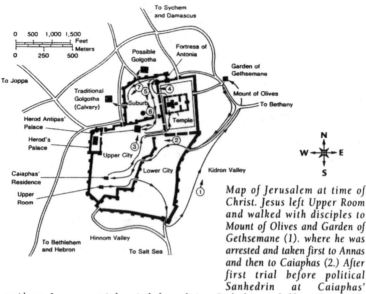

Map of Jerusalem at time of Christ. Jesus left Upper Room and walked with disciples to Mount of Olives and Garden of Gethsemane (1). where he was arrested and taken first to Annas and then to Caiaphas (2.) After first trial before political Sanhedrin at Caiaphas' residence, Jesus was tried again before religious Sanhedrin, probably at Temple (3). Next, he was taken to Pontius Pilate (4.) who sent him to Herod Antipas (5.) Herod returned Jesus to Pilate (6), and Pilate finally handed over Jesus for scourging at Fortress of Antonia and for crucifixion at Golgotha (7). (Modified from Pfeiffer et al [30])

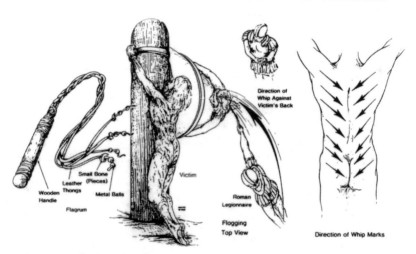

Scourging. Left, Short whip (flagrum) with lead balls and sheep bones tied into leather thongs. Center left, Naked victim tied to flogging post. Deep stripelike lacerations were usually associated with considerable blood loss. Center right, View from above, showing position of lictors. Right, Inferomdeial direction of wounds.

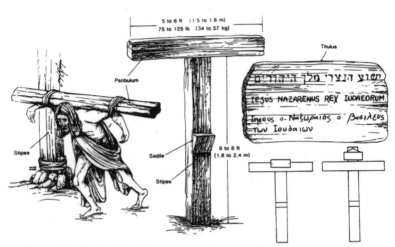

Cross and titulus. Left, Victim carrying crossbar (patibulum) to site of upright post (stripes). Center, Low Tau cross (crux commissa), commonly used by Romans at time of Christ. Upper right, Rendition of Jesus' titulus, with name and crime–Jesus of Nazareth, King of the Jews– written in Hebrew, Latin, and Greek. Lower right, Possible methods for attaching titulus to Tau cross (left) and Latin cross (right).

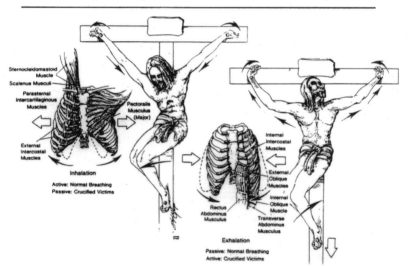

Respiration during crucifixion. Left, Inhalation. With elbows extended and shoulders abducted, respiratory muscles of inhalation are passively streched and thorax is expanded. Right, Exhalation. With elbows flexed and shoulders abducted and with weight of body on nailed feet, exhalation is accomplished as active, rather than passive, process. Breaking legs below knees would place burden of exhalation on shoulder and arm muscles alone and soon would result in exhaustio asphyxia.

The final hearing before Pilate ended a little before the sixth hour (noon), but Luke 23:44 states the actual crucifixion occurred soon after noon.

Simon of Cyrene in North Africa was pressed into service and carried Jesus' cross part of the distance when he collapsed under the weight. His selection was by chance; he entered the city from the countryside and happened to pass near the procession. Jesus was unable to bear the weight himself because of the physical beating he had absorbed at the hand of the soldiers.

The execution was carried out by Pilate's legionnaires, probably Syrians working for the Romans. They probably did not understand Hebrew, their language was Aramaic and it is presumed that they had no biblical knowledge.

If Pilate would have pronounced a verdict, it would have read: "Condemno. Ibis in crucem, lictor conliga manus Verberetur," "I sentence thee: Thou shall go on the cross. Lictor, Bind his hands. Let him be flogged."

Four soldiers were assigned to each execution (John 19:23).[138]

Executions today are usually carried out in private inside the walls of the prison in which the criminal has been confined. Not many years ago, however, they took place in public. Many generations ago the procession of death made a tour of the public streets so that the condemned person would come under the observation and scorn of the general public. Jerusalem's executions always took place outside the gate of the city.

Crucifixion was probably first begun among the Persians. Alexander the Great introduced the practice to Egypt and Carthage and the Romans learned it from the Carthagenians. It was designed to produce a slow death with maximum pain and suffering.[139]

Normally those condemned to be crucified were taken naked to the place of execution and scourged on the way there while carrying the plank. This custom was not adhered to in Jesus' case because he had been scourged before.

As there was widespread ancient belief that corpses contaminate and since Israelite law says that corpses impart impurity (Num. 5:2; 6:6-13; Lev. 21:1-4), burials were always outside the city.[140]

The soldiers gave Jesus back his own clothes (Mark 15:20) instead of the purple cloak which he had been wearing since the mocking.

Archeological evidence suggests that the low Tau cross was preferred by the Romans in Palestine at the time of Christ.[141] The weight of the cross was probably over 300 lbs. and usually the outstretched arms were tied to the cross bar. The processional to the site of crucifixion was lead by Roman military guard headed by a centurion. The guards would not leave the victim until they were certain of his death.

In many cases death was induced by hunger and thirst, heat or cold, attacks of birds and insects and in some cases accelerated by burnings, stonings, suffocation, breaking the bones or piercing the vital organs.[142]

The ligaments and bones of the wrist nailed to the *patibulum* can support the weight of a body hanging from them but the palms cannot. The driven nail would sever the large sensory-motor median nerve which would produce excruciating and fiery pain in both arms. There would be paralysis of a portion of the hand.

One of the Roman guards would pierce the body with his sword or lance through the heart or right side of the chest, a fatal wound probably taught to most Roman soldiers. The standard infantry spear was from five to six feet long. Jesus was dead before the wound to his side was inflicted.

The major pathophysiologic affect of crucifixion was a marked interference with normal respiration, particularly exhalation. The weight of the body pulling down on the outstretched arms and shoulders would hinder passive exhalation. To exhale would require lifting the body up but this would produce tremendous pain. Muscle cramps of the outstretched and uplifted arms would add to the discomfort and each respiratory effort would become agonizing and tiring and eventually lead to *asphyxia*.[143]

The evangelists did not consider death on the cross to be an honorable martyr's death; on the contrary, it must have been seen as a scandal of the first rank, the most shameful end to befall a Messiah. Had Jesus been stoned like the other martyrs, or beheaded like John the Baptist, it would have been much easier to bear. Crucifixion was viewed as a most dishonorable punishment.

"Anyone who is hung on a tree is under God's curse."
—Deut. 21:23

The three condemned men were dying on their crosses. The crowd was thinning out and the centurion noticed his soldiers whiling away tedious hours with one of their games of chance. A strange darkness began to envelope Jerusalem and the surrounding hills.

The centurion was impressed by his refusal to drink wine and myrrh. Myrrh is a spice derived from plants native to the Arabian deserts and part of Africa, probably identified with labdanum, an aromatic gum from the leaves of the sistus rose mixed with wine and drunk to relieve pain.[144]

The centurion leaned for support upon his spear, never having witnessed a death like this one. He saluted the greatness he had witnessed.

Luke reports after the trial and death of Jesus, the disciples (apostles) organized into a group and started to spread the new faith. Peter, the main spokesman, spoke of Jesus being "taken by wicked hands," crucified, and slain (Acts 2:14-37). Peter reminds the Jews they delivered Jesus up, denied him in the presence of Pilate when he was determined to let him go, but instead desired a murderer to be released (Acts 3:12-17). Peter exploited the crucifixion of Jesus as a skillful device to arouse guilt feelings of the people, and shortly thereafter his preaching came to the attention of the Jewish authorities and he is taken before the Sanhedrin. Peter and the Apostles were asked, "By what power or by what name did you do this?" (Acts 4:7).

Peter answers that he performs miracles of healing the lame "by the name of Jesus Christ of Nazareth, whom you crucified . . ." (Acts 4:10). There were a number of wonder workers, especially in the realm of medicine who were not infrequent in Jerusalem at the time, and could always attract considerable numbers of admiring followers. Peter and the apostles continued to preach "with great power" (Acts 4:33) and were able to add multitudes of men and women, new believers in the Lord (Acts 5:14), which aroused the wrath of the high priests. Unlike Jesus, the charges for which they were being tried were stated immediately. The opening question of the high priest, "We gave you strict orders not to teach in this name . . ." (Acts 5:28).

The New Testament is a rich source for evidence for this theory. Stephen (Acts 6-7) was accused of blasphemy, taken before the Council and was stoned to death outside the city. There are also records of arrests and physical punishment suffered by Christians at the hands of Jewish officials (Acts 5:18-40; 22:4; 26:10; 2 Cor. 11:24).

Discounting False Stories

Christ Dragged Through the Brook of Kidron

The dragging of Christ through the Brook of Kidron, the brook that Christ crossed with his disciples on the way to Gethsemane (John 18:1), and the plunging of Christ into a "foul pool" has received little modern scholarly attention.[145] Most accounts of the dragging Christ through the Kidron actually cite the prophecy of Ps.110:7.

The Tortures in an Underground Chamber

There is an account of the plunging of Christ into privies or cesspools in a cellar beneath the house of Caiaphas. The underground tortures in Caiaphas' house derived primarily from Biblical imagery and early art raising the possibility of a completely independent origin for this subterranean episode in the house of Caiaphas:

> "Draw me out of the mire that I may not stick fast; deliver me from them that hate me and out of the deep waters."   —Ps. 69:14

> "I am counted among those who go down to the pit."   —Ps. 88:4[146]

The Burning of Christ

John reports that the soldiers who came to arrest Christ bore lanterns and torches, and other writings of the late middle ages described the thrusting of the torches into his face so that he was burned. During the night Christ spent in prison, there are lengthy accounts of the application of red hot eggshells, irons, and plates to Christ's face, body, and private parts all in sadistic detail.

Some of this may relate to sacrificial animals burned to fulfill the precepts of the old law (Num. 19:2-5) and the prophecy of Isaiah 1:6.[147]

The Mocking of Christ: His Near Suffocation with Spittle

During the mocking of Christ at Caiaphas' house, the synoptics record that Christ was scoffed at, buffeted, and spat upon (Matt. 27:27; Mark 14:65), and late medieval authors determine that the Jews had spat into Christ's mouth so as to suffocate him.

Christ Stretched Beneath a Table and Beaten[148]

The final incident to be considered from Christ's tortures during the night of his captivity is more ingenuous than gruesome:

1. Some believe that Christ was bound to a table and beaten by drunken tormentors.

2. A number of passionate tracts recount incidents in which Christ is taken and hurled against walls and doorways as he is led from site to site.

3. As Christ is taken before Pilate, he is thrown to a stone floor (the lithostrotos) (John 19:13), or a stairway that his head smacks onto the stone floor and a large pool of blood remained there.

Christ the Man of Sorrows
Meister Francke
Co Eike Walford, Hamburg

ENDNOTES

[1] Sherwin-White, A. N. *Roman Society and Roman Law in the New Testament* (Baker Book House: Grand Rapids, MI: 1963), p. 24; Schonfield. *The Passover Plot.* (Transworld: 1967).

[2] Wingo, Earl L. *A Lawyer Reviews the Illegal Trial of Jesus.* (Wingo Publications: Hattiesburg, MS: 1954).

[3] Danby, Herbert. "The Bearing of the Rabbinical Criminal Code on the Jewish Trial Narratives in the Gospels," *JTS* 21 (1919): 60.

[4] Disdain for informer activities has roots in Leviticus 19:16, "Thou shall not go up and down as a tale bearer among the people." Daniel teaches that an informant is "one who eats the flesh of another." Penalties for being an informer included flogging, imprisonment, branding, and death. Orthodox Jews condemn the informer thrice daily in their prayers.

[5] Taylor, John E. *Biblical Archeological Review*, Vol. 21, No. 4, Aug. 1995, p. 26.

[6] Storme, Albert. *Gethsemane.* (Jerusalem: Franciscan Printing Press: 1972), p. 24.

[7] Wilkinson, John. *Jerusalem as Jesus Knew It* (London: Thames and Hudson, 1978), pgs. 127-131.

[8] Connick, C. Milo. *Jesus, the Man, the Mission, and the Message* (Prentice-Hall: Englewood Cliffs, NJ: 1963), p. 378.

[9] Some historians agree the means of betrayal was not the notorious kiss of Judas. The kiss is obviously to be understood in relation to the allegory of the deadly kiss. (2 Sam. 20:9)

[10] Emerson, William A., Jr. *The Jesus Story.* (Harper & Row Publishers: New York: 1971), p. 124.

[11] Gaechter, P. *The Hatred of the House of Annas.* (1947), pgs. 33-34.

[12] Schilder, K. *Christ on Trial.* (Clok & Clok Christian Publishers: Minneapolis, MN: 1939), p. 30.

[13] In the 13th Century, scholars began distinguishing between the "House of Annas" and the "House of Caiaphas." Probably they were not separate houses but separate meeting places. Scholars guess Annas and Caiaphas lived in different wings of the same palace. Brown, Raymond E. *The Death of the Messiah*, Vol. 1. (Doubleday: New York: 1993), p. 404; Riciotti, Guissippi. *Life of Christ.* Translated by Alba Zizzamia. (Bruce Publishing Co.: Milwaukee, WI: 1952), p. 341.

[14] Josephus tells us that whoever came before the Sanhedrin for trial was to show himself humble and assume the manner of one who is fearful and seeks mercy. It is no wonder that one of the police attendants considers Jesus' behavior to be an affront and slaps him for his arrogance in addressing the high priest.

[15] von Mayr, R. *Der Prozess Jesu*, Archiv fur Kriminal-Anthropologie und Kriminalistick, 20. (1905), pgs. 269-305.

[16] Josephus. *Antiquities of the Jews*, 18.4.2, 3.

[17] Josephus. *Antiquities of the Jews.* 13.10.6; 20.9.1.

[18] Sanders, E.P. *Jesus, the Gospels, and the Church.* (Mercer University Press: Macon, GA: 1987), p. 199.

[19] Morrison, Frank. *Who Moved the Stone?* (Lamplighter Books, Zondervan Publishing Co.: Grand Rapids, MI: 1930), p. 39.

[20] Morrison, Frank. *Who Moved the Stone?* (Lamplighter Books, Zondervan Publishing Co.: Grand Rapids, MI: 1930), p. 41.

[21] Barrett, C. K. *The Gospel According to St. John.* (London: 1960), p. 440.

[22] Cassidy, Richard J. and Scharper, Philip J. *Political Issues in Luke-Acts.* (Orbis Books: Mary Knoll, NY: 1983), p. 160.

[23] Theudas, mentioned in Acts 5:36, led one such movement also described by Josephus in *Antiquities of the Jews*, 20.5.1.

[24] "Theudas persuaded the majority of the masses to take up their positions and to follow him to the Jordan River. He stated that he was a prophet, and that at his command the river would be parted and would provide them an easy passage. With this talk he deceived many. Fadus, however, did not permit them to reap the fruit of their folly, but sent against them a squadron of cavalry. These fell upon them unexpectedly, slew many of them and took many prisoners. Theudas himself was captured, whereupon they cut off his head and brought it to Jerusalem." Josephus. *Antiquities of the Jews*, 20.5.1.

[25] Tucker, T. "The Context and Nature of the Roman Empire at the Birth of Christianity," *The History of Christianity in the Light of Modern Knowledge*. (Blackwells: London), pgs. 7-11.

[26] "The Hatred of the House of Annas," *Theological Studies*. (Woodstock Maryland: 1947), pgs. 11-13.

[27] Mazziotta, Richard. *Jesus and the Gospels*. (Ave Maria Press: Notre Dame, Indiana: 1986) p. 179; Churer. *History of the Jewish People*, Vol. 2, pgs. 225-226; Kiehl, Erich H. *The Passion of Our Lord*. (Baker Book House: Grand Rapids, MI: 1990), p. 87.

[28] There is a question as to whether *all* Sanhedrin members could have arrived in time. Only Mark says "the entire" council. The other Gospels are less clear.

[29] Sepp. *The Life of Jesus*. (Germany: 1914). This source gives particulars of forty members, but truth compels me to admit the chronology of the Talmud is so vague I cannot positively identify everyone.

[30] Richards, John E. "The Illegality of the Trial of Jesus," *Madras Law Journal*. (Charles E. George & Co.: New Orleans: 1914), p. 7.

[31] Sanders, E. P. *The Historical Figure of Jesus*. (Penguin Books: London: 1993), p. 25.

[32] Talmud, Pesachim, Folio, 57.

[33] Josephus. *The Jewish Wars*, 2.14.8; 2.15.2.

[34] Ayway, Srinivasa S. "The Legality of the Trial of Jesus," *Madras Law Journal*, Mylapore, India. (Platt & Peck Co.: New York: 1915), p. 93.

[35] The Abbey Constant Fouard. *The Christ: The Son of God*. (Longmans, Green, & Co.: London: 1951), p. 305.

[36] *Mishnah Sanhedrin*, 1.1; 7.2; *Talmud Jerusalem*, 18a & 24b.

[37] See citations in *The Death of the Messiah*, Vol. 1. (Doubleday: New York: 1993), by Raymond E. Brown, p. 366.

[38] Maier, Paul. "The Trial of Jesus and the Competence of the Sanhedrin," *New Testament Studies*, July 1964, (Cambridge University Press, 1964), p. 494.

[39] Michaels, J. Ramsey. "The Trial of Jesus," *New Testament Studies*, Vol. 36, 1990, p. 475.

[40] Robps, Daniel. *Jesus and His Times*. (E.P. Dutton & Co.: New York: 1956), p. 370.

[41] Josephus. *The Jewish Wars*, 5.4.2., Section 144.

[42] Blinzler, Josef. *The Trial of Jesus*. (The Newman Press: 1959), pgs. 112-114.

[43] Tyson, Joseph B. *The Death of Jesus in Luke/Acts*. (University of South Carolina Press: Columbia, SC: 1986), p. 122. Rulers of high priestly descent were present (Acts 4:5–6).

[44] Powell, F. J. *The Trial of Jesus Christ*. (London: 1949); Barton, G.A. *On the Trial of Jesus Before the Sanhedrin*. (Journal of Bibilical Literature 41: 1922), pgs. 205- 211.

[45] Wilson, William Riley. *The Execution of Jesus*. (Charles Scribners Sons: New York: 1970), p. 126.

[46] Sanders, E. P. *The Historical Figure of Jesus*. (Penguin Books: London: 1993), pgs. 254-258.

[47] Beinert, W. *Der alteste nichtchristliche Jesusbericht*. (Halle: 1936), p. 54.

[48] Frickey, Weddig. *The Court-Martial of Jesus*. (Grove, Weidenfeld: New York: 1987), p. 151.

[49] Thompson, George W. *The Trial of Jesus*. (Bobb's-Merrill Co.: Indianapolis: 1927), p. 9.

[50] *Mishnah Abot*, 4.8.

[51] The best example of the usefulness of cross-examination is the apocryphal "Susanna and the Elders".

[52] Chandler, Walter M. *The Trial of Jesus from a Lawyer's Standpoint*, Vol. 1. (1908), p. 238.

[53] Breed, David K. *The Trial of Christ*. (Thomas Law Book Co.: St. Louis: 1948), p. 42.

[54] *Mishnah Abot*, 4.8.

[55] *Mishnah Sanhedrin*, 4.1.

[56] *Mishnah Sanhedrin*, 4.1.

[57] Flusser, David. *Die Letzten Thee Jesu In Jerusalem*. (Stuttgart: 1982), p. 92.

[58] Ignorance of the law was a good defense to any criminal charge in Jewish law and was presumed in favor of the accused until his knowledge of the law was positively proven.

[59] *Sanhedrin* 6.1.

[60] Krummacher, F. W. *The Suffering Savior*. (Moody Press: Chicago: 1947), p. 190.

[61] *Mishnah Sanhedrin*, 7.8; Goldin, H. E. *Hebrew Criminal Law and Procedure*. (1952), pgs. 24-25.

[62] Strict observance of the Sabbath was evident in the military. A Jewish uprising against the Syrian King Antioch IV failed because of the Sabbath observance (I Macc. 2:33-36). In 64 B.C. when Pompey besieged Jerusalem, the Jews allegedly refused to bear arms on the Sabbath, thereby,

ensuring a Roman victory. Some believe the conquest of Masada by the Romans in A.D. 73 was due to the defenders' loyal and steadfast observance of the Sabbath. Landmann, Salcia A. *Jesus und die Juden*, (Munich, Germany: 1987), p. 123.

[63] Cohn, Haim. *The Trial and Death of Jesus*. (Ktav Publishing House: New York: 1977).

[64] Borg, Marcus. *Meeting Jesus Again for the First Time*. (Harper Collins: San Francisco: 1944), p. 49.

[65] Fredriksen, Paula. "Did Jesus Oppose the Purity Laws?" *Bible Review*, Vol. 11, No. 3, June 1994, p. 20.

[66] Sanders, E. P. *Jewish Law from Jesus to the Mishnah*. (Trinity Press: Philadelphia: 1990), p. 151.

[67] Winter, Paul. *On the Trial of Jesus*. (Burkill & Geza Vermes: Berlin: 1974), p. 43.

[68] Mantel, Hugo. *Studies in the History of the Sanhedrin*. (1962), pgs. 273-276.

[69] Montefiore, C. G. *The Synoptic Gospels*. New York (MacMillan: 1927), p. 357.

[70] Blinzler, Josef. *Der Prozess Jesu*. (Dritte Auflage, Regensburg, 1960).

[71] Kraeling, C. H. "Was Jesus Accused of Necromancy?" *Journal of Biblical Literature*. (New Haven, CT: 1940), pgs. 147-157.

[72] A false prophet is "he that prophesies what he has not heard and what has not been told him." *Mishnah Sanhedrin*, 11,5.

[73] Mantell, Hugo. *Studies in the History of the Sanhedrin*. (Harvard University Press: Cambridge, MA: 1965), p. 269; Burkhill, J.A. *The Competence of the Sanhedrin*. (Vigiliae Christianae: Amsterdam: 195), p. 82.

[74] Read, David W. "We Have a Law," *Novum Testamentum*, Vol. XI, July 1969, p. 188; BT Sanh.44a *The Baraita*.

[75] Josephus. *Antiquities of the Jews*, 18.8.3.

[76] "If (the cleansing of the Temple) is not expressly mentioned, it may be due to the fragmentary and casual character of the particulars that have come down to us." Kopling, H. *Fundamental Theology*, Vol. 2 (Regensburg: 1974), p. 640.

[77] Bammel, Ernst. *The Trial of Jesus*. (SCM Press, Ltd.: London: 1970), p. 73.

[78] Cohn, Haim. *The Trial and Death of Jesus*. (Ktav Publishing House: New York: 1977). The rending of the high priests' garments was expressly contrary to the law (Lev. 10:6; 21:10), but was a common method of expressing violent grief and horror at what was deemed blasphemous or impious. All that heard a blasphemous speech were obliged to rend their clothes and never to sew them up again.

[79] *Mishnah Sanhedrin* 7.5.

[80] Schilder, K. *Christ on Trial*. (Clok & Clok Christian Publishers: Minneapolis, MN: 1939), p. 121.

[81] Jesus is the only person who uses the phrase, and uses it more often than any other, explaining who he is (including "Son of God" and "Messiah"). Jesus was smart enough to use the phrase as both generic and angelic. He was a rational teacher who wished to convey a single meaning. Jesus speaks of the exaltation of the Son of Man and the crowd replies impatiently, "We have heard from the Law that the Christ will remain forever, so how can you say, "The Son of Man must be lifted up? Who is this Son of Man?" (Jn. 12:34) The crowd understood both the terms "Messiah," and "Son of Man."

Jesus was the master of the parable—the comparison—and comparative speech was his particular strength. He could portray the kingdom of God in terms of a growing seed, (Mt. 13:31; Mk. 4:30; Lk. 13:18) a woman making bread, (Mt. 13:33; Lk. 13:20) or a merchant out to close an attractive deal. (Mt. 13:45) You could understand the kingdom in terms of such realities and ordinary activities. Jesus genuinely related his own activity and the activities of those around him to the kingdom of God.

The Son of Man was Jesus' way of talking about himself as a person who had access to the very throne of God, the place of another angelic person. Jesus took a classic passage from the Bible (Dan. 7:13-14) in which a "Son of Man" is clearly the agent of final judgment, blended with an Aramaic idiom of his time, and appropriated it to himself. Chilton, Bruce. *A Galilean Rabbi and His Bible: Jesus' Use of the Interpreted Scripture of His Time*. (Wilmington: Glazier: 1984); Chilton, Bruce. "Who Is He?" *Biblical Review*, Vol. XII, No. 4, Aug. 1996, pgs. 35-39.

[82] Yoder, John H. *The Politics of Jesus*. (William Eerdmans Publishing Co.: Grand Rapids, MI: 1972), p. 59.

[83] Buttrick, David G. *The Mystery and the Passion*. (Fortress Press: Minneapolis, MN: 1992), p. 155.

[84] Cullman, Oscar. *Dieu et Cesar*, 1956, p. 31.

[85] "Thou has said," appears in the Talmud and is the equivalent of "You are right," Tosefta Kelim, Baba Kamma 1:16. This evasive and ambiguous reply which could be an affirmation or a denial is in all probability a corruption of the Hebrew expression, "ken dibbarto," is no where else to be found in Hebrew literature as equivalent to an affirmation. In the Aramaic language there was no literal way to simply say "yes." To answer in the affirmative said, "You know it is." Asked if he himself was going to betray Jesus (Mt. 26:25), Caiaphas asked, "Are you the Christ, the Son of God?" Jesus' response was the same: "You know that I am!" Catchpole, D.R. *The Answer of Jesus to Caiaphas*, NTS 17 (1970), pgs. 212-226.

[86] Foster, R.C. *The Final Week*. (Baker Book House: Grand Rapids, MI: 1962), p. 206.

[87] Sherwin-White, A.N. *Roman Society and Roman Law in the New Testament*. (Baker Book House: Grand Rapids, MI: 1963), p. 49.

[88] Cornfeld, Gaaylah. *The Historical Jesus*. (MacMillan Publishing Co.: New York: 1982), p. 163.

[89] Josephus. *The Jewish Wars*, 5.5.8., Section 241.

[90] Gabbatha in Hebrew and Lithostroton in Greek, though the two words do not mean the same thing. *Lithostroton* means "a paved area." *Gabbatha* is not certain, but the underlying Aramaic root means "to be high, to protrude." Benoit, Pierre. "Pretoire Lithostrothon et Gabbatha," *Revue Biblique*, 59 (1962), pgs. 548-550.

[91] Maier, Paul L. *Pontius Pilate*. (Doubleday & Co.: New York: 1968), p. 219.

[92] Blinzler, *Zum Process Jesu*, p. 69; Bernard, J. H. *A Critical and Exegetical Commentary on the Gospel According to St. John*, Vol. 2. (T & T Clark Co.: Edinburgh: 1928).

[93] Krimsky, Joseph H. *Jesus and the Hidden Bible*. (Philosophical Library: New York: 1951), p. 68.

[94] The theory that Jesus was mixed up with the Zealot movement of armed resistance has never lacked proponents. There is very wide agreement that there was a religious issue between Jesus and his own people which went far deeper than an attack on the collaborating priestly aristocracy; that he brought a theological challenge of the most fundamental kind. Still, there is no positive evidence that the Roman verdict was justified in the sense that Jesus actually was a Zealot. Sweet, J.P.M. *The Zealots and Jesus*; Bammell, Ernest, and Mouley, C.P.D. Jesus and the Politics of His Day. (Cambridge Press: London: 1984), p. 1.

[95] Wilson, William Riley. *The Execution of Jesus*. (Charles Scribners Sons: New York: 1970), p. 129.

[96] Sherwin-White, A.N. *Roman Society*, pgs. 15-45.

[97] By entering a house in which the leaven had not been removed they would have been incapacitated from eating the Passover that evening.

[98] It is historical fact Emperor Tiberius had no scruples about humiliating his subordinates. Pilate was weak as well as wicked. He was afraid (Jn. 19:8) and lacked the courage of his convictions. Chapel, Clovis J. *Faces About the Cross*. (Abingdon Cokesbury Press: New York: 1973), p. 113.

[99] "Did Jesus Speak Aramaic?" *Expository Times*. (Edinburgh: 1944), p. 95; Blinzler, Josef. *The Trial of Jesus*. (The Newman Press: 1959), p. 171.

[100] Josephus. *The Jewish Wars*, 2:12.1., Section 224.

[101] A good illustration of the attitude of Roman officials toward questions of native religious infractions is found in the cases of Gallio, Paul, and the Jews of Corinth (Acts 18:12-17).

[102] Wilston, C. W. "The Roman Law of Treason Under the Early Principate," *Journal of Roman Studies*, 45 (1955), pgs. 73-81.

[103] Justinian, *Digestes*, 48.4.3.

[104] Wilson, William Riley. *The Execution of Jesus*. (Charles Scribners Sons: New York: 1970), p. 135.

[105] Strauss, Dr. David Freundrick. *The Life of Jesus Critically Examined*. (Swamsonnenshein & Co.: London: 1906). Translated from German by George Elliott, 5th Edition), p. 674. The "fact" of this dream is totally unattested to by history or tradition. Many scholars believe it was fabricated after the events for the sake of heightening its effect. The Greek Orthodox Church canonized her as "Procula," and the Ethiopian church recognized June 25 as "St. Pilate and St. Proculla's Day." Waymauch, Edwin M. "Historical Notes on the Trial and Crucifixion of Jesus Christ," *Christianity Today*, Vol. XI, No. 14, April 9, 1971, p. 8.

[106] Mommsen, T. *Romische Strafrecht*. (Leipzig: 1899), pgs. 356- 357.

252   The Trial of Christ

[107] Josephus. *Antiquities of the Jews*, 18.2.3, Section 36.

[108] Schilder, K. *Christ on Trial*, Vol. 2. (Clok & Clok Publishers: Minneapolis, MN: 1939), p. 395; For a survey of positions, see *The Gospel According to Luke*, by J. A. Fitzmyer (Doubleday: Garden City, NY: 1985), pgs. 1478–1480.

[109] Their food was cooked in utensils coated with lead and the wine they drank was supplemented by a grape syrup that had been boiled in lead containers. This syrup which prevented further fermentation and added color and fragrance made drinking wine the major source of lead poisoning. Nriagu, Jerome O. "Occasional Notes, Saturnine Gout Among Roman Aristocrats: Did Lead Poisoning Contribute to the Fall of the Empire?" *New England Journal of Medicine*, 308.11, Mar. 17, 1983: pgs. 660-663.

[110] Goguel. *The Life of Jesus*, Vol. 2., p. 521.

[111] Edwards, Dr. William D. "On the Physical Death of Jesus," *Journal of the American Medical Association*," March 1986, Vol. 255, No. 11.

[112] This information draws heavily on my personal interview with Dr. Charles A. Crenshaw, a prominent physician who attended to JFK at Parkland Hospital, Dallas, TX, in 1963, and who was Director of the Department of Surgery, John Petersmith Hospital, Fort Worth, TX.

[113] Lumpkin, R. "The Physical Suffering of Christ," *Journal of Medical Associates of Alabama*, 1978, Vol. 47, p. 8.

[114] "Without a private revelation, it is impossible to know exactly the number and severity of the blows which the Savior received in this atrocious scourging." Ludolph the Carthusian.

[115] McHugh, Isabel & Florence. *The Trial of Jesus*. (The Mercier Press, Ltd.: England: 1959), p. 222.

[116] Nothing could be more horrible than the brief description of it given in the letter of the Church of Smyrna on the martyrdom of St. Polycarp; Eusebius, Hist. Eccl. IV, xv, 4. Tiberius had a centurion of a famous cohort scourged; Caligula inflicted the same punishment on his quaestor. Paul was beaten three times with rods (2 Cor. 11:25).

[117] Josephus. *The Jewish Wars*, 2.21.5. Section 612.

[118] Davis, C.T. "The Crucifixion of Jesus: The Passion of Christ from a Medical Point of View," *Arizona Medical Journal*, Vol. 22, (1989), p. 183.

[119] Authorities in Caesarea punished agitators with scourging and imprisonment. Flaccus scourged the Jews of Alexandria and many died during the punishment and the rest only recovered after a long period of disablement.

[120] Florus had Jewish citizens scourged in front of his judgment seat and then crucified. Josephus. *The Jewish Wars*, 2.14.9. Section 306.

[121] The only reason for the words "Pilate then took Jesus..." would be to convey that the accused was taken from the scene to another place.

[122] McHugh, Isabel & Florence. *The Trial of Jesus*. (The Mercier Press, Ltd.: England: 1959), p. 229.

[123] *Pesachim*, 7.6.

[124] Bandit, translated by the Jewish historian Josephus, probably means Zealot.

[125] Bammell, Ernest and Mouley, C.P.D., "The Titulus," *Jesus and the Politics of His Day*. (Cambridge Press: London: 1984), p. 354.

[126] "The King of the Jews," (Mk. 15:26); "This is the King of the Jews," (Lk. 23:38); "This is Jesus, the King of the Jews," (Mt. 27:37); "Jesus of Nazareth, the King of the Jews," (Jn. 19:19). According to Codex Sinaiticus, Codex Alexandrinus, and Codex Bezai, three of the most ancient Greek manuscripts of the New Testament from the fourth and fifth centuries A.D., it is clear three languages were used. Bivin, David and Blizzard, Roy, Jr. *Understanding the Difficult Words of Jesus*. (Destiny Image Publishers: Shippinsburg, PA: 1994), p. 8.

[127] Suetonius, *Caligula*, 32:2.

[128] *Mishnah*, Sanh. 6:1-2; 4-6.

[129] Neusner, Joseph. *The Mishnah, Introduction and Reader*. (Trinity Press: Philadelphia: 1992), pgs. 155-157.

[130] Josephus. *Jewish Wars*, 5.146.

[131] Bahat, Dan. "Does the Holy Sepulchre Church Mark the Burial of Jesus?" *BAR*, June 1986, pgs. 26-45.

[132] O'Connor-Murphy, Jerome. "The Geography of Faith: Tracing the Via Dolorosa," *BAR*, December, 1996, pgs. 33-53.

[133] Tiede, David L. *Prophecy and History in Luke-Acts*. (Philadelphia: Fortress Press: 1980), pgs. 65-125.

[134] Eusebius, *Ecclesiastical History*, 17.

[135] *Vita Const.*, III.25-40. This fourth century ecclesiastical historian was present, as a boy, in A.D. 336 when the Holy Sepulchre and the site of Golgotha were "discovered" by Bishop Macarius of Jerusalem. They were beneath a temple of Venus which had been erected by the Romans after the desecration of the city. Beneath this temple there was a cave, and when the Empress Helena found out about it, she lost no time, with the assistance of fellow Christians, in finding the true cross, and the "crown of thorns" and the spear with which the side of Christ was pierced.

Macarius was not an archeologist but the Macarius Calvary, now visible within the city walls, led 19th century archaeologists to be more impressed with the site favored by General Gordon, the hero of Khartoum, which lies just outside the Damascus gate of the present-day old city or Place of the Skull.

[136] Eusebius, *Ecclesiastical History*, 4, 26. 13-14; Taylor, Joen E. *Christians in the Holy Places*. (Clarendon Press: Oxford: 1993), p. 116.

[137] National statistics show an average of ten years between the crime and execution.

[138] The simple soldier's pay was miserable, his annual income paid in three installments amounted to 227 denarii. A Palestinian day-laborer by comparison, earned one denarus a day. Batz, K., and Mack, R. *Sachtexte Zur Bibel*. (Munich: Lahr: 1985), p.27. Thus, when the four soldiers were allowed to share in the clothing of the crucified, no matter how shabby, this was deemed a pay supplement and was a prophecy fulfillment. "They divide my garments among them and cast lots for my clothing." (Ps. 22:18)

[139] Depasquale, N.P. "Death by Crucifixion," *American Heart Journal*, 1963, Vol. 66, p. 434. The earliest example of crucifixion of record is probably that of Pharaoh's chief baker, said by Josephus to have been crucified.

[140] The Mishnah is explicit: Burial in towns surrounded by a wall is forbidden, Kelim 1.7. Also see the Dead Sea Scroll known as the Temple Scroll. An exception was royal burials. Some kings were buried in the City of David such as David (I Kings 2:10), Jehoshaphat, JRAM, Uzziah, Jotham, Ahaz, and Hezekiah. The burial of later kings is often noted, but is never located in the City of David.

[141] Barbet, P. *A Doctor at Calvary: A Passion of Our Lord Jesus Christ as Described by a Surgeon*, (Doubleday Image Books: Garden City, NY: 1954), pgs. 12-18.

[142] Stroud, Dr. William. *The Physical Cause of the Death of Jesus Christ*. (London: 1862), p. 52.

[143] Johnson, C.D. *Medical and Cardiological Aspects of the Passion and Crucifixion of Jesus*. (Bol. Assoc. Med.), 1978.

[144] Stroud W. *Treatise on the Physical Cause of the Death of Christ and its Relation to the Principles and Practice of Christianity*, 2nd Ed. (London: Hamilton & Adams: 1861), pgs. 28-156.

[145] The prophecy of Ps. 110:7 that "He will drink of the brook beside the way," has long been recognized.

[146] Jameson, Anna. *The History of Our Lord*, New Edition, Vol. 2. (London: 1892), pgs. 110-113.

[147] "From the sole of the foot unto the top of the head there is no soundness therein, only wounds, and bruises, and swelling sores."

[148] Foreman, Dale. *Crucify Him: A Lawyer Looks at the Trial of Jesus*. (Zondervan Publishing House: Grand Rapids, MI: 1990), p. 179.

"Surely this man was the Son of God!"

—Mark 15:39

CHAPTER SEVEN

Conclusion

"He said to them, 'This is what I told you while I was still with you: Everything must be fulfilled that is written about me in the Law of Moses, the
Prophets and the Psalms...this is what is written: The Christ will suffer and
rise from the dead on the third day, and repentance and forgiveness of sins
will be preached in his name to all nations, beginning at Jerusalem."

—Luke 24:44-47

H E HUNG FROM A ROUGH-HEWN CROSS. Blood ran down his legs. A crown
of thorns perched at a crazy tilt on his bowed head. He had been
beaten by the Roman soldiers and nailed for three hours to a hideous wooden
cross. Every few seconds, as his lungs filled with blood, he gasped for breath.
His body convulsed.

With great effort, he arched his back to gain enough air to speak. Those
nearby leaned forward to catch his last words. Whom would he curse?

He spoke, but he did not curse. Instead he cried an awful and unsettling question, "Eloi, Eloi, lama sabachthani?" ("My God, my God, why have you forsaken me?" (Matt. 27:46; Mark 15:34).

The question is a troubling one for Christians. Luke and John say more that Jesus also said, "Father, forgive them, for they do not know what they are doing" (Luke 23:34).

To a lawyer, such a statement is called a "dying declaration," a relatively trustworthy statement because human experience has shown that people seldom die with a lie on their lips. Death is a "moment of truth" and at that moment Jesus did not curse. He blessed.

John reports what the Jewish national officials believed: that the death of one man might avert political disaster for the whole nation. He came to Jerusalem to bring the nation nearer to God, yet lost life because of the mistaken fear he might bring the nation to destruction.

So zealous were the Sadducees to save their nation from destruction that they sold themselves outright. The high priests not only reported activities of the malcontent, but even arrested and interrogated them.[1] And Caiaphas held the high priesthood for more than a decade, when one normally did not rule for more than a year. He was a henchman, carrying out Pilate's whims.

If Pilate made reference to a formal offense in sentencing Jesus, it was against the majesty of the people of Rome, a political rebel against Roman authority, the customary designation for treason.[2] Pilate condemned Jesus without reference to a formal statute citing only his supposedly revolutionary activity as a challenge to the peace of the country.[3]

Historians have developed many explanations for Jesus' death. Four are most common:

1. *The misunderstanding theory.* Jesus, a mystic dreamer claimed messiahship and preached the kingdom of God in a spiritual, nonpolitical sense. The masses were disappointed and their political longings frustrated. The Romans were quite clear Jesus was a menace and took action accordingly (Mark 12:17; John 18:37);

2. *The messianic claim theory.* Most Jewish authors believe that Jesus claimed to be the Messiah, particularly at his entry into Jerusalem. They believed he aimed to restore national independence despite the uniform denial of this by all four (Jewish-authored) Gospels;

3. *The popular unrest theory.* The effect of Jesus upon people rather than any deliberate claims which provoked police action was important. Political aspirations were present,[4] but there was no messianic claim. He was executed as a rebel together with others who were executed on the same charge; and

4. *The Zealot Theory.* This theory believes John the Baptist was a zealot leader, praised by Jesus. Jesus originally took a more pacifist line, but stirred by his own fervent eschatology and dejected by his failure in Galilee, he sought a verdict in Jerusalem. He entered the city and occupied the temple by armed force while supporters seized the Tower of Siloam (Luke 13:1-4). The rebellion was put down, but Jesus was arrested and executed as a rebel.[5] At least one of Jesus' disciples was known to be a Zealot. Jesus committed some acts which Zealots would have approved.

The words of Jesus, taken as predicting the temple's destruction, was taken as a threat of political upheaval.[6]

Who Was to Blame?

Assessing responsibility for this catalog of illegalities, injustices and errors draws us to more than a dozen culpable parties.

In the first days of the church, Christians did not see Jesus' crucifixion as a necessary stage in God's redemptive plan and an ultimate victory. They regarded it as an unparalleled tragedy.[7] And they blamed this tragedy on the Jewish people who rejected their Messiah.

The earliest statement which puts the blame for the death of Jesus on *Jewish Leaders* is the moving scene of two disciples conversing with their risen Master. They say to their fellow-traveler on the road to Emmaus:

> "About Jesus of Nazareth—He was a prophet, powerful in word and deed before God and all the people. The chief priests and our rulers handed him over to be sentenced to death, and they crucified him." [8]
>
> —Luke 24:19,20

One must understand that religious people could have disliked Jesus. Jesus' death had nothing to do with Judaism.

The traditional Christian answer has been that the authorities were not truly religious but were hypocrites, or intolerant ultra-legalists and did not

Above:
Christ Before Caiaphas
Giotto, ca. 1305
Arena Chapel Padua, Italy

Below:
Christ Nailed to the Cross
Gerard David
The National Gallery, London

hesitate to be callously brutal. In Jesus' time, religious opposition often led to violence. Jews hated and killed one another over religious issues.

High priests were responsible for many violent deeds. In late Second Century Alexander Jannaeus massacred 6,000 Jews at the Feast of Tabernacles over a challenge by Pharisees to his legal qualifications to hold the priestly office, and later crucified 800 while their wives and children were butchered before their eyes.[9]

A desire on the part of some fellow Jews for severe action against Jesus, a troubling religious figure, and eventually against those in Judaism who came to accept Him, was not unthinkable.

Acts records Simon Peter's address to the assembled Jewish crowd, stating Jesus was "crucified at the hands of lawless men" (Acts 2:23) and Jesus was he "whom you (all the Jews within hearing) crucified."[10]

Matthew's words that "all" the Jews cried out, "Let his blood be upon us and upon our children," is thought by many historians to be a "terrible verse, a horrible invention...one of those phrases which has been responsible for oceans of human blood, and a ceaseless stream of misery and desolation."[11] Some historians believe these words are completely fictitious, not a statement by the Jews at the trial but a chilling summation of the Christian insistence of the Jewish national guilt.[12]

Luke offers the very first commentary on Roman versus Jewish responsibility.

> Men of Israel . . . you handed him over to be killed, and you disowned him before Pilate, though he had decided to let him go. —ACTS 3:12-13

In Thessalonians, the very earliest writing in the New Testament, Paul states Jews "killed both the Lord Jesus and the prophets" (1 Thess. 2:15).

The trial of Jesus was conducted exactly as Roman law would dictate in the case of a provincial coming under the personal investigation of a Roman governor.[13]

No ranking scholar today is sure that later Talmudic Law for Sanhedrinal court procedure applied at the trial of Christ. Even if it did, it disregarded or compromised on the basis of civil emergency. Unhappily, lynchings, judicial or otherwise, take place in the most ordered societies, such as the stoning of Stephen.

Josephus records in A.D. 62, only twenty-nine years after the crucifixion, that the high priest and Sanhedrin stoned to death James, the half brother of Jesus, and the first Christian bishop of Jerusalem in the absence of the Roman governor Albinus who was later so angry at this execution that the high priest Ananus, son of Annas, was deposed.[14]

Responsible Christian theology emphasizes that it was God—not any Jewish prosecution—who was ultimately responsible for the crucifixion since all mankind was involved in and affected by the events swirling around the cross, not just one or another ethnic group.[15]

Justin Martyr wrote that Jesus, "endured all things which the devils instigated, the senseless to inflict upon him."[16] Justin wrote that Jews crucified Jesus, not Pilate.[17]

Perhaps the most interesting example in non-Gospel literature is found in the Gospel of Peter dating to the second century.[18] It is the earliest existing account of Jesus' trial outside the Gospels. The trial events are described with an extremely anti-Jewish bias, and in describing the hand washing by Pilate states: "of the Jews no man washed his hands."

A full and complete review of biblical literature, however, will not allow any kind of anti-Semitic blame for Jesus' execution. As Edmund Burke once wrote:

"I do not know the method of drawing up an indictment against a whole people."

The Christian scriptures name many others besides the Jewish people. Three are named in Acts 4:27: *Herod*, *Pontius Pilate*, and *the Gentiles*. The fifth is *Satan*. Three more named are the *Father*, the *Son*, and the *Holy Spirit*.

Judas Iscariot must bear some responsibility for what has become recognized as the world's most repulsive betrayal.

The body of *disciples* were not without blame in that none came forward with compelling evidence in his favor. That also could be true of some whom Jesus healed. No one came to his defense.

The *Sanhedrin* was guilty of allowing a series of illegalities to proceed unchallenged, and those who were present were open to serious blame for closing their eyes to the demands of their own judicial system.

Herod was responsible for not asking what the charge was, and then for a whole series of mockeries opposed to the concept of justice. He found none of the accusations proven, yet made no effort to release Jesus.

Pilate was guilty of dreadful crimes against Jesus, against the Roman system of justice [19] he represented, against mankind, and ultimately against himself. Hand washing could never remove his indelible guilt.

Roman government records reveal no interest in denying Roman responsibility. From their point of view, the case was too unimportant. Christianity was a contemptible superstition. Tacitus did not know the name of Jesus of Nazareth and reported briefly that the religion got its name from Christ, an executed criminal.

An ironic reaction to the Gospel reports surfaced in 1972 when a motion was presented by Christian theologians to the Israeli Supreme Court recommending the nullification of the judgment pronounced against Jesus of Nazareth. The Chief Justice politely explained that regrettably, he could not consider the motion because of a lack of jurisdiction, and referred the petitioners to an Italian court.

The *Jerusalem mob* was guilty in that their bloodlust blinded them to the reality of Jesus' claims and deafened them to the voice of their own conscience.

The ultimate blame lay with *Annas* and *Caiaphas* and other members of the high priestly family. Jesus was a threat to their standing as temple administrators, especially in matters of trade which had grossly enriched them.

Caiaphas believed the teachings of Jesus had fostered a secret and subversive movement.[20] But by their judgment of Jesus, the Sanhedrin judged themselves.

Christianity teaches that in the death of Jesus, God delivered the world from sin. No blame can attach to God for allowing Jesus to die on the cross for our sins, or to the instruments God chose and directed to attain his ends. Since *his death was foreordained by God, no criminal liability can cling to anyone who carried out God's will.*

The Jews fulfilled prophecies by condemning Jesus because "they knew him not." Jesus had to die. If not, the prophecies would be unfulfilled.

His words on the way to the cross warn of the doom awaiting Jerusalem which had turned its back upon divine mercy and brought upon themselves exposure to judgment and wrath:

"Daughters of Jerusalem, do not weep for me; weep for yourselves and for your children."   —Luke 23:28

The Jewish leaders thought the final vanquishing of the Galilean was a triumph for them.

Personal Reflections

After thirty years of law practice, *The Question* continues to discomfort me. "How can you defend a person you know to be guilty?" I no longer go through the mental gymnastics of a first year law student explaining himself, but I do occasionally turn to a well-thumbed page in Sir William Blackstone's *Commentaries on the Laws of England* (1765). The line leaps off the page:

> "It is better that ten guilty persons escape than that one innocent suffer."

This is the answer to *The Question* and basis of this book. The trial of Christ represents the ultimate innocent suffering.

The trial of Jesus continues to this day and will continue to the end of time, not as an actual but a symbolic trial.[21] The death on Golgotha historically viewed was not the inevitable result of certain tragic consequences, nor a simple miscarriage of justice. *It was a judicial murder.*[22]

While Jesus was dying on the cross, he prayed for forgiveness of his enemies (Luke 23:34). This attitude should be constantly remembered by Christians. It alone makes clear how unChristian it would be on the part of Christians today to harbor feelings of dislike and enmity towards the descendants of those who incurred guilt through what happened on Good Friday on Golgotha.

The old doctrine of the inherent evil in all men can be found in the events that brought about the death of Christ. He was a noble, true and kind man, friend of the friendless, defender of the weak, tender caretaker of the aged, lover of little children, with character pure and spotless, but was convicted and crucified as a criminal. Mankind is sinful and unclean and is still sinning against God in word and deed.

Mankind is on trial. Jesus met his judges, accusers, and the multitude. They rejected him and chose Barabbas.

So has it ever been. Those who refuse to acknowledge the claims of Christ condemn themselves, for they choose the evil and reject the good. Today the cross of Christ both condemns and saves mankind.

When will mankind heed the words of Jesus?

> "But seek first his kingdom and his righteousness, and all these things will be given to you as well."   —Matt. 6:33

The choice before the world remains:

Is it Christ or Barabbas?

"Jesus did many other things as well. If every one of them were written down, I suppose that even the whole world would not have room for the books that would be written."

—John 21:25

Conclusion

"For even the Son of Man did not come to be served, but to serve, and to give his life as a ransom for many."   —Mark 10:45

For 2000 years, Jesus' followers have left their footprints on every part of the earth. Now we must choose. The choice is not to accept Jesus as some good man, great teacher, or some idealist. Jesus of Nazareth was either the chosen Messiah of the Jews, or he was a fraud. There is no middle ground. You must accept him or reject him.

The teachings of Jesus have changed the world. In 2000 years not a day has gone by when the influence of this itinerant teacher from Nazareth has not been felt. As a trial lawyer, trained to be skeptical and critical, it is improbable that any fraud or false Messiah could have made such a profound impression for good.

The trial of Jesus goes on everyday until he returns. He calls us to be actors in the drama, defenders of the faith to give God our best fruits, labors, and love:

"You must be on your guard. You will be handed over to the local councils and flogged in the synagogues. On account of me you will stand before governors and kings as witnesses to them."   –Mark 13:9

But listen. The bailiff has summoned a new jury for the daily retrial of Jesus. Twelve new impartial jurors file into the box and sit down ready to hear the evidence. Will they believe in Jesus or not?

The judge calls the first witness. What a shock! He has just called out your name!

QUESTIONS FOR BIBLE SCHOLARS

1. Did Jesus leave Galilee for Jerusalem to avoid Herod (Luke 13:31) or to accomplish his death in accordance with a divine plan?

2. Why was Jesus identified with a kiss from Judas when he was well-known as a daily teacher in the synagogue?

3. Was there sufficient time for all the events to have occurred at various places in Jerusalem within one day?

4. Why was it necessary for Annas to first question Jesus, as he was no longer chief priest?

5. Were *all* of the members of the Sanhedrin present, or only part?

6. Were Nicodemus and Joseph of Arimathea given notice to attend the Sanhedrin trial and if so, why didn't they speak out?

7. Once the high priest tore his garments, were not others present under the obligation to follow his example?

8. Was there any record of any formal sentence by the Sanhedrin?

9. Once Jesus was brought to the governor's court and delivered into Roman custody, did the detachment of Jewish Temple Police stay or depart?

10. If Jesus were tried before Pilate, would he have not been tried in the Praetorium where the Jews would not go? If so, Jesus actually was tried in private.

11. Why did the Roman governor jump up and down on four occasions from his seat of judgment? Why did he go at odd intervals into the courtyard to talk with a mob?

12. If the Jews did not believe in crucifixion, why would Pilate (John 19:6) tell the people, "Take him yourselves and *crucify him*. I find

no guilt in him." Pilate "handed Jesus over to them to deal with as they wished." Who is the "them," if not the Jews?

13. Since Pilate would have been surrounded by his imperial court, officers, troops, and clerks, isn't his running out and reporting his deliberations on how to deal with a criminal unbelievable? How could Pilate, with any sense of human justice, abdicate his responsibility in passing sentence and cower in the presence of people?

14. If the Sanhedrin lacked the authority to execute Jesus, does that fact alone explain why the Jewish officials took Jesus to Pilate?

15. Why would Pilate be so deeply interested in attesting his innocence in the execution of Jesus by washing his hands?

16. Exactly who were the gathered interested onlookers by whom the Roman governor let himself be influenced?

17. How could Pilate's wife learn about the sudden early morning trial in time to dream about Jesus and make a report to her husband?

18. While Pilate was questioning the onlookers and citizens, why did the chief priests try to persuade, since there was little sympathy for the chief priests?

19. Since the Romans attached great importance to dreams, such as Calpurnia's dream of Caesar's impending assassination, why did Pilate not listen to Claudia Procula's dream of Christ?

21. If Pilate wanted to pardon Jesus, why didn't he do so?

22. Why was the choice confined to releasing either Jesus or Barabbas? What, for instance, of the other two convicts who were crucified with Jesus?

23. Why was Barabbas given as a choice since he had been responsible for a murder committed in the course of an insurrection, a dangerous but notable resistance fighter? Why should he be compared to Jesus?

24. Is there any independent historical data of any Roman law establishing that at Passover a custom existed to release a prisoner?

25. Why did Pilate suggest to the people that Jesus be pardoned since it does not appear that the provincial governor had such power? Only the Emperor had the power to grant pardons.

26. Was Jesus made to carry the entire cross or just the crossbar?

27. Was Golgotha located on a high hill as often depicted, or on more level ground outside the city walls?

28. Why would Roman soldiers cast lots for Jesus' clothes, which suggests he was wearing clothes that were worth something?

29. Why did Pilate who had consistently been arbitrary and heavy handed suddenly become, in Jesus' prosecution, meekly submissive to the will of his subjects?

30. If the Sanhedrin lacked the authority to execute Jesus, does that fact alone explain why the Jewish officials took Jesus to Pilate?

ENDNOTES

[1]   Zeitlin, Solomon. *Who Crucified Jesus?* (Block Publishing Co.: New York: 1964), p. 156.

[2]   Buse, I. *St. John and the Passion Narratives of St. Matthew and St. Luke.* (NTS 7 (1) (1960), pgs. 208-212).

[3]   Guigenbert, C. *Jesus.* (New York: 1956), p. 471. "It is not likely that Pilate, or any other procurator, would have troubled to base his decision on a statute. He was responsible for the maintenance of order and would take what measures he thought necessary to that end, by virtue of his general powers."

[4]   Winter, Paul. *On the Trial of Jesus.* (Berlin: 1961), p. 138. Jesus was a nationalist and had politically-inclined friends. "Rather than the content of his teaching, it was the affect which his teaching had on certain sections of the populous that induced the authorities to take action against him," p. 135.

[5]   Eisler, R. *The Messiah Jesus and John the Baptist.* (London: 1931). Even Biblical experts who do not follow this theory do admit his movement was closely parallel to and at times overlapping with Zealot aims and principles.

[6]   Mattuck, I. I. *The Trial of Jesus.* (London: 1929).

[7]   Wilson, William Riley. *The Execution of Jesus.* (Charles Scribners Sons: New York: 1970), p. 76.

[8]   Paul also puts the blame for Jesus' death on the Jews, 1 Thess. 2:14-15.

[9]   Josephus. *Jewish Wars*, 1.4.6; *Antiquities of the Jews*, 13.13.5; Brown, Raymond E. *The Death of the Messiah,* Vol. 1 (Doubleday: New York: 1993), p. 394.

[10] Peter says to Jewish authorities, "The God of our fathers raised Jesus whom you killed by hanging on a tree" (Acts 5:30), "whom you crucified" (Acts 2:36), and Jesus as "whom you disowned and handed over to be killed" (Acts 3:13-16). These references emphasize "the Jews" as the people who through their officials murdered Jesus.

[11] Montefiore, H. W. *Josephus and the New Testament.* (1960), pgs. 139-160.

[12] Wilson, William Riley. *The Execution of Jesus.* (Charles Scribners Sons: New York), p. 81.

[13] Maier, Paul M. "Who Is Responsible for the Trial and Death of Jesus?" *Christianity Today*, Vol. 18, No. 14, April 12, 1974, p. 9.

[14] Josephus. *Antiquities of the Jews*, 20.9.1.

[15] Maier, Paul. "Who Is Responsible for the Trial and Death of Jesus?" *Christianity Today*, Vol. 18, No. 14, April 12, 1974, p. 11.

[16] *Apology*, I. 63:10.

[17] *Dialogue with Trypho*, 17:1.

[18] *Gospel of Peter*, I.1; James, M. R. *The Apocryphal New Testament.* (Oxford: 1924), p. 20.

[19] Catchpole, David R. *The Answer of Jesus to Caiaphas in New Testament Studies*, #17 (1970-71), p. 139.

[20] Stevenson, Herbert F. *The Road to the Cross.* (Revell Co.: Westwood, N.J.: 1962), p. 108.

[21] Powell, Frank J. *The Trial of Jesus Christ.* (Paternoster Press: London: 1949), p. 153.

[22] McHugh, Isabel & Florence. *The Trial of Jesus.* (The Mercier Press, Ltd.: England: 1959), p. 293.

APPENDIX

Glossary of Legal Terms, People & Places

Adjuration: Means "to cause to swear" (I Kings 8:31); an act or appeal wherein a person in authority imposes upon another the obligation of speaking or acting, imposed upon one without his consent and binding in the highest degree. When it was connected with a question, it made an answer compulsory (I Kings 22:16; 2 Chr. 18:15).

Allocution: The opportunity of a condemned man to speak his final words.

Annas: The high priest and political boss of Jerusalem, appointed in A.D. 7 by the Procurator Coponius and deposed around A.D. 16. His five sons became high priests. Later when Peter and John were subsequently arrested, Annas was prominent among their examiners (Acts 4:6). His family grew immensely wealthy through the temple trading booths.

269

Annas could not be called a religious man, as he subscribed to the creed that there was no life after death, nor did he believe in a spiritual world. To him the temple was a convenient meeting place where unfair exchanges could be made to his personal benefit.

Annas was outraged, humiliated beyond endurance, and determined to "get even" with Christ. The cleansing of the temple by Jesus the previous Monday was a direct challenge to this power and authority of Annas and his group of Sadducees. Annas and Caiaphas entered into the conspiracy with Judas Iscariot to betray Jesus.

Apocrypha: Fifteen religious books in Greek and Hebrew not admitted to the Hebrew canon of scripture, but included in the Septuagint and Latin Vulgate.

Aramaic: A Semitic dialect which in Jesus' time was the current speech of the people of Israel.

Bar Kochba: The leader of the second Jewish revolt against Rome (A.D. 132-135), who was hailed by Rabbi Akiba as the expected Jewish Messiah.

Barabbas: Often described as a thief, bandit, revolutionary, insurgent, a rebel against the Roman occupational forces, a rioter in an uprising in which someone was murdered, for which he was arrested for the crime. In certain circles he was regarded as a local hero. It is long thought that the Jerusalem populous demanding the execution of Jesus, described as "crowds", may have been followers or friends of Barabbas who came to beg for amnesty for their hero, but had to fend off Pilate's attempts to release Jesus instead.

Older Greek texts of the New Testament call him Jesus Barabbas. Pilate twice refers to "Jesus who is called Christ," (Matt. 27:22) as if to distinguish the two.

Blasphemy: It is derived from the Greek and means slander, defamation or in general, abusive language. According to Tannaitic Law, a man who uses abusive language against God can be put to death by a court.[1] Blasphemy, if created in ignorance, thoughtlessness, or weakness of the flesh might be atoned for, but if committed with a "high hand" was punished by stoning (Lev. 24:13).

1. The speaking (slander) evil of God to "curse the name of the Lord" (Isa. 52:5; Rom. 2:24).

2. Attributing some evil to God or denying him some good that we should attribute to him;

3. Or giving the attributes of God to a creature (which form the blasphemy charge the Jews aimed at Jesus) (Matt. 26:65; Luke 5:21; John 10:36).

Blood Money: Money paid to informants to help arrest or convict suspected criminals.

Ben Caiaphas: The last of four high priests appointed by the Roman Procurator Valerius Gratus. Valerius was procurator from A.D. 15 to 26, and his appointment of Caiaphas must have occurred in A.D. 26. Caiaphas held office from A.D. 18 to 36 when he was removed by Vitellus, the legate of Syria. His administration lasted eighteen years, belonged to the party of the Sadducees.

His close friendship with Pontius Pilate was grounded on the proposition that they had much in common, a deep hatred for Christ.

Caiaphas disgraced the high office of high priesthood. Although biased and prejudiced, he continued to serve and preside at the trial, having previously taken an oath under the existing Jewish laws to assume an attitude of impartiality towards every accused person to manifest complete indifference to the results of any trial, and to not serve as presiding officer should there ever arise a case where there existed prejudice or enmity towards the accused.

The remains of Caiaphas were discovered in November 1990, during the building of a water park in Peace Forest on the outskirts of Jerusalem.[2]

Caesar: The name of a Roman family prominent from the third century B.C., subsequently the title taken by each of the Roman emperors. Tiberius Caesar reigned from A.D. 14-37 (Luke 3:1). "Caesar" is mentioned by Jesus (Luke 20:22-25) referring to both Tiberius and any earthly ruler.

Capital Offenses: Capital offenses in Jewish law included blasphemy, adultery, rape, incest, idolatry, murder. They are divided into absolute and relative.

1.   *Absolute* crimes had mitigating factors which could alter the severity of the sentence: such as: striking a parent, blasphemy, Sabbath breaking, witchcraft, adultery, rape, incest or unnatural connections, kidnapping, idolatry, false witness.

2.   There were thirty-six *relative* crimes in the Pentateuch where the penalty was "cutting off from the people," a form of excommunication, generally a breach of *morals* (willful sin, incest, unclean connections); *covenant* (uncircumcision, neglect of the Passover, Sabbath breaking, work done on the Sabbath Day); or *ritual* (eating unleavened bread, eating blood, eating the sacrifice in an unclean condition, slaying an animal elsewhere other than at the Tabernacle door, touching holy things illegally).

Capital penalties employed by Jews included crucifixion, stoning, hanging, death by sword, spear, arrow, or beheading, burning, strangling, and cutting off. Others were borrowed from foreign lands: beheading, dichotomy (cutting into pieces), or death by torture.

Secondary or corporal punishments were of a less severe nature: retaliation (such as extracting an eye for an eye, Exod. 21:24), money compensation, corporal stripes of thirty-nine blows; (2 Cor. 11:24), or imprisonment.

Imprisonment was not recognized, but "custody" (Lev. 24:12) occurred until a decision concerning his case had been made. After the exile, imprisonment was a common punishment in cases of debt (Matt. 18:30), being chained to other prisoners, or by putting feet or hands in stocks (Acts 16:24).

Claudia Procula: Granddaughter of Emperor Augustus who married Pilate ten years before they came to Judaea, an increasingly empty childless union which would have avoided historical record but for one momentous event. She dreamt about Jesus on the night before his death and sent her husband a message that could have changed history. The desperate intervention of a woman who loved Christ secretly—or a calculating response to use her husband to promote her social ambitions? Declared saint by the Greek Orthodox church.

Crucifixion: The victim is tied or nailed to a wooden cross. Death was hastened by breaking their legs, as was done in the case of the robbers crucified with Jesus (John 19:32).

The preliminary cruelties of scourging and compelling him to bear his cross were common (John 19:17). Infliction seems neither to have been the legal scourging after sentence nor examination by torture (Acts 22:24), but rather a scourging before sentence to excite pity and procure immunity from further punishment (Luke 23:22; John 19:1). Often a medicated cup was given the victim before nailing to deaden the pangs (Prov. 31:6) of wine mixed with myrrh.

Since there were instances of persons surviving for nine days, Jesus was watched according to custom by a party of four soldiers and their centurion (Matt. 27:54; John 19:23). Death often took four to six days, but in Jesus' case only six hours (John 19:33).

Court: On the advice of Jethro, Moses initiated a system of jurisprudence over the Israelites and appointed judges and finally a supreme court under himself and his successors. There was no appeal to a higher court (Exod. 18:25). The office of judge was an elective one eventually chosen from the Levites and held in high regard. The profession of law developed in which its members were called lawyers, scribes, or doctors of the law (Luke 2:46).

Diaspora: Jewish community living outside Palestine. The flight and enslavement of a million Jews outside of Jerusalem accelerated their spread throughout the Mediterranean. Scholars date the Diaspora from the destruction of Herod's Temple.

Essenes: A Jewish religious community which lived at the northern end of the Dead Sea (a pre-Christian sect), who owned and produced the Dead Sea Scrolls.

They had general features of simplicity and moderation, were all free, mutually working for each other, owned no slaves, and swearing was forbidden. They bathed in cold water before each meal or after coming in contact with a member of a lower class of the order.

Essenes held the fundamental Jewish view of the world in common with the Pharisees. The Sabbath was strictly observed. They turned to the sun while praying in opposition to the Jewish custom of looking toward the temple. They disappeared from history after the destruction of Jerusalem.

Flagellation: A punishment known as scourging, often a punishment for delinquent clerics, administered by the judges and was limited to a certain number of blows, either a single-lash whip or a multi-lashed flagellum.

Flagellation was a prelude to the crucifixion. The temple police limited it to the customary forty blows, less one, such as Paul suffered on at least five occasions (2 Cor. 11:24). Other apostles received flagellation at least once (Acts 5:40).

Gabbatha (Praetorium): An elevated pavement (John 19:13) or an open space in front of Herod's palace.

Gamaliel: Known as "the Ancient," a worthy Israelite whose name is spoken of with honor in Acts and the Talmud, acquired a great reputation for his scientific knowledge (Acts 5:34; 22:3). He died nineteen years after the death of Christ.

Among his disciples were Barnabas and Stephen. When the Sanhedrin members considered putting the apostles to death, it was Gamaliel who prevented the death sentence.

Gethsemane: The place of Jesus' arrest across from the Kidron Valley. An olive grove at the foot of the Mount of Olives, to which Jesus was accustomed to retire, (Luke 22:39), a garden (and cave) in a secluded spot several hundred yards northeast of traditional sites now commonly identified.

The traditional site is not far from the road, near the bridge over the Kidron and laid out a neat gardens. Large olive trees exist today and are no doubt ancient, but Emperor Titus destroyed all the trees around Jerusalem during the siege in A.D. 70.

Golgotha (Calvary): Outside the city walls of Jerusalem where Christ was crucified and in the vicinity where he was buried, a conspicuous spot perhaps near the highway. The name was due to the cranial shape of the rock. Thought to be located at the Church of the Holy Sepulcher or a hill, (Jeremiah's Grotto), about 250 yards northeast of the present Damascus Gate. Eusebius was the earliest historian who gives any information on the subject. A temple to the goddess Venus was built over it, and later Constantine erected a church.

Herod Antipas: (21 B.C.—A.D. 39) Son of Herod the Great, Ruler of Galilee and Perea. Regarded as sly, ambitious, luxurious, but not as able as his father. Jesus said, "Go and tell that fox, behold I cast out demons," (Luke 13:32). His administration was characterized by cunning and crime, he was intensely selfish and utterly destitute of principle.

Herod the Great: (73 B.C.—4 B.C.) Emperor of Rome, known for his cruelty, who was responsible for beheading John the Baptist who was in a nearby prison and whose head was requested by Salome after she danced before the nobles. He consumed more than a gallon of hard wine daily and was a habitual drunkard.

His father was named Procurator of Judea by Julius Caesar in 47 B.C., was subsequently appointed governor of Galilee by his father. Marc Antony gave Herod the position of Tetarch of Galilee. An anti-Roman insurrection in Palestine forced Herod to flee to Rome in 40 B.C.

He married Hasmonean Princess Mariamne, who became one of nine wives. Herod I supported his friend Marc Antony in his struggle against Augustus for the Roman throne—even though Antony's mistress Cleopatra persuaded Antony to annex part of Herod's kingdom.

Herod was personally unstable, perhaps insane. He murdered Mariamne and her whole family and disowned and killed his firstborn son Antipater. He ordered the infamous *massacre of the innocents*, the murder of all male infants in Bethlehem.

Herod married ten women, murdered seven of them whom he had become bored with. When he died, he left a last will and testament causing the segregation of the kingdom among his three sons.

Herodians: A party among the Jews which comprised the political supporters of Herod the Great and his house—notably Herod Antipas, his son.

James: The brother of Jesus (according to Josephus) put to death in Jerusalem in A.D. 62 by stoning.

John: The Gospel of John is believed by many to be the deepest and most wonderful book in the New Testament, simple, direct, and penetrating, understood by common people, called by many the "greatest book in the world." The Apostle John was known to the High Priest and entered the High Priest's residence in the company of Jesus (John 18:15), he was a Jew from Palestine, and a beloved apostle, and introduces himself in his writings.

Joseph of Arimathea: A secret disciple fearful of publicly committing himself, whose unused grave was surrendered to Jesus. He was a wealthy, devout member of the Sanhedrin, and one of the few friends of Jesus within that body. Though apprehensive about a negative vote before the Sanhedrin, Joseph had the courage to go before Pilate to petition to remove the body of Jesus from the cross.

He was a respected member, an honorable counsellor and Sanhedrin member (Mark 15:43), and because of his adherence to the law and integrity of life, a good and just man (Luke 23:50).

He showed even greater love and kindness when he wrapped Jesus' crucified body in linens, and assisted Nicodemus in sweetening the linens with spices.

Josephus, Flavius: A Jewish historian born in A.D. 37 and commander of the Jewish forces in Galilee. After being captured he was attached to the Roman headquarters. Author of three famous historical writings.

Reluctantly drawn into his people's revolt against Rome in A.D. 66, Josephus surrendered to the Romans and sought to win Vespasian's favor by predicting that he would one day become emperor. The prediction came true in A.D. 69, and Josephus now in Imperial favor was attached to the Roman army during the siege of Jerusalem. He was stigmatized as a traitor by his people, but later in Rome he devoted his time to writing their history.

Judea: The Latin name of a central part of Palestine annexed by the Romans as a province after the deposition of Herod the Great's son Archelaus in A.D. 6.

Judas: Called "the traitor", he was a healer of the sick and travelling companion of Jesus. Jesus honored Judas, healed Judas' mother of leprosy, and made him treasurer because he wanted to show his trust and confidence. The only Judean among the disciples, he had been repeatedly honored by Jesus and sent upon holy missions. Greed and love for money was his undoing, and he was highly disappointed when he began to realize Jesus had no possible intention of ever setting up an earthly kingdom. Worldly pomp and power were his dreams and hopes. Portrayed as a zealot disappointed at Jesus' failure to lead a mass movement or rebellion against Rome, great resentment and bitterness set in. Jesus wiped and cleaned his feet, and Judas Iscariot may have been, next to Peter, one of the most trusted disciples.

Judas was not needed for the trial, only as an informant in the arrest. Some think he was reacting to Jesus' rebuke when he criticized the woman with the anointment. When a woman named Mary came to pour rich ointment on the feet of Jesus, Judas complained, "Why wasn't this perfume sold and the money given to the poor? It was worth a year's wages" (John 12:5). John comments that Judas said this "He did not say this because he cared about the poor but beacuse he was a thief" (John 12:6). Others think Judas acted out of greed for the money that Jesus' enemies offered him.[3]

The Law of Moses: A divine rule of life mediated through Moses to govern God's covenant and chosen people, Israel, regulating their common everyday conduct. The Mosaic Code of laws included the Commandments, laws stipulating the Israelites' social life, and those directing worship.

Mosiac laws have often been compared with other legal codes of early time. Such as the Code of Hammurabi[4] (1700 B.C.), from Babylon, the Hittite Code[5] (1450 B.C.), and the Assyrian Code[6] (1350 B.C.).

The Ten Commandments are the fundamental laws and are a summary of the whole moral code founded in the nature of God and in the permanent relation of men on earth.

The Mosaic Law given orally to the people and unto Moses during the two 40 day periods on Mt. Sinai, may be divided into moral, civil, and ceremonial law:

1. The moral law is the Ten Commandments. It applies to the broad moral principles for conducting life generally. Every person was expected to memorize these precepts.

2. Civil law gives specific instruction about daily social relationships, rights of property, care of the poor, administration of justice, training of children, punishment of criminals, and many other matters.

3. The ceremonial law deals with religious matters, most of it concerning priestly functions at the tabernacle.

Lawyer: A lawyer conversant in the law of Moses (Matt. 22:35; Luke 7:30), for which he is a professional interpreter (Matt. 22:35; Mark 12:28). Lawyers joined with the Pharisees in rejecting John the Baptist, considered themselves above the need for instruction from Jesus, but when they did communicate with him tried to puzzle him by means of difficult questions

(Matt. 22:35; Luke10:25). Jesus denounced them in severe language for laying heavy burdens on the people and in keeping people back from the key of knowledge (Luke11:45-52).

Luke: A physician, Gentile, and traveling companion to Paul. Written before Acts while Paul was imprisoned at Cesarea around A.D. 58—60. The book is addressed to a man named Theophilus, probably a Gentile Christian, and the material is obtained from earlier documents and from information obtained by Luke personally.

Mark: The second book of the four Gospels is not necessarily the second in order of composition. It is the shortest of the four Gospels, but the brevity of events does allow him to still give a generous amount of detail, the story moving forward rapidly, dwelling on the last week of Jesus' ministry. The Gospel was written shortly after Peter's death around A.D. 65 to 68, shortly before the fall of Jerusalem, evidently written primarily for Gentiles.

Mishnah: A collection of Hebrew legal interpretations and traditional precepts (means "instruction") completed around A.D 200; forming the core of the Talmud. Jewish legal interpretations and traditions codified by Rabbi Judah, forming the core of the Talmud.

The Mishnah consists of six orders, and is divided into sections or chapters. The whole Mishnah contains 63 tractes with 525 chapters.

These were basic attempts at orderly arrangement and collection of opinions by various rabbis on questions that are more or less connected with each other concerning folklore, legends, history, interpretations of Biblical passages, sermons. The Talmud is like notes and jottings made by students at rambling lectures or round table discussions.

Nicodemus: A secret disciple who paid for the embalming of Jesus (John 19:39). A Pharisee member of the Sanhedrin, one of the three richest men of Jerusalem, and convinced by the miracles of Jesus that Jesus was a teacher "come from God." Under cover of darkness he came to Jesus seeking the plan of eternal life.

Nicodemus, speaking to the Sanhedrin said, "Our lot is not to judge a man, unless at first hears from him and knows what he is doing" (John 7:51). Nothing further is known of Nicodemus from Scripture.

Nicodemus is always mentioned with the label "the same that came to Jesus by night." He came at night because it was the best time for both Jesus and himself to relax and have a quiet, uninterrupted conversation about spiritual matters. Nicodemus had teaching duties during the day and Jesus was active in his ministry. Nicodemus, the cautious inquirer and man of spiritual perception, (John 3:2) sought out Christ and listened.

Oath: To take an oath or swear, call upon God, or to severe one's self to act after a manner of God. Each oath contains two elements: (1) an affirmation or promise, and (2) an appeal to God as the punisher of falsehoods.

The oath was often by the lifting up of the hand or laying their hands on the head of the accused, or under the thigh of the person to whom the promise was made while looking towards the temple.

The mischief which may arise from a rash oath was well illustrated when Herod made an oath against his will to murder John the Baptist (Matt. 14:3-12).

"An oath should be given in truth, in judgment and in righteousness" (Jer. 4:2). Some interpret Matt. 5:34 as totally forbidding all oaths thus our current laws allow such witness to "affirm" rather than "swear." By the time of Christ, the Old Testament law regarding oaths (Exod. 22:11), was perverted by the scribes. Jesus condemned indiscriminate and light taking of oaths saying that men should be so transparently honest that oaths between persons are unnecessary. Oaths were recognized by the apostles who called upon God to witness to the truth of what they said.

Old Testament: The Hebrew Bible composed of three categories of Scriptures:

1. The first five books of "instruction," called the Torah, attributed to Moses (Genesis, Exodus, Leviticus, Numbers, Deuteronomy);

2. Twenty-one books of the "prophets" six of which are the historical Chronicles (Joshua, Judges, Samuel, Kings); record of the oracles of the three major prophets (Isaiah, Jeremiah, and Ezekiel) and the twelve minor ones (Hosea, Joel, Amos, Obadiah, Jonah, Micah, Nahum, Habakkuk, Zephaniah, Haggai, Zechariah, Malachi);

3. The thirteen books called the "writings" (Ruth, Chronicles, Ezra, Nehemiah, Esther, Job, Psalms, Proverbs, Ecclesiastes, Song of Solomon, Lamentations, Daniel).

Pentateuch: One of the five books of Moses, the first of the three divisions for the ancient Hebrew Cannon, called the Law or Torah. They include: *Genesis, Exodus, Leviticus, Numbers, Deuteronomy.*

Moses wrote the law, gave it to the priests, commanding the Levites to "take this book of the law and place it beside the arch of the covenant of the Lord your God, that it may remain there as a witness against you."

Perjury: To swear falsely or to lie under oath, commonly known as forswear (Matt. 5:33). The crime of perjury was strongly condemned, and a person who bore false witness was given the same punishment that was due the crime to which he testified (Exod. 20:7; Deut. 19:16).

Pharisees: An exclusive sect non-political party at the time of Jesus numbering around 6000. Means "separated" because they separated themselves from the great portion of Israel they believed were unclean.

Pharisees united themselves closely with the association that made a duty of the laws punctilious observance. They looked at political questions from a religious point of view. They acted under two different religious views: (Divine providence), believing that the chastisement of God must be willingly submitted to, and the harsh government and the heathens must be willingly borne; and (Israel's election), Israel must acknowledge no other king than God alone as the ruler of the house of David.

Pharisees were of seven kinds: the Shechemite—who simply kept the law for what he could profit from; the humbling Pharisee—who appeared always humble and hung his head; the bleeding Pharisee—walked with his eyes closed in order to not see a woman, and thus often injured himself; the mortar Pharisee—wore a mortar shaped cap to cover his eyes, so that he might not see any impurities; the What-Am-I-Yet-To-Do Pharisee—who did not know much about the law, but always asked "What is my duty now? And I will do it" (Mark 10:17); the Pharisee from Fear—kept the law because he was afraid of future judgement; the Pharisee from love— obeyed the Lord because he loved him with all his heart.

There was a right and left wing, one interpreting principles rigidly and the other more liberal. At the time of Christ, the leader of the two schools were the famous Gamaliel and Hillel. They were often in disagreement. Three hundred points of law upon which they were opposed have been recorded.[7]

Pilate: Pilate, a native of Seville, was a traitor to the cause of the Spaniards, his father having served as a famous general on the side of the Romans. He courted and married Claudia, whose mother was the daughter of Augustus Caesar, and thus gained the appointment of procurator or governor of Judea by the then Emperor Tiberius Caesar.

He was responsible for the cruel execution of hundreds of innocent Jews and was a man of extreme violence. He feared the ever present possibility that some might report him to his political benefactor, the Emperor, which would obtain his removal from office, so he kept his ear to the ground to avoid any rumbling or outbursts of dissention.

Pilate was a man of considerable experience and was directly responsible to the Roman Emperor, and not to the Roman Senate. He climbed a ladder of offices including military commands and held office for ten years. He built a better water supply and constructed a new aqueduct, taking the money from the temple treasury.

He was completely unsympathetic to the Jews, was contemptuous of what he called their irrational and fanatical prejudices which they called principles. Pilate killed himself after he was banished to Vienna, but some authorities say he resided near the lake of Lucerne, now called Mount Pilatas. Pilate made an official report to Tiberius of the trial and condemnation.

Philo Judaeus: Philo Judaeus was born about 25 B.C. and lived in Alexandria at the beginning of the Christian Era. He wrote describing events that occurred in A.D. 40. He wrote two long treatises and died between A.D. 45-50. He was from a wealthy family, later appointed Roman procurator in Palestine in A.D. 46, and made prefect of Egypt by Nero.

Priest: An authorized minister who officiates and ministered at the altar and taught the people the law of God.

Punishment: Punishment was a penalty due for sin inflicted for the satisfaction of justice. Some punishment, such as chastisement, was intended to reform the offender. Other punishments were inflicted with the view towards the prevention of crime by deterring others. Some were from purely moral considerations in the sense of justice.

The "majesty of the law" must be maintained, and punishment bear an adequate proportion to the crime committed, neither too little or too much.

In ancient peoples, often regarded as primitive, "blood revenge" existed as a primitive custom (Gen. 27:45) to inflict greater injury than that which he avenged, but under the Mosaic Code punishment was made to correspond to the heinousness of the offense and would fall only upon the guilty party without extending to his children. Under Mosaic Law, "then do to him as he had intended to do to his brother" (Deut. 19:19).

Rend: Refers to the tearing of one's clothes as a sign of grief and signifies contrition of heart and not mere outward signs of grief (Joel 2:13). Caiaphas rent his robe upon hearing Jesus' blasphemy.

Sadducees: Sadducees were aristocratic, wealthy persons of rank and from the rank of priests. They were distinctive in many of the positions they took regarding the law, ritual, and doctrine. They refused to believe in a resurrection of the body in a future life (Matt. 22:23; Mark 12:18; Luke 20:27). With the fall of the Jewish state the Sadducees altogether disappeared from history.

Sanhedrin: A term used by the rabbis, both for the Supreme Council and the Court of the Jews in Jerusalem. The rules are found in the Trachtates Sanhedrin and Makkot of the Mishnah. The Sanhedrin in the form of Jesus' day probably began with the election of Simon to the high priesthood (142 B.C.). It is today's equivalent of a combination of the Supreme Court and Congress.

Scribe: A public writer employed to write at dictation and draw up legal documents, a copier of the law and other parts of Scriptures.

Simon the Cyrenian: Compelled to bear the cross of Christ. The father of Alexander and Rufus (Mark 15:21).

Suetonius: A Roman historian, born in A.D. 120, a court official under Hadrian, an annalist of the Imperial house.

Stephen: A preacher in Jerusalem's Hellenistic synagogues. Enraged by his unorthodox preaching, Stephen was subsequently stoned to death by a crowd that included the brilliant young Pharisee Saul of Tarsus, later to be known as Paul. The death of Stephen heralded a wave of persecution in Jerusalem.

Synoptic Gospels: The term used to identify the first three New Testament Gospels because they can be read together when laid side by side.

Talmud: A great corpus of Jewish religious learning consisting of the Mishnah and the Gemara. Two versions of the Talmud were completed, the Palestinian Talmud in the fifth century A.D., and the Babylonian Talmud in sixth century.

A recording in writing of traditional oral law, second only to the written laws which are the sacred scriptures, but in theory considered to be almost on par with the Scriptures.

Twenty four cartloads of the Talmud were burned on June 17, 1242. The Babylonian Talmud was first printed in Venice in 1520.

Tetrarch: One who rules over a fourth-part of a kingdom of province. Eventually the word was used loosely for a petty subject prince, even though the land was not divided among four rulers. Romans used the term as a title for a prince to whom they granted a small territory but were unwilling to dignify with the authority and rank of a king.

Tiberius Caesar: Caesar held the high office of Emperor of Rome during the trials of Jesus. Any Roman citizen had the right of appeal on a capital offense directly to the Emperor. Paul was given that privilege after his conviction, but since Jesus was not a Roman citizen his trial appeal went to the Roman governor, Pilate.

Titilus: A sign carried in front or around the neck of a condemned man, later nailed to a cross specifying a crime.

Torah: The law is known in Hebrew as the "Torah" or pentateuch, the first of the three traditional divisions of the Hebrew Bible. The other two divisions of the Bible are "the Prophets" and "the Writings".

Witness: Men were called upon to witness an event (Gen. 23:10-18). The concurrent testimony of at least two witnesses was required under the

Mosaic Law to establish guilt of a capital crime (Num. 35:30; Deut. 17:6; Heb. 10:28). The witness, before his testimony was given, was adjured to tell the truth and conceal nothing. It was a sin for him to withhold evidence in his possession (Lev. 5:1; Prov. 29:24). False witness-bearing drew the same penalty that he had attempted to get imposed on the accused (Deut. 19:16-19).

Zealots: A group of small unorganized bands that worked throughout the procuratorial period for the immediate overthrow of the Romans. They offered scattered fanatical resistance.

ENDNOTES

[1] Talmud, Keritut XII.

[2] *Biblical Archeology Review*, Vol. 18, No. 5, Oct. 1992, pgs. 30-76. After the flesh had decomposed, relatives gathered the bones and collected them in an ossuary apparently reflecting a belief in resurrection for which purposes the bones were stored. Ossuaries were used for the secondary burial. In the initial burial, the body is laid out in a recess carved in the wall of the burial cave. After the flesh decomposes, the bones are collected and placed in an ossuary made of limestone, decorated, and inscribed. This occurred for approximately the First Century, and after the Roman destruction of Jerusalem were rarely used. Brodi, R. "Caiaphas and Cantheras," *Schwartz, Agrippa I, The Last King of Judea*, App. 4, pgs. 190-195 and 203-208, Mishna, Parah 3:5.

[3] Schmidt, Carl. "Judas Iscariot," *The New Schaff-Herzog Encyclopedia of Religious Knowledge*, Volume XI, Samuel H. Jackson. (Baker Books: Grand Rapids, MI: 1977), p. 244.

[4] Wood, Leon J. *A Survey of Israel's History*. (Zondervan Publishing House: Grand Rapids, MI: 1970).

[5] Mendenhall, "Ancient, Oriental and Biblical Law," *Biblical Archeologist*, May 1954.

[6] *Law and Covenant in Israel and the Ancient East*. (Pittsburgh: Biblical Colloquium: 1955).

[7] O'Brian, Patrick. *Daily Life in the Time of Jesus*. (Hawthorn Books: New York: 1962), p. 437.

To Order Additional Copies of

THE TRIAL
OF
CHRIST

please call

1-417-887-1155